IMAGES
of America

ROCK SPRINGS

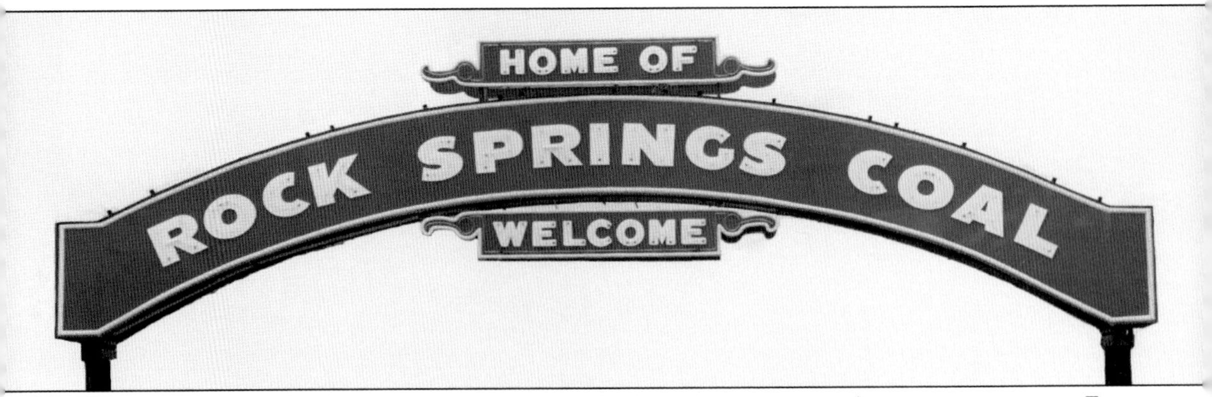

The ubiquitous Rock Springs Coal sign was moved several times as the community grew. First placed to be visible from the Union Pacific Railroad tracks, the sign was near the depot downtown. It later was moved to greet visitors traveling U.S. Highway 30, then to College Hill to greet students at the community's new college. In the early 1990s, the discarded sign was rescued by Liesel Shineberg, an ardent preservationist who found it in the scrap pile behind the city shops. Today the sign again greets visitors to the historic downtown area. (Courtesy New Studio.)

On the Cover: From left to right, John Zembo, Earl Pulley, and John Nelson, real cowboys from nearby ranch outfits, pose in front of the new Rock Springs City Hall. Pulley is wearing a fine Stetson and angora chaps, and they all sport typical working cowboy attire. Nelson's lariat was intended for roping livestock and wild horses. The city hall was designed by Salt Lake City architect Martin Didriecus Kern and built of native sandstone in 1894. Rock Springs had a population of about 5,000 individuals at that time. (Courtesy Nelson family.)

IMAGES
of America

ROCK SPRINGS

Russel L. Tanner
and Margie Fletcher Shanks

ARCADIA
PUBLISHING

ISBN 978-0-7385-5642-0

Published by Arcadia Publishing
Charleston, South Carolina

Printed in the United States of America

Library of Congress Catalog Card Number: 2008921583

For all general information contact Arcadia Publishing at:
Telephone 843-853-2070
Fax 843-853-0044
E-mail sales@arcadiapublishing.com
For customer service and orders:
Toll-Free 1-888-313-2665

Visit us on the Internet at www.arcadiapublishing.com

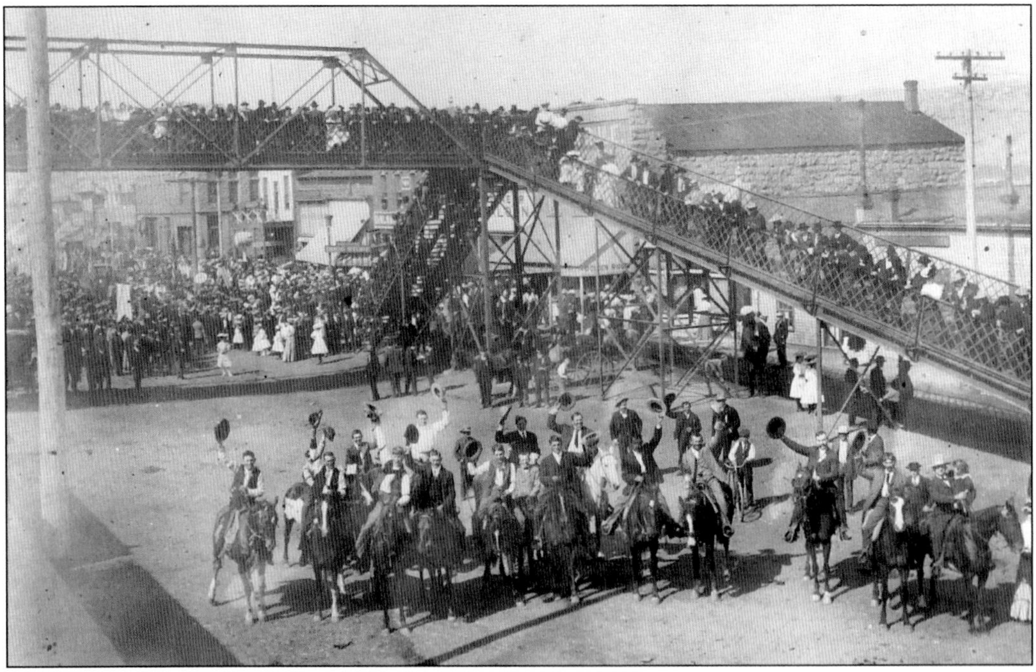

The cause for this robust celebration is not known, but it seems almost everybody in town turned out for this photograph. It was taken at the pedestrian overpass connection of South Front and North Front Streets with a safe way to cross over the several sets of railroad tracks that divided Rock Springs from the town's inception. This picture was taken between the 1890s and 1910s judging by the lack of automobiles and the types of attire worn by the people. The occasion might have been Wyoming statehood on July 10, 1890, perhaps the opening of the pedestrian viaduct itself, or it might have been a rodeo that attracted this large crowd. (Courtesy Sweetwater County Museum.)

Contents

ACKNOWLEDGMENTS

This book is the culmination of collaboration among many people and institutions. The authors would like to thank the people of Rock Springs, Sweetwater County, and the state of Wyoming for providing their assistance and inspiration to this project. We can honestly say that everyone approached for help was not only willing to assist but became excited by the prospect.

The staffs of several institutions were particularly generous in their assistance, including the Rock Springs Historical Museum (RSHM), the Sweetwater County Historical Museum (SCHM), Western Wyoming Community College and the Union Pacific Coal Company (UPCC) Archives housed there, the American Heritage Center at the University of Wyoming, and the Wyoming State Archives in Cheyenne. The people at all of these agencies provided invaluable support of our efforts. We would like to extend special thanks to the Sweetwater Travel and Tourism Board and the Sweetwater Board of Cooperative Education Services for believing in this undertaking and providing financial support for the production of this book.

A very special mention of appreciation is due Diane Whiteman Butler, owner of the New Studio. Diane willingly provided not only photographs from the vast collection of the New Studio but also scanned those and other images for us. We hope this book will increase public awareness and appreciation of the resources available at the New Studio. Former owners of the New Studio, Oliver and Mary Snow Tebedo, also provided assistance and should be recognized for their preservation of the photographic archive originating with the Mike August family, early owners of the New Studio.

We are beholden to the late Henry Chadey, founder of the Sweetwater County Museum. His wife, Helen Putz Chadey, and son Michael Chadey provided tremendous moral support for this project and access to photographs, family records, and contacts. Helen also introduced us to Karen Spence McLean, who gladly shared a lifetime of research and records on the coal camps that comprised the greater Rock Springs community.

Many other people provided assistance of various kinds, including Ruby Enyart Lawrence, David Kathka, Charles Love, Albert Dudley Gardner, David Johnson, Henry Kovach, Bernice Moon Kovach, Robert Fletcher, Bernadine Craft, Albert Allias, Joan Parks, Judy Von Rembo, Thomas Bunning, Norm Dudzik, and many others. Our families—especially Ronald Shanks, Daniel Krza, and Willard and Beverly Adams Tanner—deserve special thanks for their patience and encouragement throughout this effort.

INTRODUCTION

This book covers about the first 100 years since Anglo Americans began to migrate through the region along a natural corridor crossing the Great Continental Divide. Any discussion of Rock Springs, Wyoming, must begin with a description of the awe-inspiring landscape of the region. The community is situated in the Rock Springs Uplift, a geological feature created when pressure from beneath forced a low mountainous region to tilt upward, exposing layers of ancient lake sediments.

The surrounding region is generally called the Red Desert. This high, cold desert setting witnesses very active weather patterns during the winter and dry summers. Temperature extremes fluctuate greatly on both a daily and a seasonal basis. It is not unheard of for there to be rain, snow, and bright sunlight in the same day. And there can be minus 40 degrees Fahrenheit temperatures in winter matched by summer highs nearing 110 degrees. The reason for the active weather is the near-constant wind that buffets the region as a result of its location in a small depression right on top of the Great Continental Divide. The extremes of this setting, including the wind, have developed a community of robust individuals adapted to deal with adverse conditions.

The active geological and geographic processes produced mineral deposits integral to the economy of the people living in Rock Springs and the surrounding areas of the Green River Basin. The basin within the Great Divide itself has had primary significance, for it provides the easiest natural corridor across the Rocky Mountains. This feature allowed the region to host trans-regional Native American trails, pioneer emigration routes, the first transcontinental railroad, and today's ever-more crowded Interstate 80 highway full of 18-wheelers hauling all manner of goods from coast to coast and Americans driving their automobiles.

"All wealth comes from the earth," well-known Rock Springs business leader Leonard Hay liked to say. Leonard's family were the original settlers of Rock Springs: the Blair brothers Archie and Duncan were station attendants at the Rock Springs Overland Stage Station in the 1860s. Nowhere is the fact of all wealth originating in the earth more true than in Rock Springs. The community is set in a picturesque high-desert environment characterized by dormant volcanic cones like Boar's Tusk and active sand dunes. This setting is the result of a unique geological history dating back nearly 60 million years. And this environment formed of ancient lake sediments later pierced by igneous uplifting then eroded again by eons of wind produced a mineral-rich region in a high, cold desert setting ideal for sheep raising. It is situated in a basin atop the Rocky Mountains that facilitated east-west passage across the North American continent first by fur traders, then pioneers to Oregon, the Mormon religious exodus, and gold seekers headed for California, followed shortly by the first transcontinental railroad.

Coal, created by the ancient lakeside environment, fueled the trains that carried other minerals and agricultural products to markets and brought manufactured goods to this frontier outpost, which developed around the large spring where the stagecoach station had first been located. Today natural gas also derived from these ancient sediments is serving as the nation's relatively clean bridge fuel to the future. The Sweetwater County Commission granted permission for a large wind-generation facility to be located on the high ridges north of Rock Springs. In the near future, even the wind that shaped this environment from dead volcanoes and propels moving sand dunes will be a source of energy for export to the rest of the United States. Indeed, all wealth in Rock Springs comes from the ground.

But the community that developed in this unusual setting is likewise unique. A gathering of English and Scottish sheep ranchers was mostly replaced by the Basque herders brought from Spain and France, who mingled with a plethora of other European immigrants from Czechoslovakia, Prussia, Slovenia, Croatia, and Serbia as well as Italy, Greece, Holland, France, Finland, and Germany to mine the coal that fed the trains and now feeds the electrical generators at the Jim Bridger Power Plant. There were also Chinese miners and railroad workers who added even more diversity to the blend. When national immigration laws turned away Chinese workers, laborers from Japan were brought in to help. As mines in the Midwest closed down, black miners came also came to Rock Springs, adding their own richness to the melting pot. And when coal began to play out in the 1950s, another mineral, trona—a source of sodium carbonate compounds—came to the rescue and provided jobs for more generations to hold on until coal returned to prominence as a fuel for electrical power generation.

The resulting town of crooked streets that connected more than a dozen mining enclaves to each other and to the railroad running through the middle is now characterized by ethnic diversity seldom seen in a comparatively small community.

But the Doughboy statue in Bunning Park makes it clear these are not the first of Rock Springs men and women who returned to the "Old Countries" in the service of the United States. Veterans' memorials are comprised of stone markers bearing the names of Rock Springs and Sweetwater County soldiers, many who still today have foreign-sounding names.

It is this richness we hope to present to readers in a book of photographs with supporting text that tells the story of Rock Springs, where all wealth does indeed come from the earth, whether dug from the seams of ancient sediment or harnessed from the formidable wind that echoes across the Continental Divide, where the lay of the land made it the easiest way across North America, the place where the ties binding our nation together are bound together.

The book presents historical photographs to convey a sense of the history of the Rock Springs community. While it is our intention to have our facts completely correct in the book, this is not a critical historical essay of the place. It is, as the title indicates, images of Rock Springs. These images were gleaned from literally thousands considered in the various archival resources as well as photographs and documentary information provided by many individuals. It would be impossible to discuss all aspects of this unique community in a single book, but we hope the reader will come away with an appreciation for how life was between about 1860 and 1960 in what must have been a smoky little town.

The 1970s marked another boom in the continuing cycle of booms and busts experienced by Rock Springs, and now in the early 21st century, yet another boom is occurring. We will leave it to future generations to review the history of this latest period of the town's history.

One

Red Desert Corridor

Passage across an Ancient Landscape

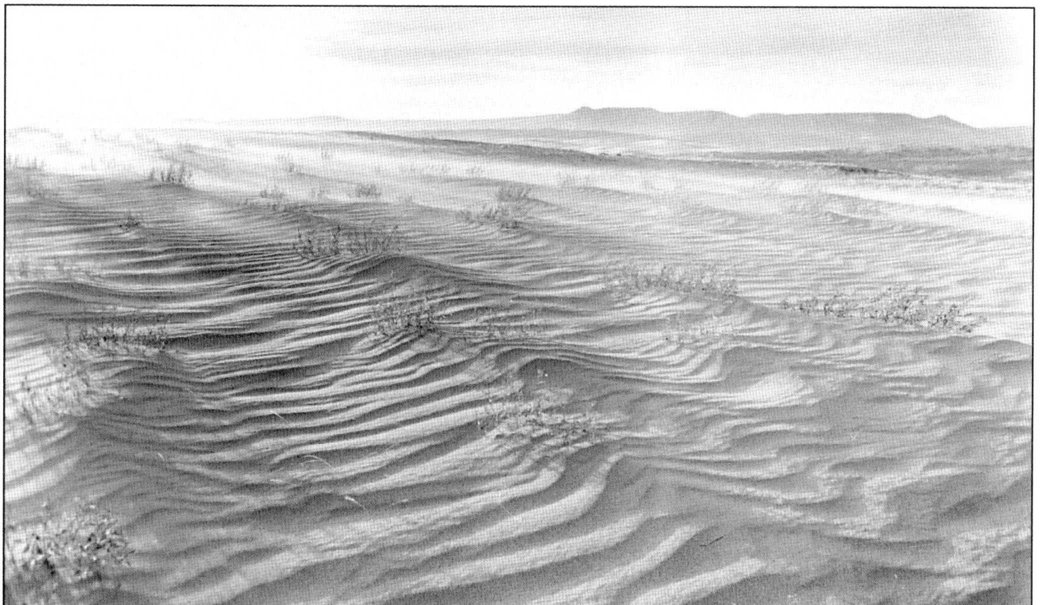

The Killpecker Sand Dunes are the largest continually migrating sand dunes in North America. They are but one of the unique geological features characterizing the setting of Rock Springs in the Red Desert of Wyoming. This diverse setting sculpted by nature attracted people from around the world not because it is beautiful, though it is, but because of the geological processes and geographic situation as a narrow passage over the Great Continental Divide created vast wealth "from the earth." (Courtesy SCHM.)

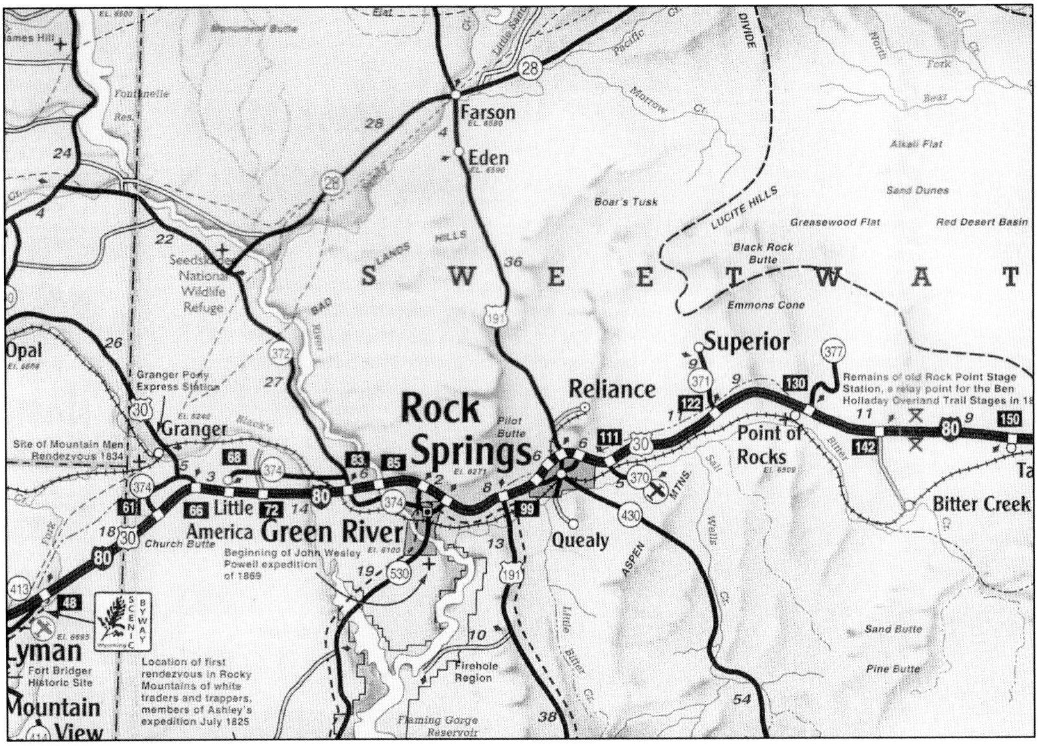

This map shows Rock Springs and surrounding communities. The area around Rock Springs is commonly known as the Red Desert. This high desert environment, together with the corridor across the Rocky Mountains provided by the Great Divide Basin, strongly influenced the way Rock Springs and southern Wyoming developed. (Courtesy Wyoming Department of Transportation.)

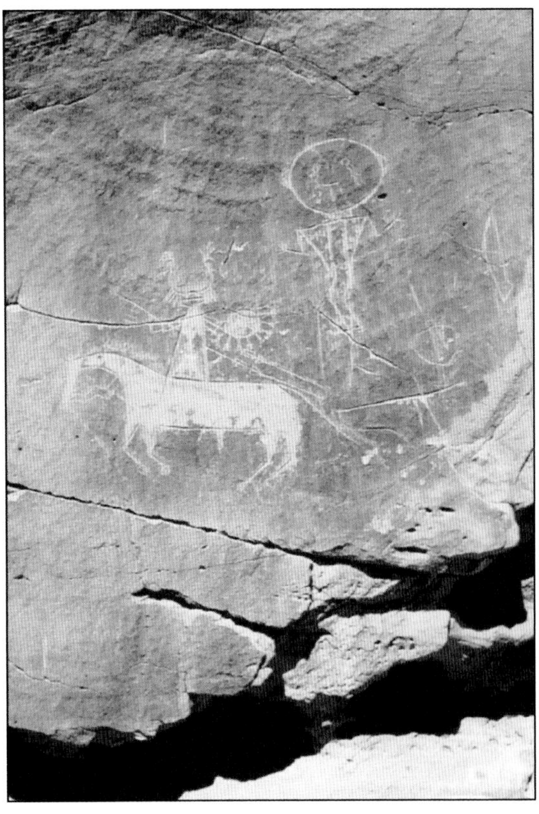

These drawings, called petroglyphs, made by Native Americans probably in the 18th century, are thought by some anthropologists to be representative of early horse trading and spirit beings of the Shoshone and Comanche cultures. These are but a few of many places where evidence of pre–Anglo American cultures is evident, representing over 10,000 years of occupation of the Red Desert region. (Courtesy Russel L. Tanner.)

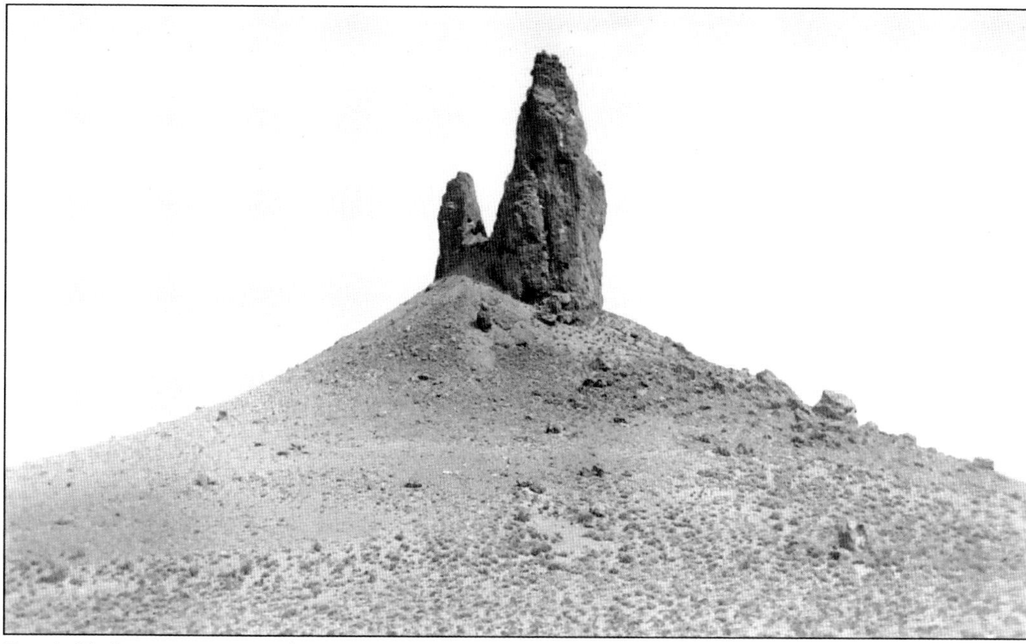

Boar's Tusk, an ancient volcanic tower, is a prominent landmark about 20 miles north of Rock Springs. This impressive landscape feature resulted three million years ago when igneous rock was forced upward through the Eocene lake sediments but never erupted onto the surface. In the intervening years, the lake sediments have weathered, primarily by wind erosion, to expose the ancient volcanic neck today called Boar's Tusk. (Courtesy SCHM.)

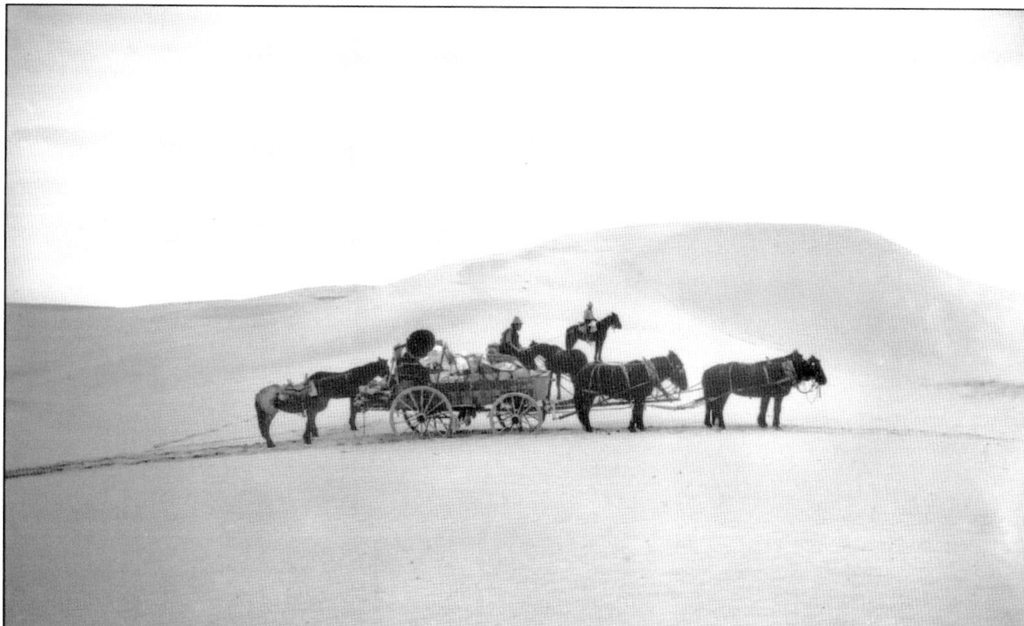

A freight wagon traverses the treacherous Killpecker Sand Dunes north of Rock Springs headed for the goldfields in the South Pass region. Heavily laden wagons sometimes became mired in the sand and had to be abandoned. Gold mining in the South Pass area has been a sporadic enterprise since 1868. (Courtesy SCHM.)

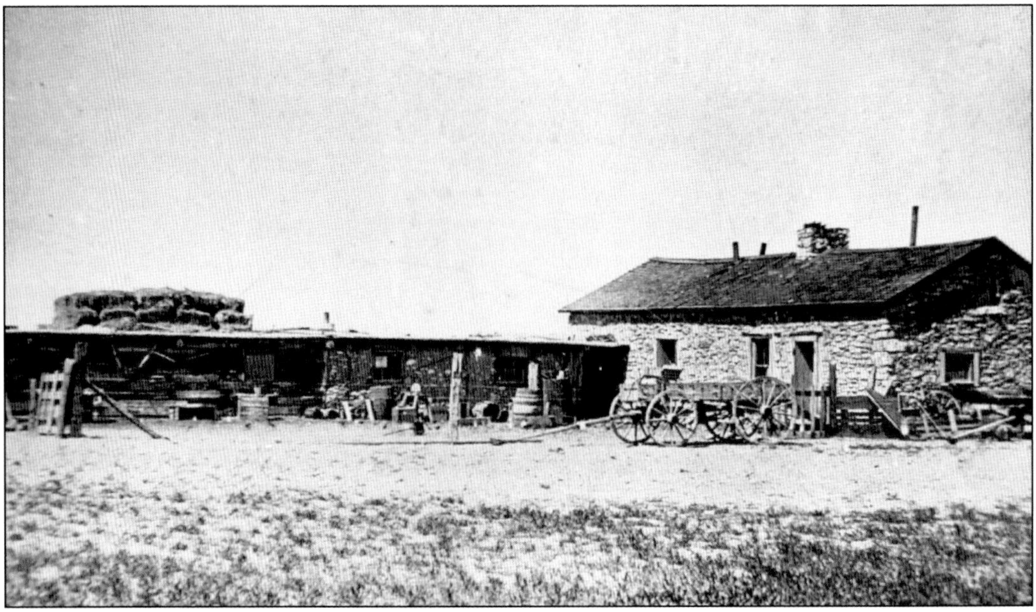

The Granger Stage Station, shown in this c. 1900 postcard, likely looks much like the Rock Springs Stage Station on Ben Holladay's Overland Stage line would have appeared. These small stone "stations" were constructed by Holladay's company in 1862 when the Overland stagecoach and mail operations were moved south from the main emigration trail corridor, which traversed South Pass about 100 miles to the north. (Courtesy the Russel L. Tanner family.)

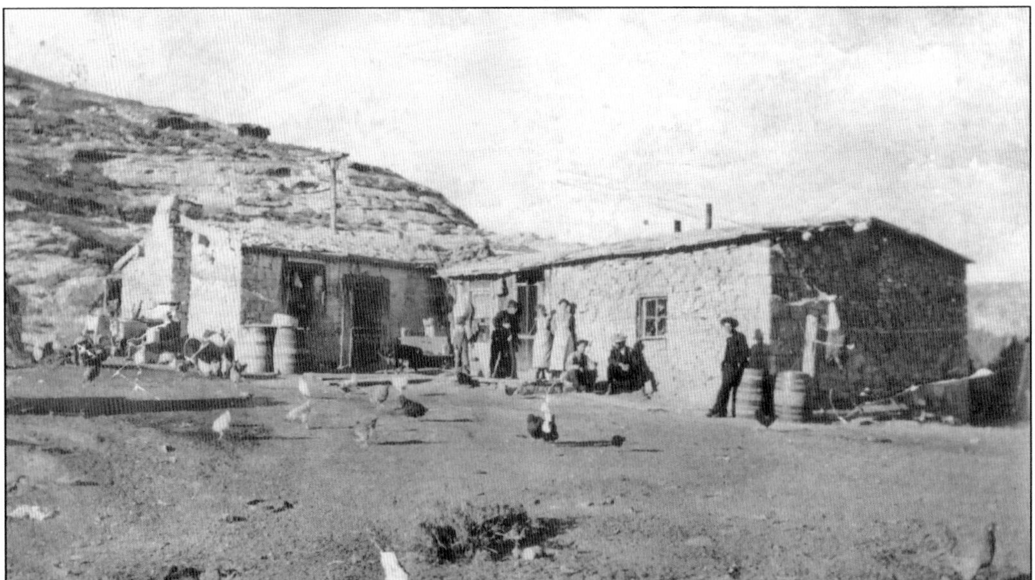

The Point of Rocks Stage Station, 24 miles east of Rock Springs, is what remains of one of Ben Holladay's Overland Stage stations. It also served as a connecting point between the Union Pacific Railroad and the gold mining towns in the South Pass area, via the Point of Rocks to South Pass Freight Road. Gold mining efforts along the Sweetwater River about 120 miles to the north went through a series of booms and busts between 1867 and the 1950s. South Pass City today is a state historic park. (Courtesy Wyoming State Archives.)

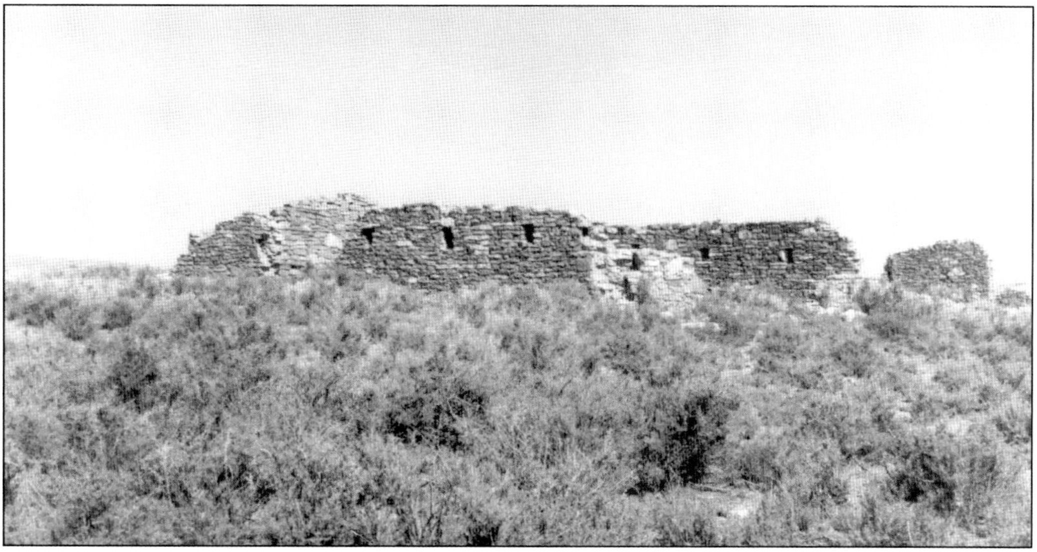

Midway between Fort Halleck and Fort Bridger, both official military posts, was situated Fort LaClede, shown here. There is no historical record of LaClede being an official military facility. However, troops under Col. Patrick Conner were sent to escort stagecoaches and freight wagons on Ben Holladay's Overland route during the Civil War. Fort LaClede seems to have been an enlarged stagecoaching station, likely given this strategic location. Only these ruins of the old "fort" remain today. (Courtesy Wyoming State Archives.)

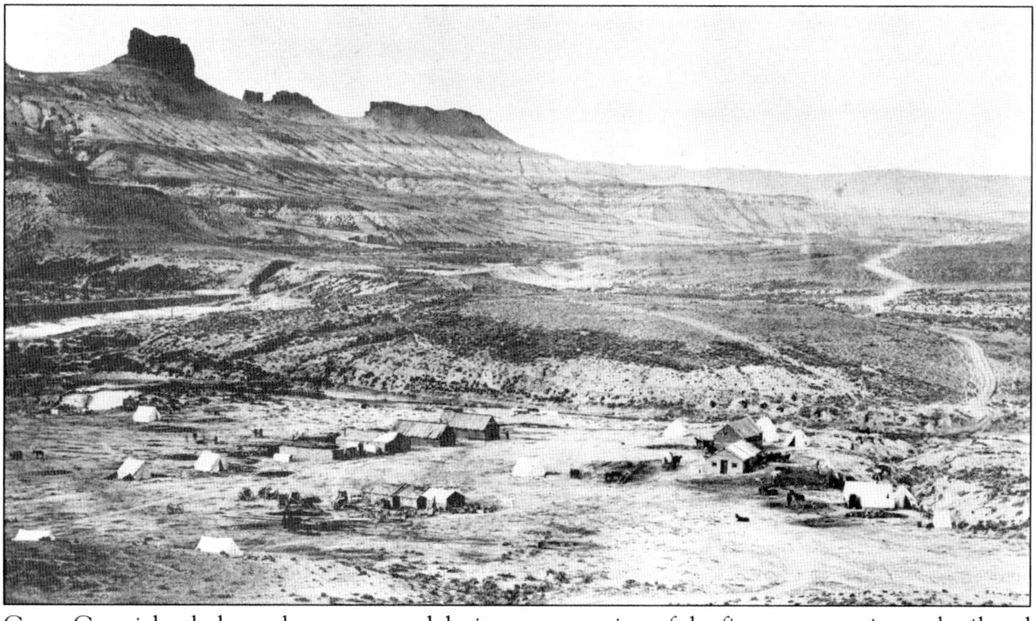

Camp Carmichael, shown here, operated during construction of the first transcontinental railroad during 1868. It served as the base of operations for preparation of the rail grade and cutting of several of the passages through hills, necessary to maintain a relatively level grade for the railroad. "Billy Buck" Tittsworth served as a meat hunter providing bison, mountain sheep, bear, and other wild meat served to construction workers at Camp Carmichael and wrote about the experience in a little journal called "Outskirts Episodes." (Courtesy American Heritage Center, University of Wyoming.)

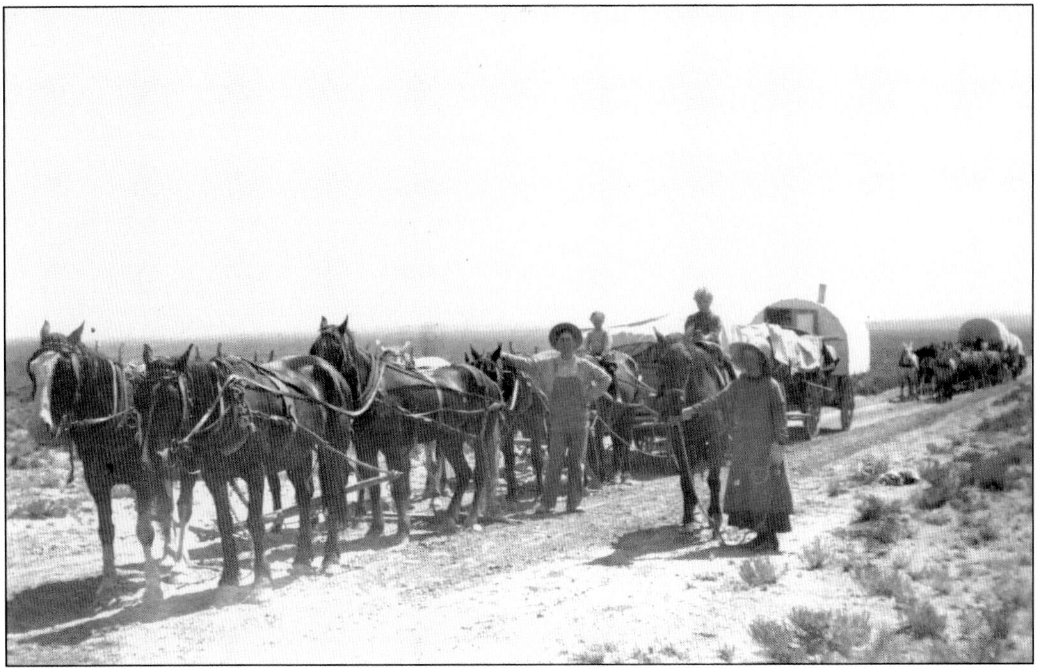

The emigration to the western United States that began in the 1840s actually never has ended. The diary of one ranch woman north of Rock Springs recalls a couple of families of emigrants camping on her ranch in 1916. This picture from the early 20th century shows several families making the trip west on one of the several trails through the Red Desert. (Courtesy SCHM.)

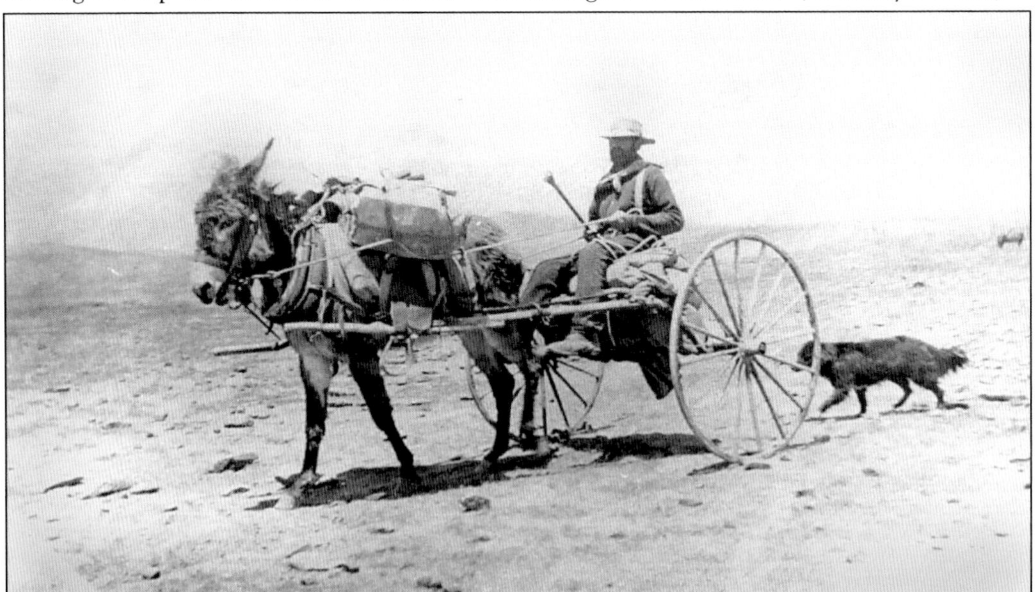

Sometimes a heavily laden burro pulling a small buggy would suffice to carry supplies to a remote sheepherder camp in the Red Desert. The camp tender, like the fellow shown here, would bring supplies to the herders who lived in a small wagon as they kept watch over flocks rotating between the desert winter range and summer forage in the Wind River Mountains or Uinta Mountains. (Courtesy SCHM.)

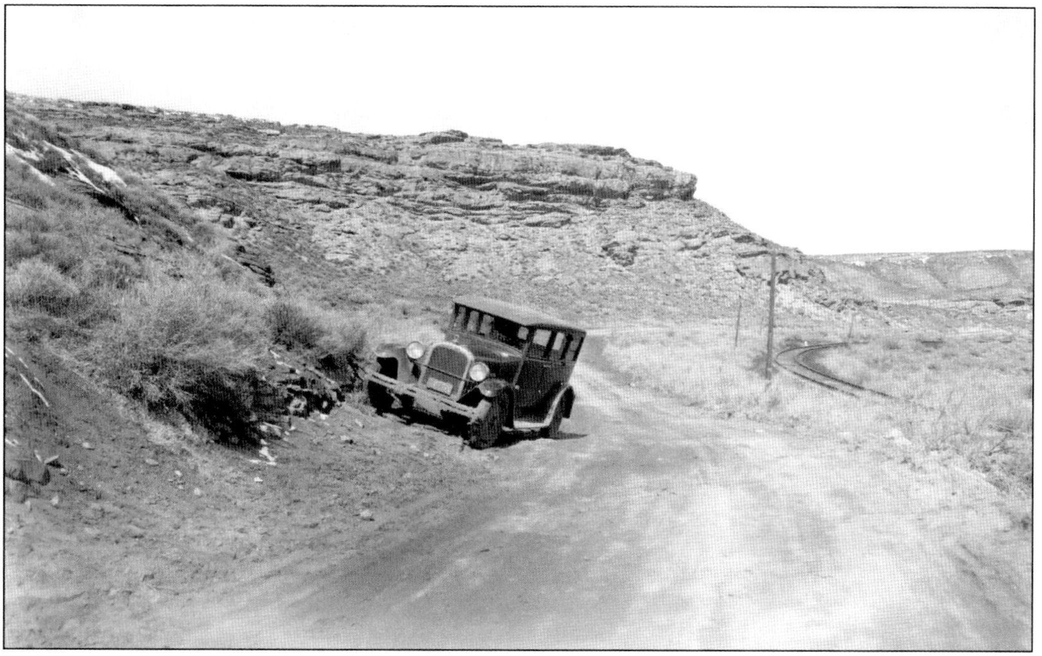

A 1920s-era Ford automobile is parked along the "flat bladed" road from the railroad section camp at Thayer to the mining area known as Superior several miles east of Rock Springs. This road is typical of thousands of miles of roads used by people in the West before asphalt paving was affordable for county governments. (Courtesy New Studio.)

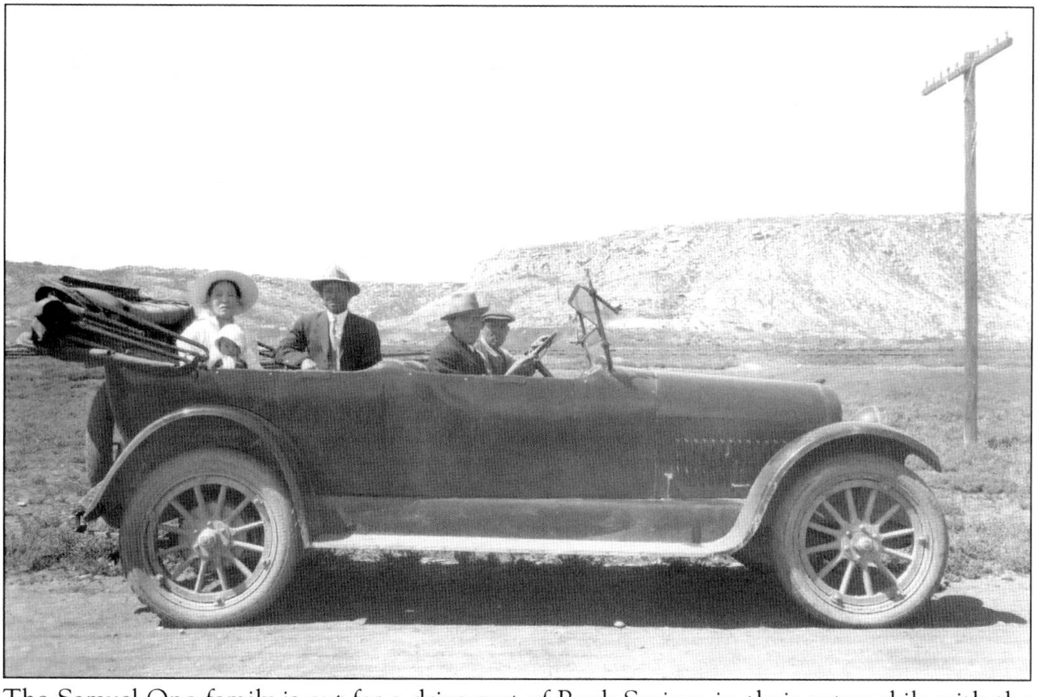

The Samuel Ono family is out for a drive east of Rock Springs in their automobile with the convertible top down in 1920. Ono was one of many Japanese American coal miners in the early 20th century. Daughter Yoko sits on her mother's lap. (Courtesy New Studio.)

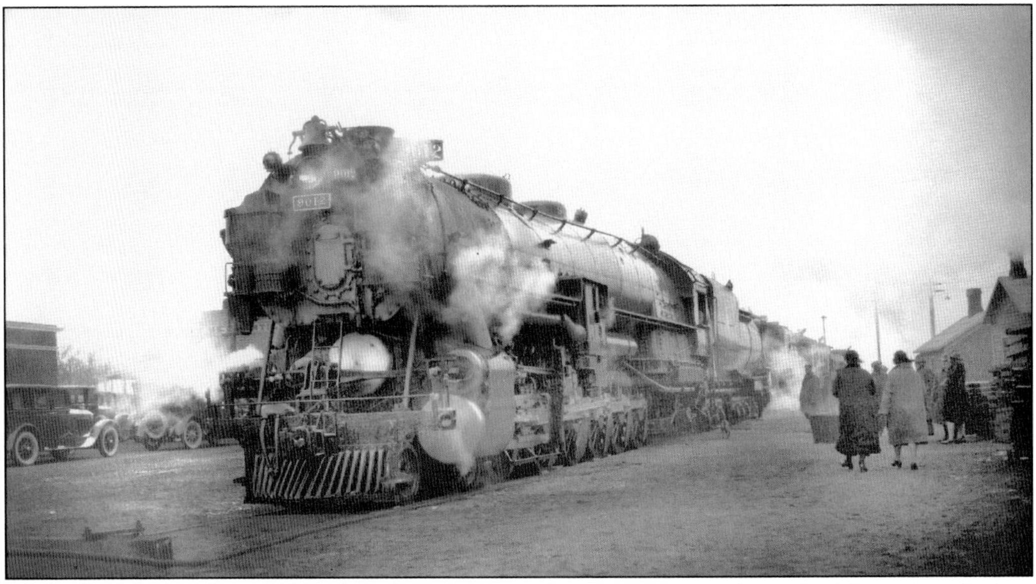

Union Pacific 9012 is typical of the huge steam engines operating along the Union Pacific line through Rock Springs. More importantly, the Rock Springs area provided more coal for Union Pacific than any of the company's other mining regions. Rock Springs coal was known across the country for its high British Thermal Unit (BTU) and high carbon content, ideal for many industrial uses. (Courtesy New Studio.)

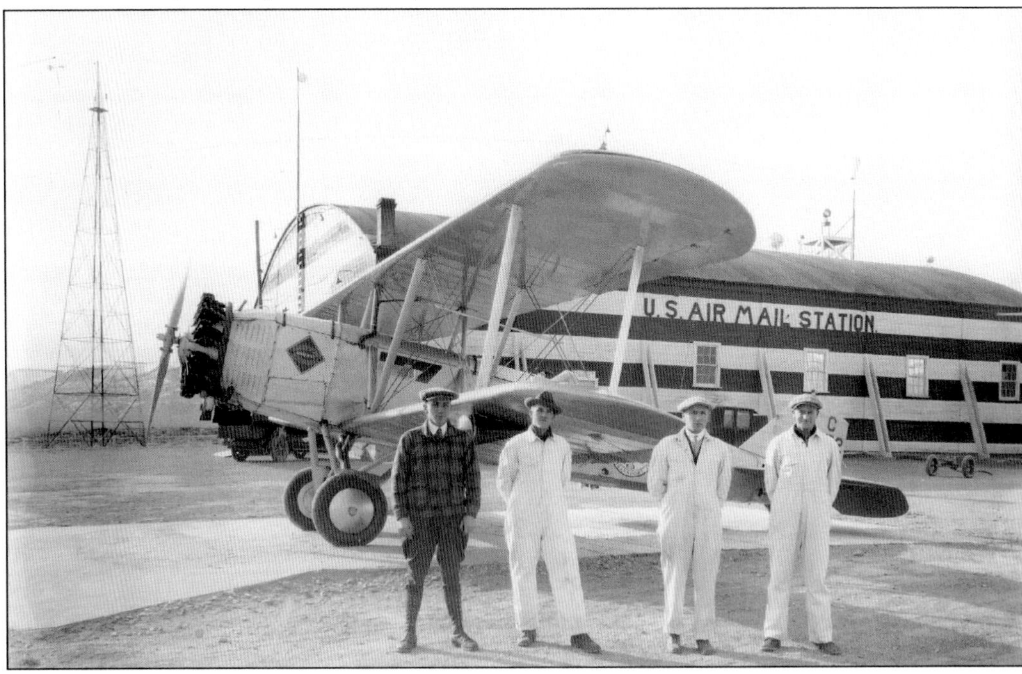

The U.S. Air Mail Service used Boeing 40A planes like the one shown here to carry mail across the country. Rock Springs was a major stop along the transcontinental route from the late 1920s through the 1930s. An unidentified air mail official (left) is shown with, from left to right, mechanics Raymond Aho, Frank Garnick, and Nitzi Garnick, all wearing white coveralls. (Courtesy New Studio.)

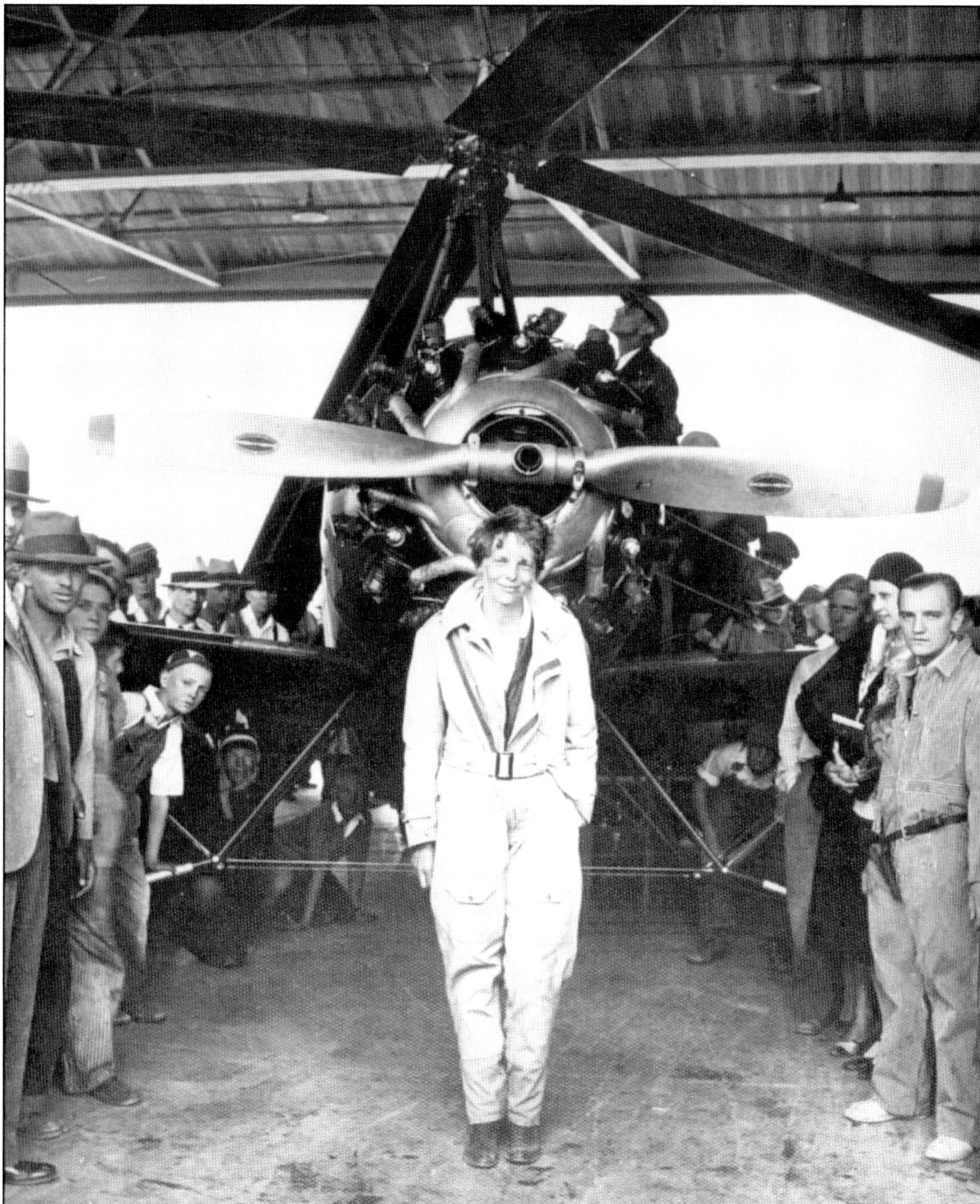

Famed aviator Amelia Earhart landed at Rock Springs Air Mail station at 1:30 p.m. on June 4, 1931, during the Beech-Nut Transcontinental Tour. She was flying an autogiro, sort of an airplane-helicopter hybrid. The female pilot attracted a large crowd of fans at the airport. (Courtesy New Studio.)

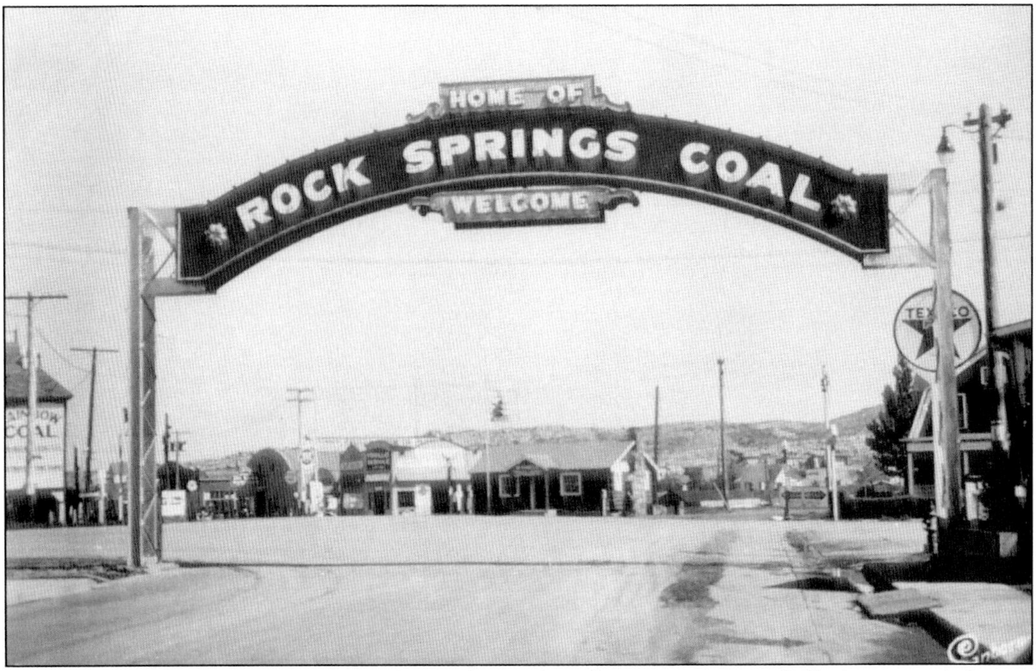

The omnipresent Rock Springs Coal sign, located at the intersection of Elk Street and Center Street, welcomes travelers along U.S. Highway 30, a precursor of Interstate Highway 80. Note Rainbow Coal, at left, which was the last coal tipple standing in Rock Springs until it was torn down in the early 1960s. The sign was later restored back near its original location on C Street. (Courtesy New Studio.)

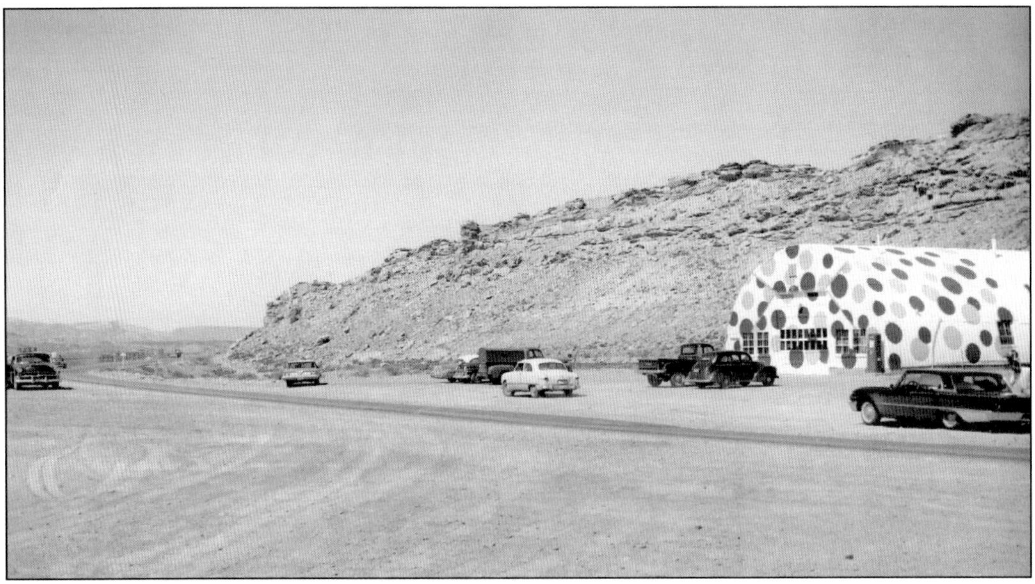

Until the population boom of the 1970s, the Wonder Bread warehouse marked the west edge of Rock Springs. The balloon-festooned Quonset-style garage is still there on Dewar Drive, but the city has expanded well beyond this point. Dewar Drive is the original route of U.S. Highway 30, part of the transportation corridor that now includes Interstate Highway 80, arguably the busiest highway across the United States. (Courtesy New Studio.)

Two

WEALTH FROM THE EARTH

MINING AND RANCHING

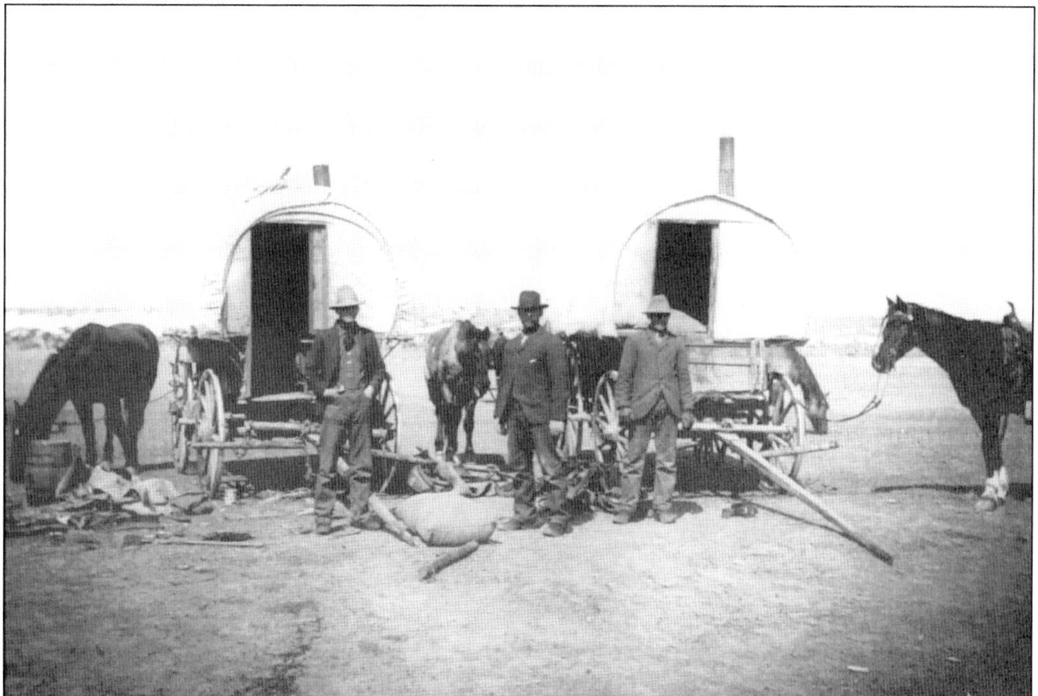

Usually called "sheepcamps," these canvas-topped wagons provided cooking and sleeping quarters for both cattle and sheep tenders on the harsh Wyoming plains. Although cattle raising was successful some of the time, the Red Desert area proved to be ideal winter range for sheep. These herders with O. C. Papworth's outfit might have been called "stockmen," indicating their employment at various times herding either sheep or cattle. Although there was animosity between sheep and cattle ranchers in nearby areas, eventually many larger ranch operations raised both in order to increase their potential for financial success. (Courtesy SCHM.)

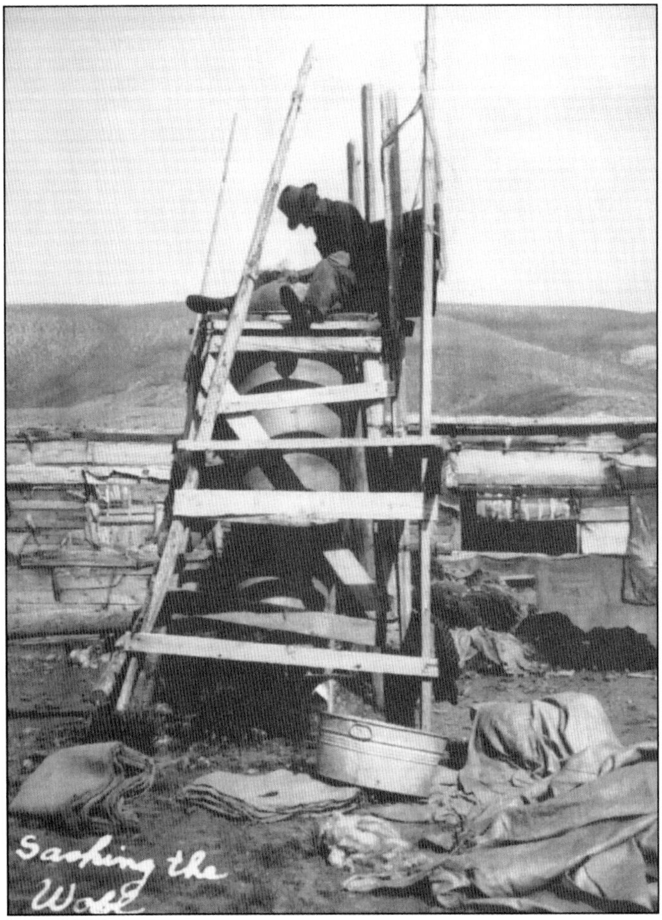

A worker is shown soaking wool. Wool freshly shorn from range sheep is quite dirty with suint (perspiration) and infested with all manner of insects. Oftentimes the price received for wool could be increased by soaking the wool in lye soap to clean it and to remove some of the natural lanolin that gave the wool a greasy appearance and feel. (Courtesy SCHM.)

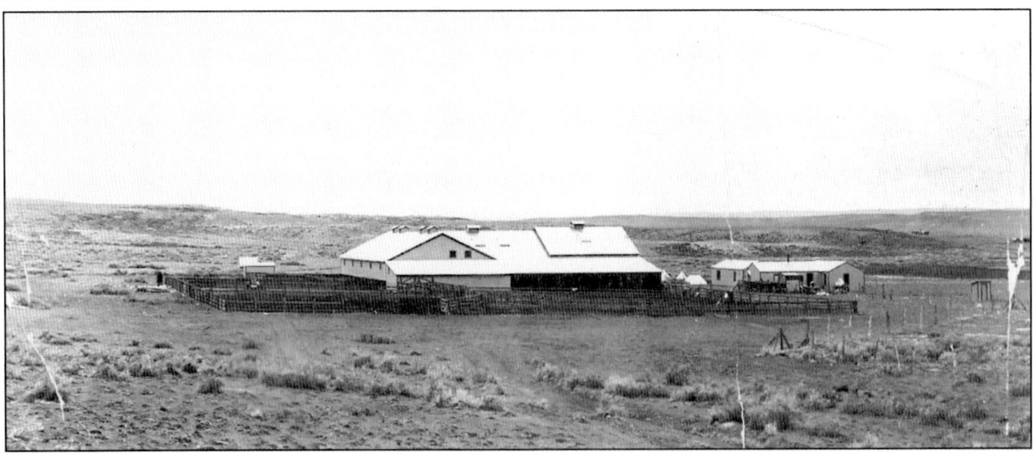

The size of the *c.* 1915 Boyer Sheep Ranch shearing facility indicated the importance of sheep grazing in southwestern Wyoming. At this facility in 1918, some 89,000 sheep were shorn using what was called the Australian method, using an electric generator to power shearing machines. Unfortunately, a typical early spring snowstorm hit the area east of Rock Springs, and nearly all of the sheep shorn at the Boyer facility died, which quickly caused stockmen to reconsider their shearing schedules. (Courtesy the Boyer family and Western Archaeological Services.)

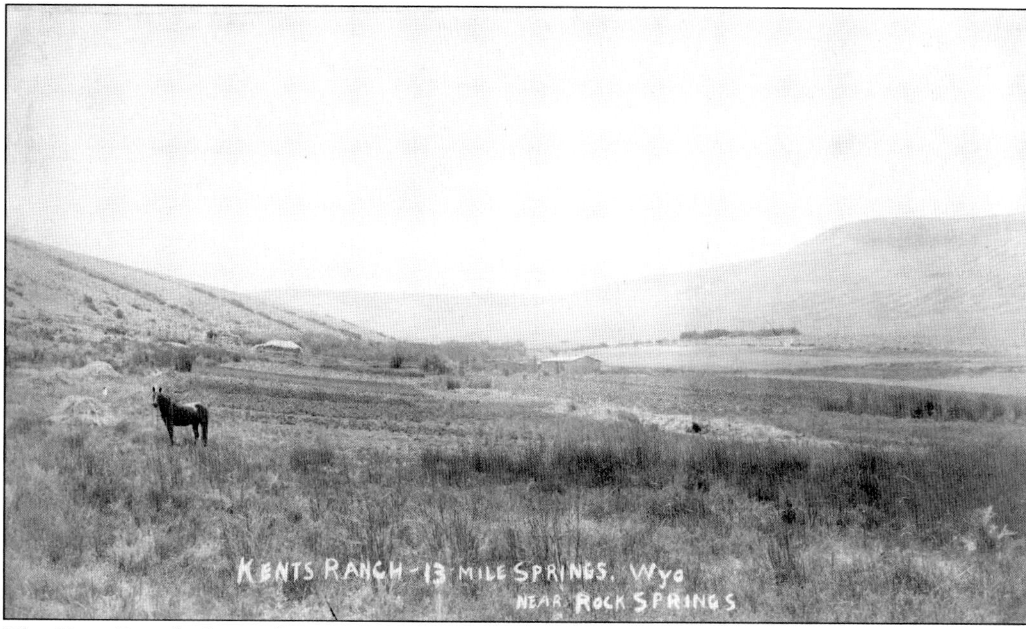

The Kent Ranch shown here was originally homesteaded and later became part of one of the large livestock operations that grazed both sheep and cattle on the open range of the Red Desert. Livestock raising and mining were the ways of making "wealth from the earth" in Wyoming. (Courtesy SCHM.)

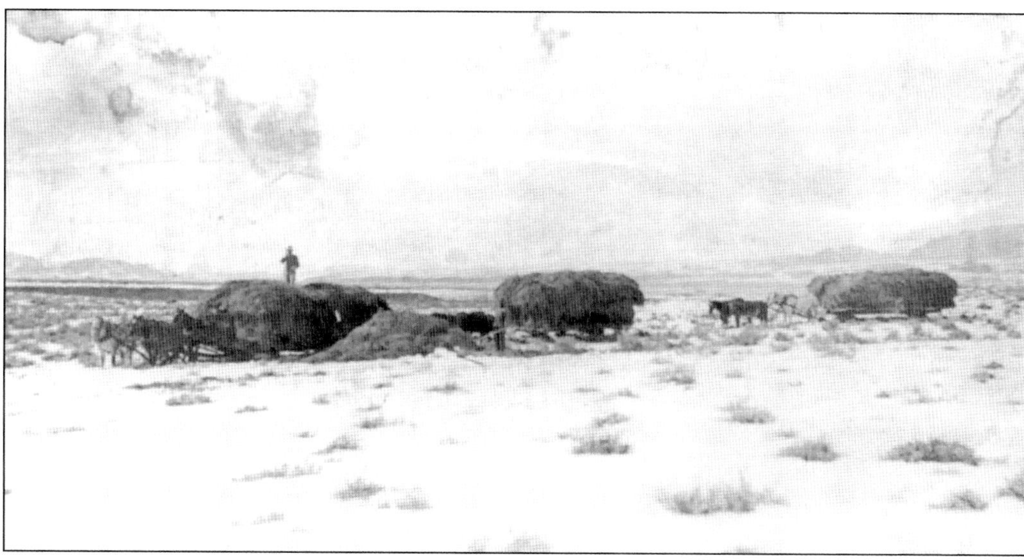

Local stockmen usually had to feed cattle in the wintertime. Hay was taken on wagons to cattle in pastures often far from ranch headquarters, as shown here. Sheep usually did not require any supplemental feed because they could forage on native grasses and forbs, thus making them a more attractive stock for ranching operations in this region. (Courtesy SCHM.)

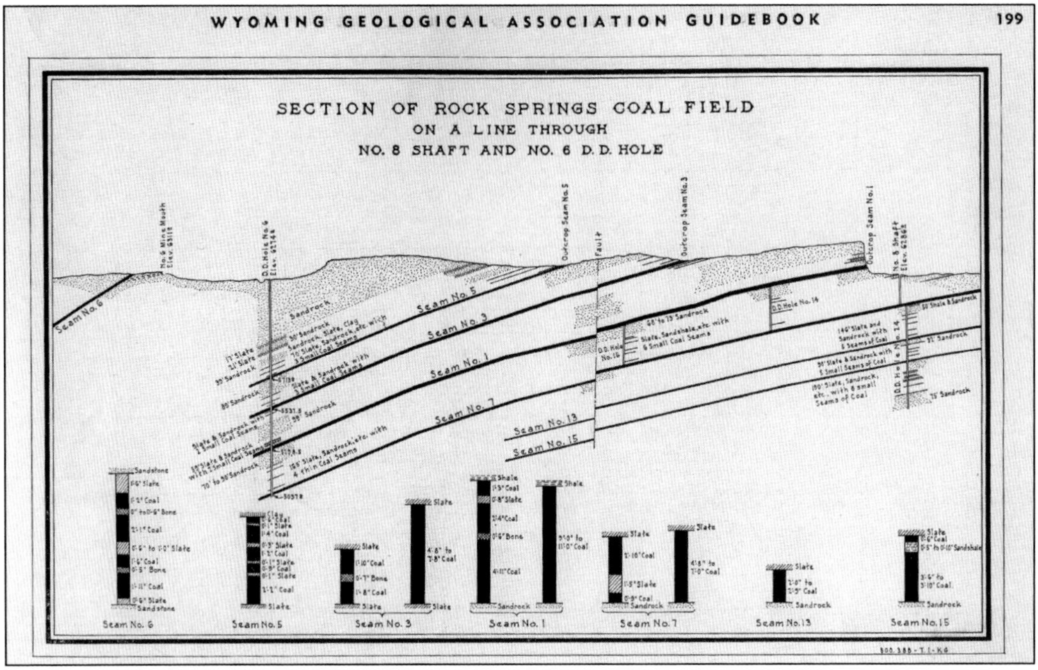

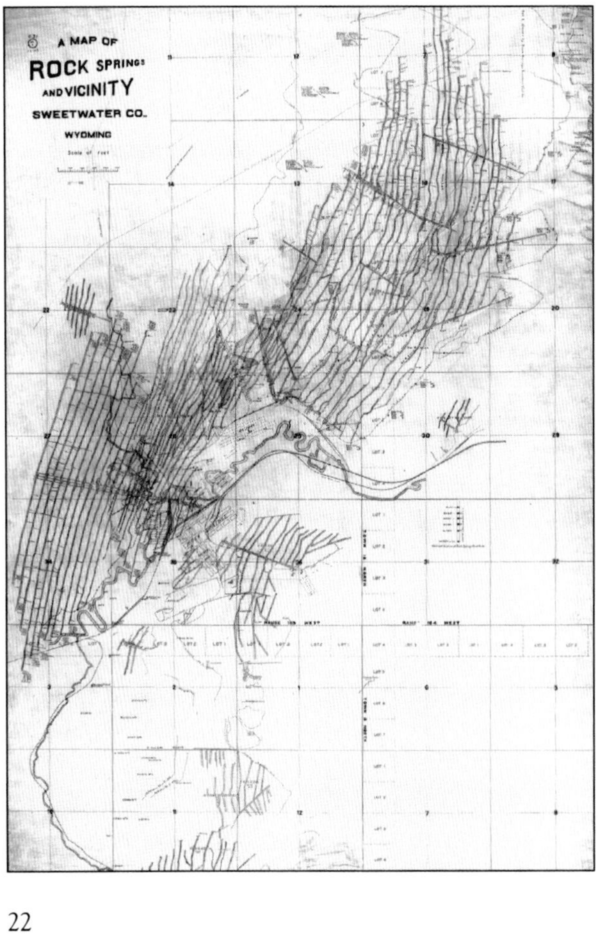

This diagram of the geological strata of the Rock Springs Uplift indicates the many seams of coal where mining could be productive. Over 20 mines tapped these seams with underground tunnels between 1870 and 1960; today large, open-pit mines are operated to access coal from even deeper seams.

This map of coal mine tunnels in Rock Springs and the vicinity dates to about 1930. The central downtown Rock Springs area is shown just left of the center of the map. Eventually almost all of the town would be undermined, and remedial methods are still being implemented to prevent old mine drifts from collapsing and placing businesses and residences in peril. The Abandoned Mine Lands program funded by coal taxes has benefitted Rock Springs in this regard. (Courtesy New Studio.)

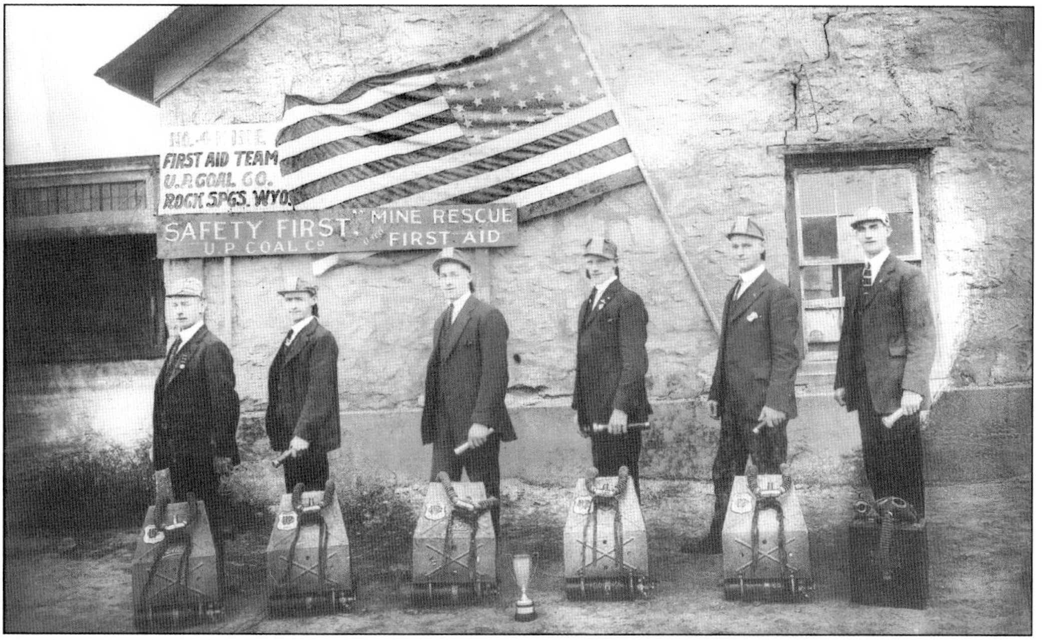

Coal mining has always been dangerous work. Mine rescue and first aid teams were trained by mine companies and labor unions to assist in times of mine disasters. This team from the Number Four Mine, seen here with their emergency air-supply packs, won the competition among Union Pacific Coal Company mines and was awarded the trophy, shown between the third and fourth rescue team members from the left. (Courtesy New Studio.)

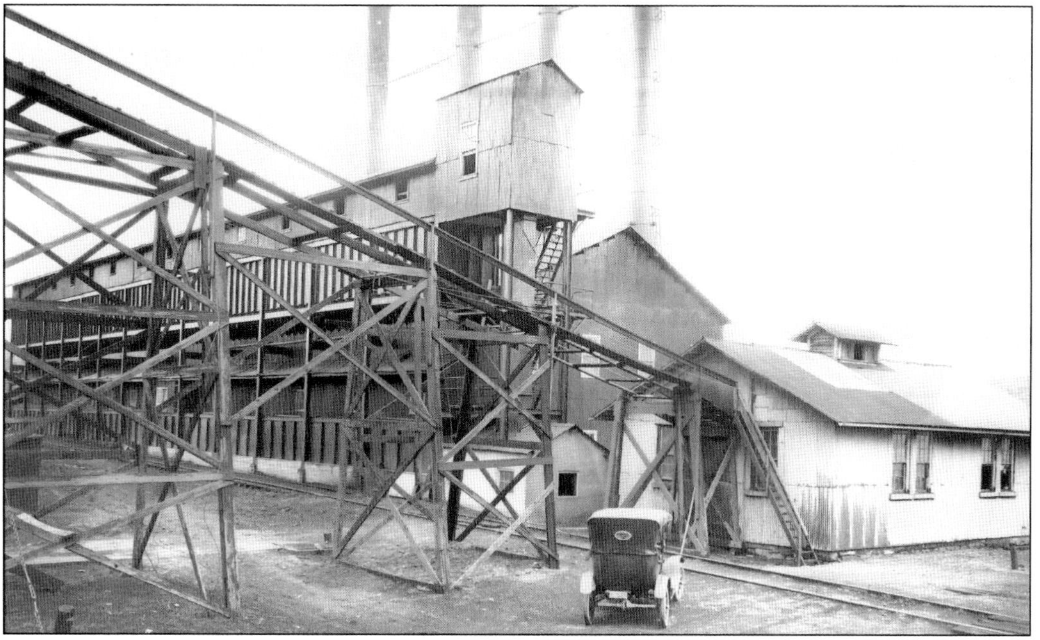

By the 1910s, electricity was generated by the Union Pacific Boiler Plant. The boilers are shown here next to the mine tipple; the tipple supplied coal to power the boilers that generated electrical power to run mining equipment. The steam plant was located in what is now eastern Rock Springs. (Courtesy WWCC UPCC Archive.)

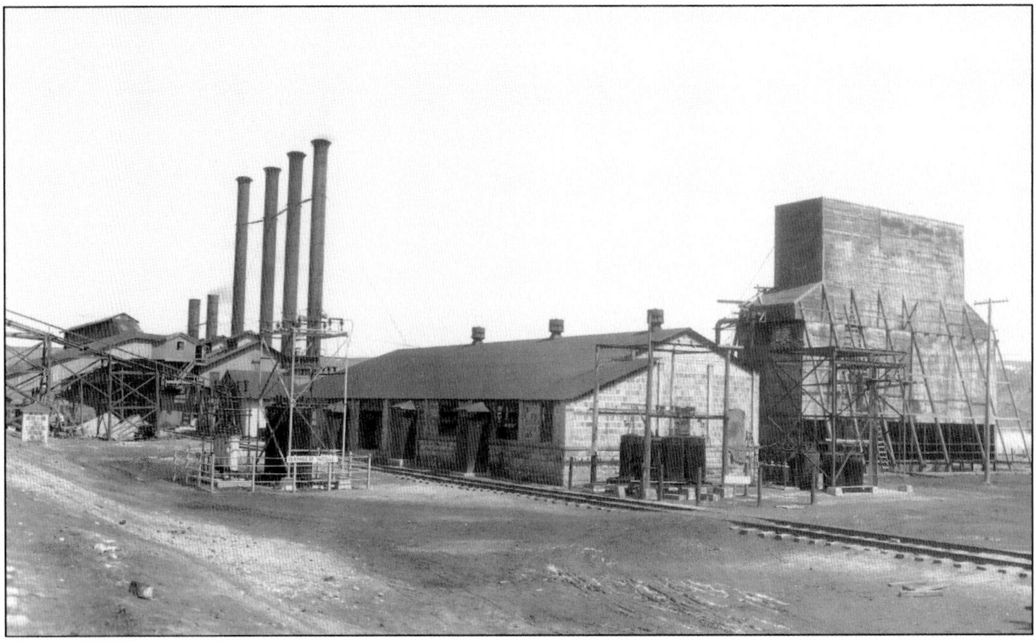

This view of the steam plant shows the maintenance facility and cooling towers to the right. Cooling towers are like giant radiators used to cool boiler water so it could be recycled. Since water had to be pumped to Rock Springs nearly 20 miles from the Green River, water conservation was an early concern. (Courtesy WWCC UPCC Archive.)

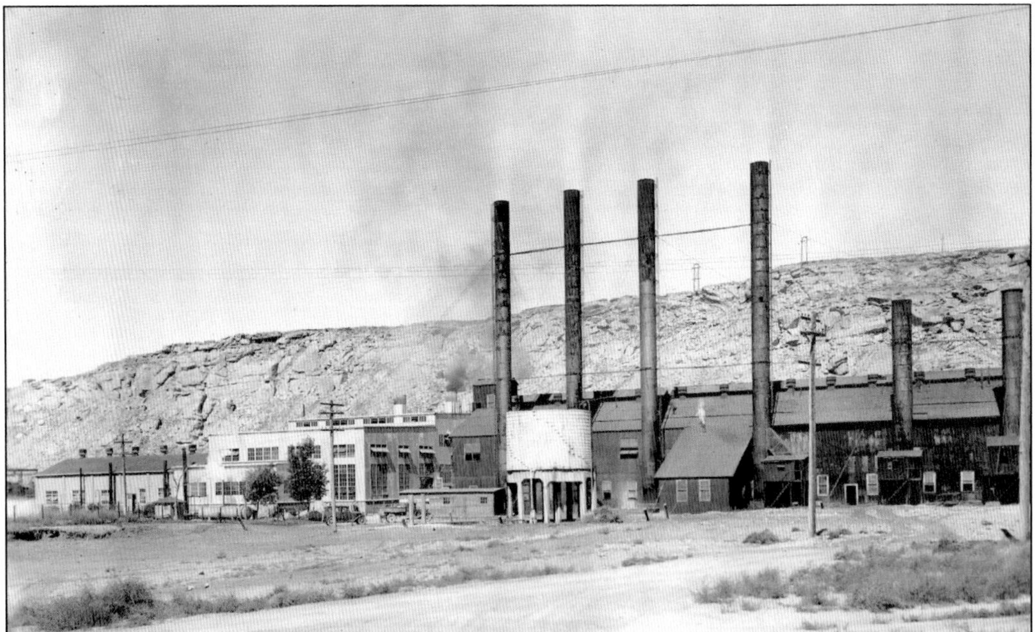

Electricity was generated for residential use as well as for mine equipment. The old power plant was torn down in the 1970s, although the boilers, where the smoke stacks are in the center of the photograph, were removed long ago when Rock Springs was added to the electrical power grid serving the western United States. (Courtesy WWCC UPCC Archive.)

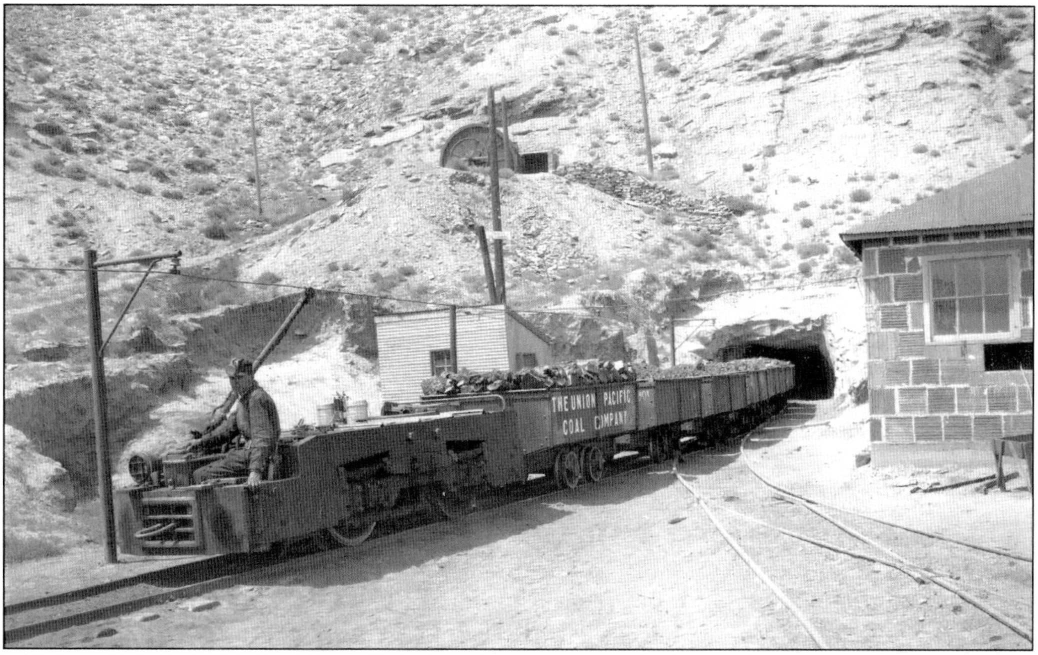

The ore train shown in this photograph was one of many that carried coal from deep within the mines to tipple facilities, where it was processed for shipment or for local use. The power plant generated electricity to power these electric trains as well as other mining equipment. Earlier ore carts had been pulled from the mines by horses and mules. (Courtesy WWCC UPCC Archive.)

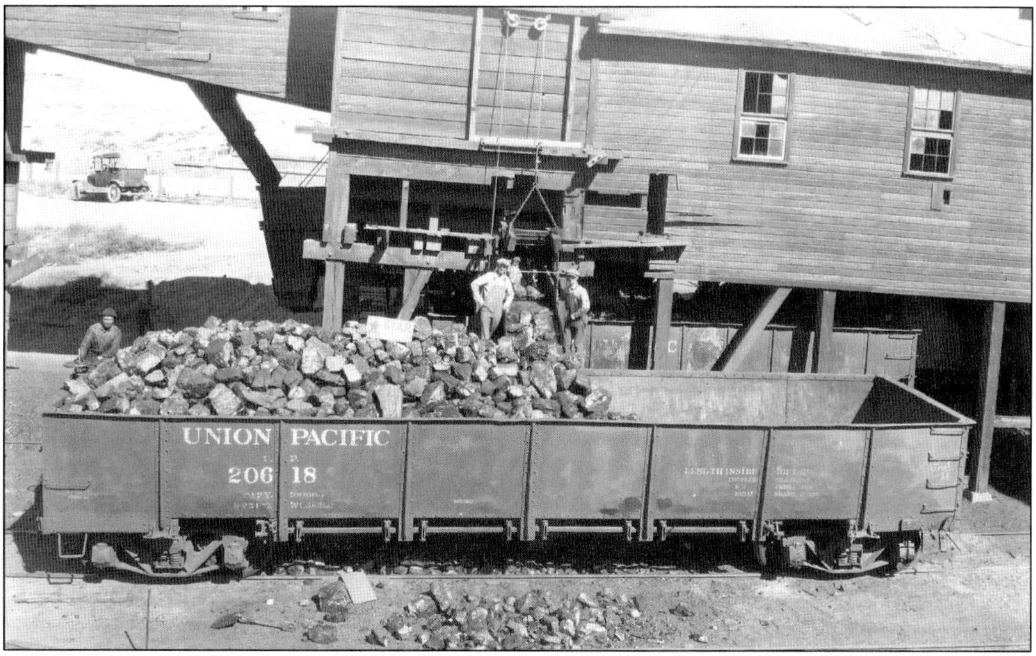

A Union Pacific Railroad coal car is being loaded with Rock Springs coal for shipment across the nation to run railroads, factories, and electrical generating plants across the nation. The Rock Springs area was arguably the largest coal-producing region in the western United States in the early 20th century. (Courtesy WWCC UPCC Archive.)

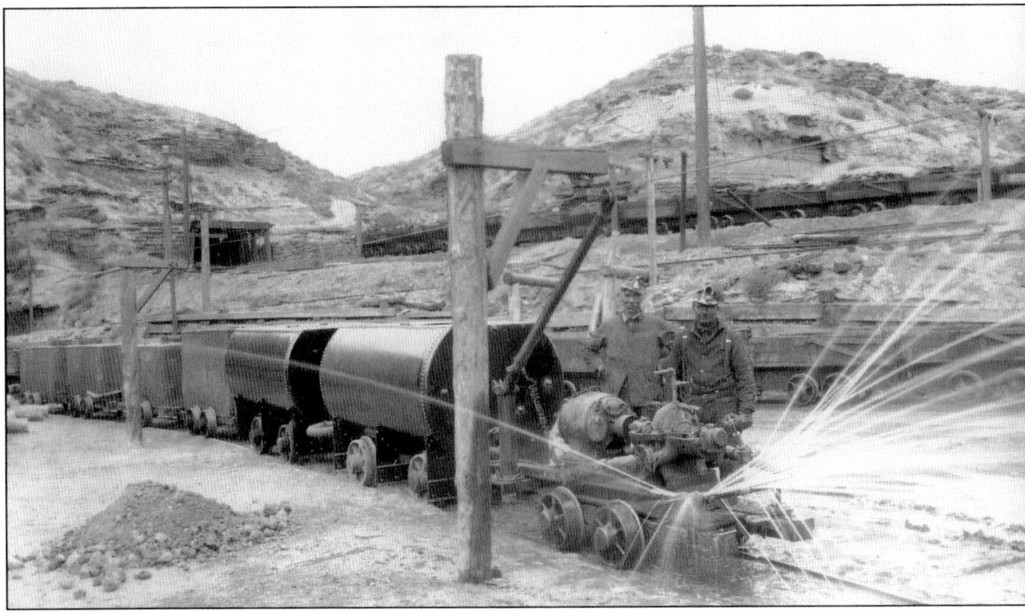

Water sprayers, like the one shown here, were used to keep down dust in the coal mines. Coal dust in confined areas could be extremely explosive, posing a significant danger to miners and mine operations. Coal dust was also deleterious to miners' health, causing a respiratory disease known as black lung, which afflicted numerous miners. Sprayers like this were only marginally effective in preventing miners from having to breathe coal dust. (Courtesy WWCC UPCC Archive.)

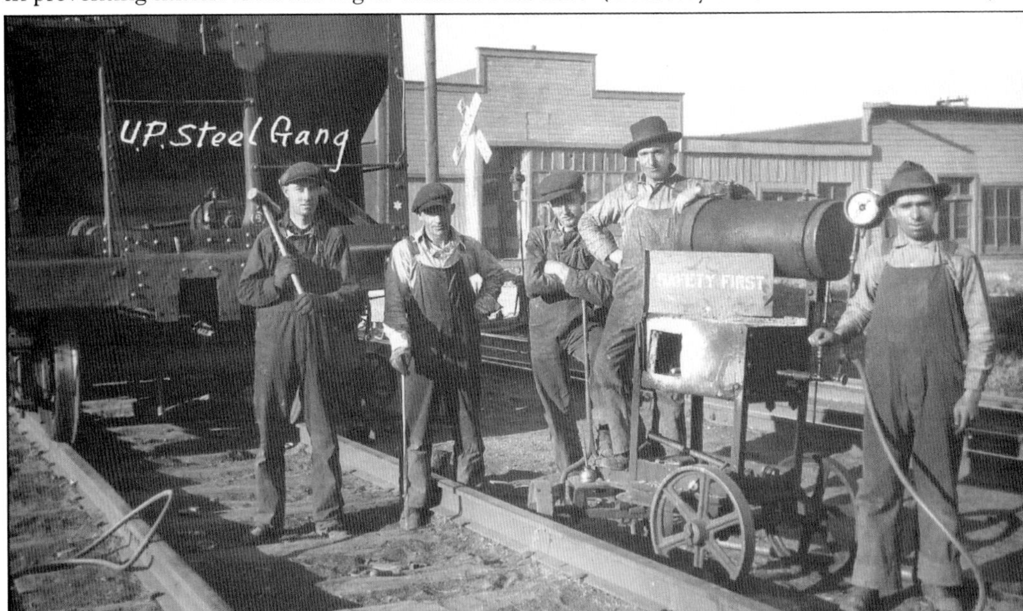

Once coal was mined from the ground, transportation of the vital fuel became the province of the Union Pacific Railroad. This crew of workers was called a "steel gang" because it was their job to lay the steel rails on which trains ran. Rails were nailed with spikes to wooden ties placed on a prepared bed of well-tamped gravel to facilitate a level grade capable of supporting the vast weight of railroad cars loaded with coal. (Courtesy New Studio.)

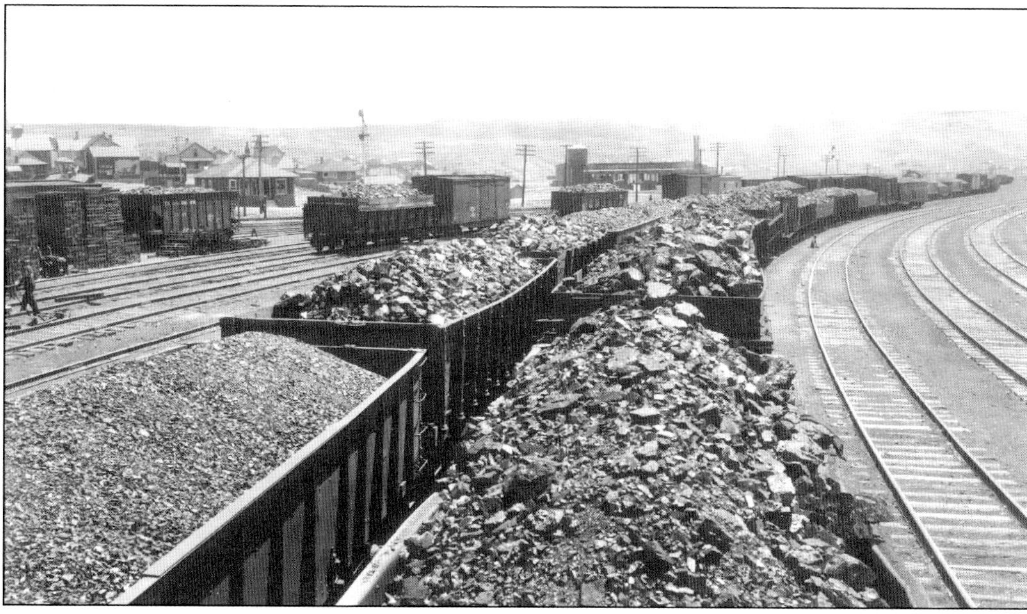

Huge trains of coal cars like those shown here carried coal across the nation. These cars each held upwards of 100,000 pounds, or 50 tons, of coal. From 1875 to 1930, mines in the Rock Springs area produced more coal than any other mining region where the Union Pacific Coal Company operated. UP Coal had mines elsewhere in Wyoming, Utah, Colorado, and Washington state. (Courtesy WWCC UPCC Archive.)

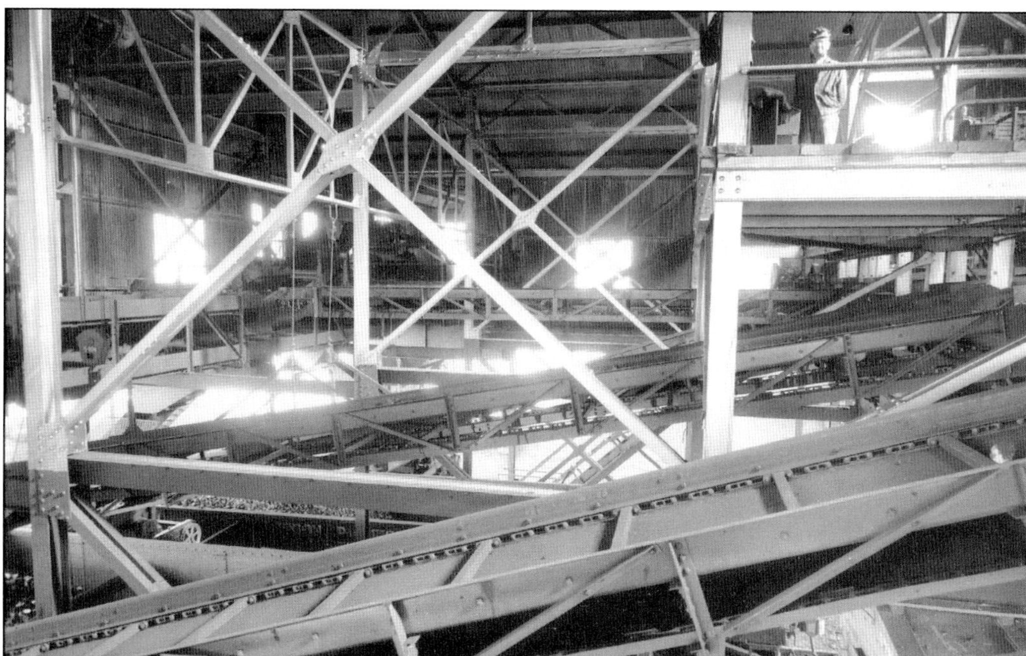

Each mine had a tipple where coal was screened according to size and where slate and other impurities (called "bony") were removed before the coal was loaded into railroad cars. For over 50 years, Rock Springs mines produced between 500,000 and one million tons of coal. (Courtesy WWCC UPCC Archive.)

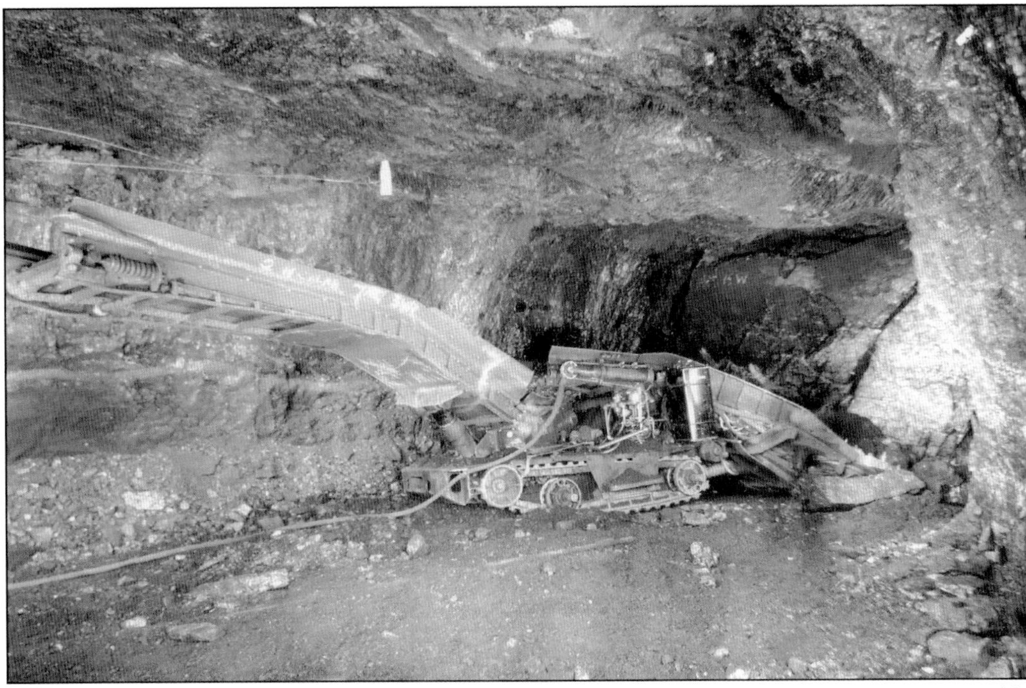

This equipment, called a loader, was manufactured by the Joy Mining Equipment Company. It is like a large funnel attached to a conveyor to move coal from a block that had been fractured by blasting and put it into a mine car to be hauled to the surface. (Courtesy WWCC UPCC Archive.)

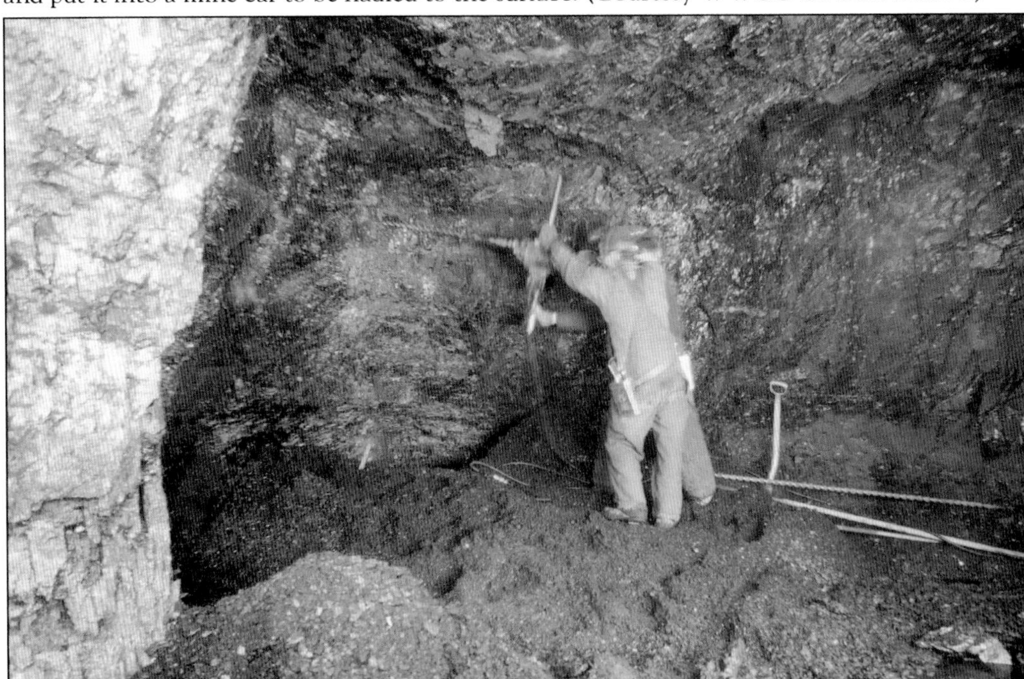

The miner shown here is drilling holes into the coal seam so explosives can be placed to fracture a large block of coal, which would then be loaded and transported to the surface. Drilling and blasting were jobs requiring extreme skill on the part of miners. (Courtesy WWCC UPCC Archive.)

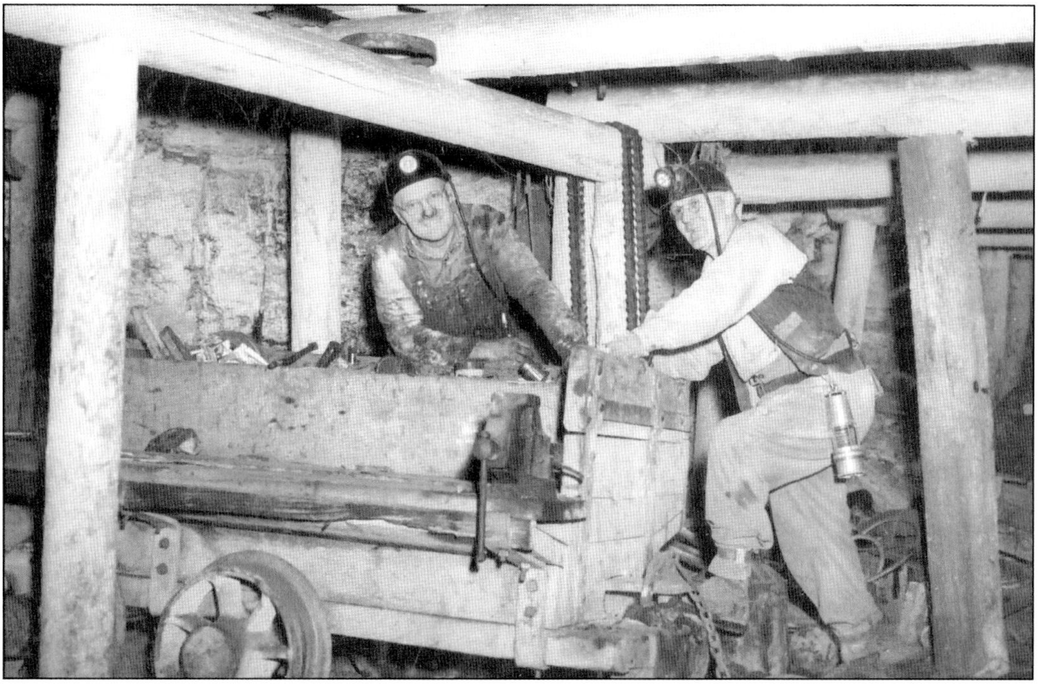

Mine foreman James Law (left) and miner Dominic Coletti pose with a mine car loaded with equipment. Note the mine shoring above the miners and the carbide lamps worn on their helmets. (Courtesy WWCC UPCC Archive.)

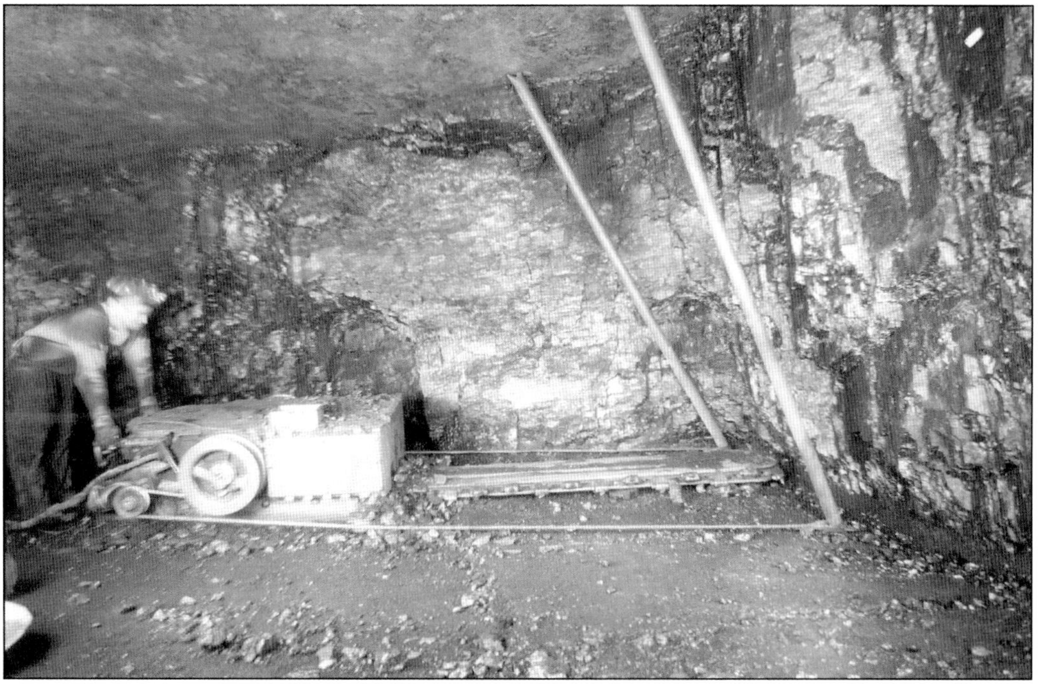

This miner is using a cutter, which is like a large chain saw, to undercut the coal seam in preparation for blasting, which would fracture the huge block of coal so it could be removed. (Courtesy WWCC UPCC Archive.)

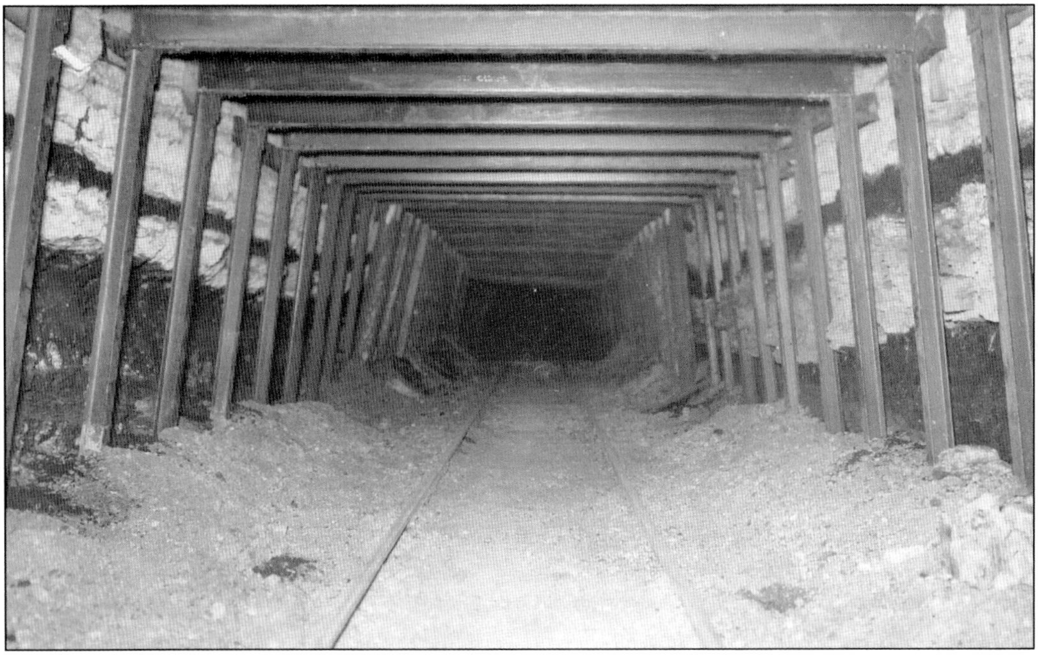

This picture shows the mine tramway at the Winton mine north of Rock Springs. The tramway had to be well supported with steel beams because it was the main tunnel through which coal was removed from the mine. (Courtesy WWCC UPCC Archive.)

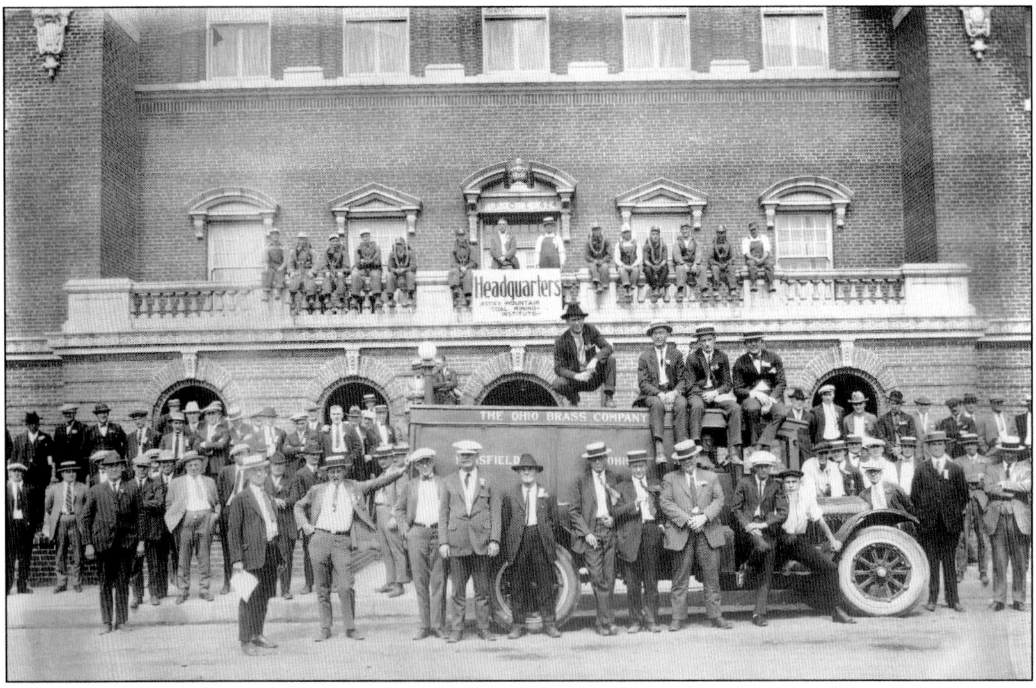

The large industrial operations in and around Rock Springs have always attracted numerous support businesses. This photograph is of the Rocky Mountain Coal Mining Institute meeting at the Elks Building in Rock Springs in the late 1920s. The truck carried brass fittings and piping supplies from the Ohio Brass Company, a major vendor of mining equipment. (Courtesy New Studio.)

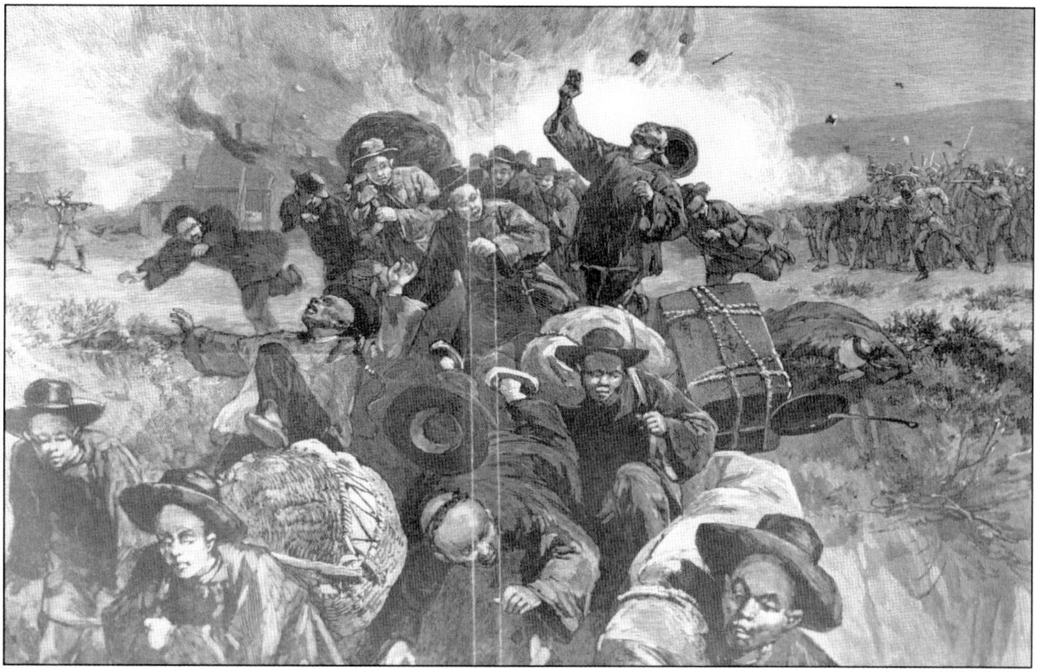

Perhaps the darkest day in Rock Springs history occurred on September 2, 1885, when white miners attacked the community of Chinese miners in the culmination of a labor dispute. Before the fracas was over, many Chinese had been killed—some accounts say 28, others as many as 40—and the Chinese village of some 80 cabins had been burned. The Chinese were driven into the Wyoming desert. This illustration from *Harper's* magazine supposedly shows the chaos of what came to be known as the Rock Springs Massacre. (Courtesy American Heritage Center, University of Wyoming.)

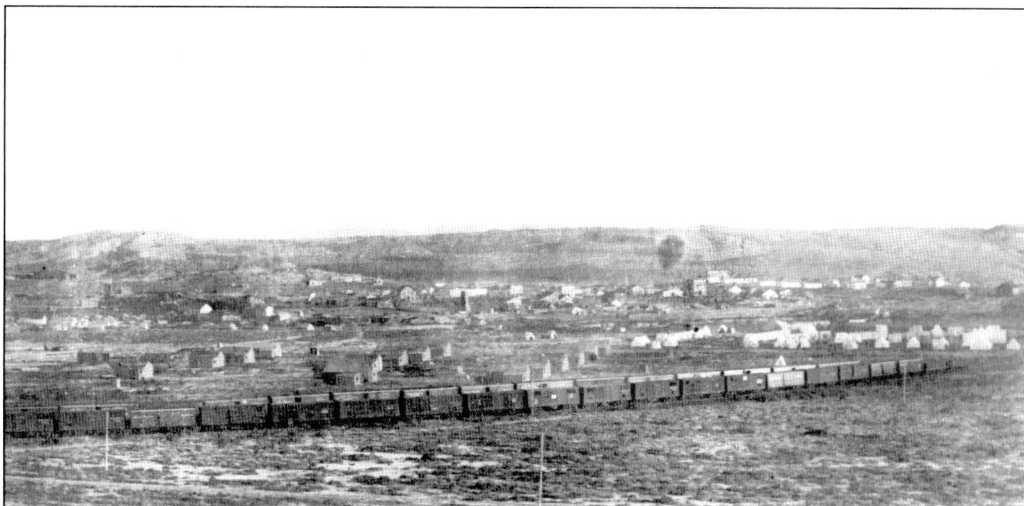

Coal company officials requested intervention from Wyoming governor Francis E. Warren, and soon U.S. Army troops were detached to Rock Springs. The army encampment known as Camp Pilot Butte stayed in Rock Springs until 1911 to ensure the safety of Chinese miners and to protect coal company assets. The importance of coal to the U.S. economy may be indicated by this use of federal soldiers. (Courtesy New Studio.)

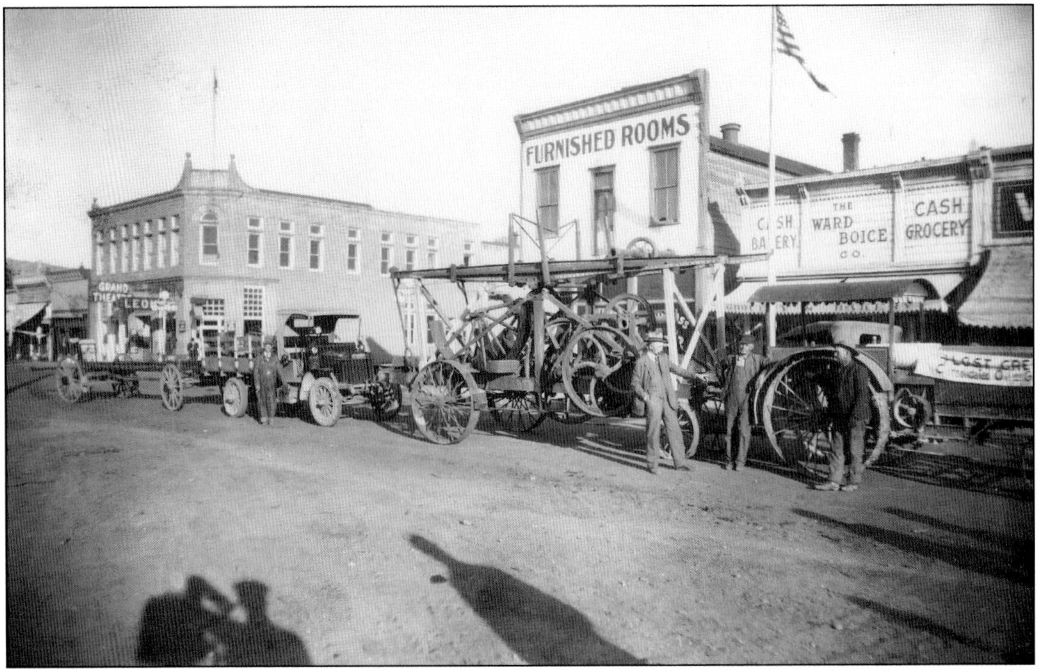

The early 20th century saw a new source of wealth from the earth being exploited in the Rocky Mountain west. This c. 1915 photograph shows one of the first "pump jacks" installed in the region being transported to newly developing oil fields near Rock Springs. Eventually oil and natural gas production would become a significant part of the region's economy. (Courtesy New Studio.)

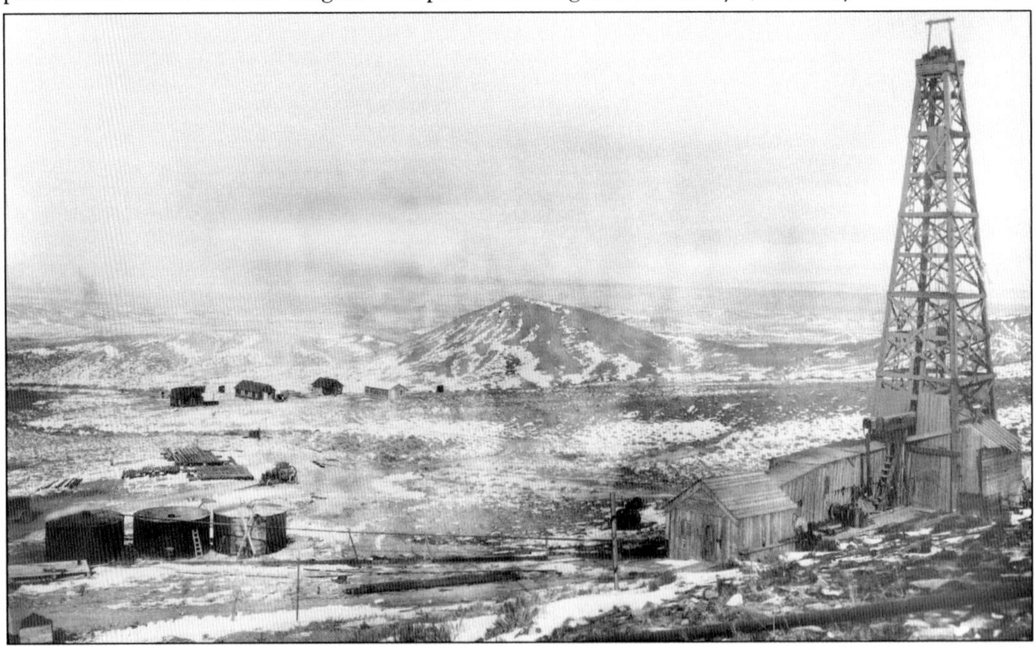

The 1920s saw oil discoveries at various locations: South Baxter Basin and Powder Wash south of Rock Springs. A Utah Oil Refining Company well shown here uses a pump like that shown above to hoist oil from deep underground reservoirs for transport to refineries being built in the Salt Lake City area. (Courtesy New Studio.)

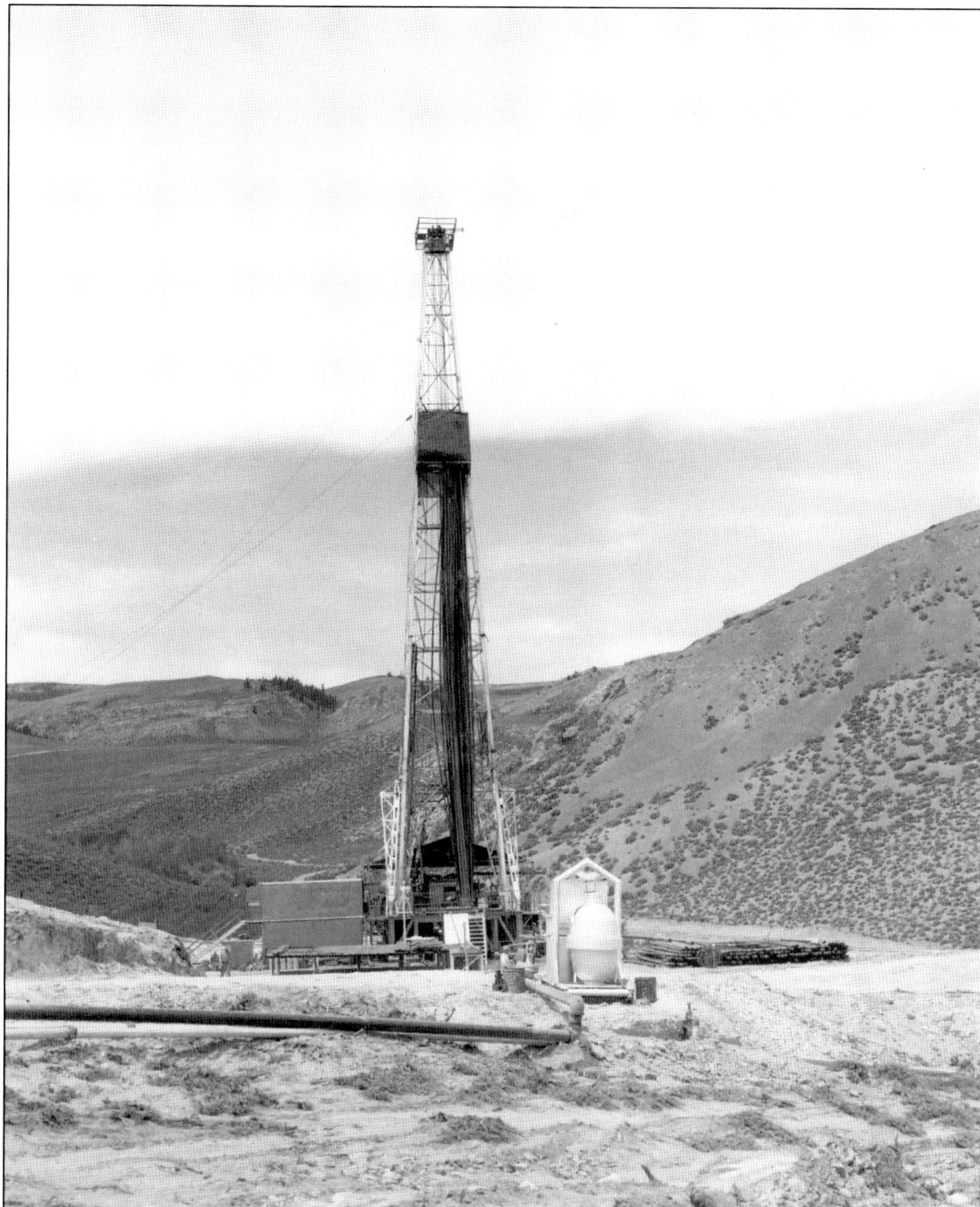

While oil production has been an important part of the Rock Springs economy for over 100 years, natural gas produced from the deep geological strata is the commodity that breathed new life into the minerals industry of Wyoming beginning in the 1950s. This drill rig was operated by General Petroleum Corporation in 1957. (Courtesy New Studio.)

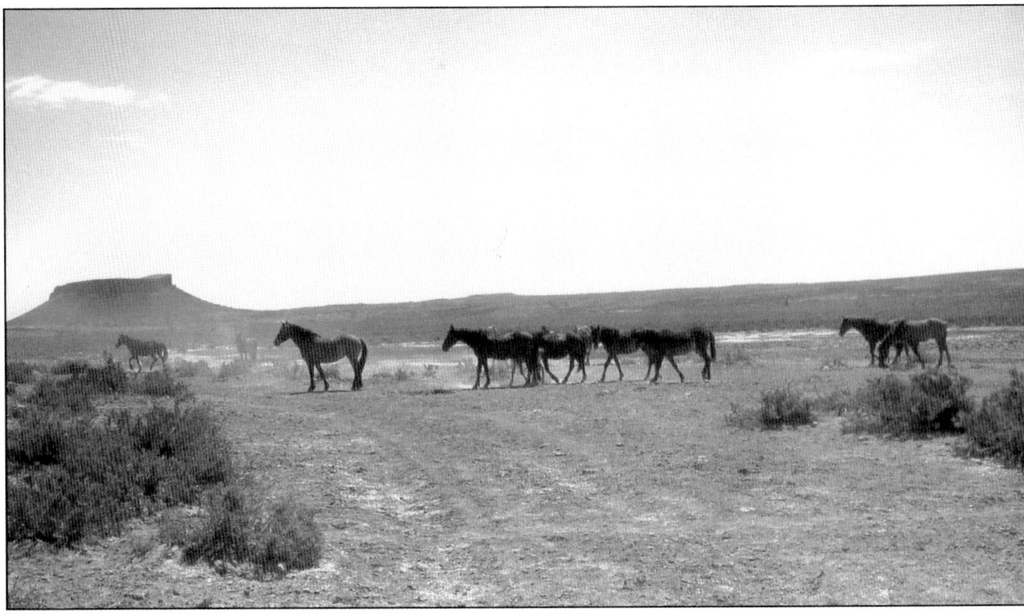

Wild horses roam the regions around Rock Springs. Thoroughbred stallions were brought in by ranchers like Charles Jameson to breed with the fast, sturdy horses used by Plains Indians in order to create hearty horses that could be sold to the U.S. Army in the years leading up to World War I. Following the war and during the Depression, some ranchers turned free large draft horses they had used for plowing fields and other heavy labor. The horses roaming the Red Desert today are descendants of this mixture. (Courtesy Russel L. Tanner.)

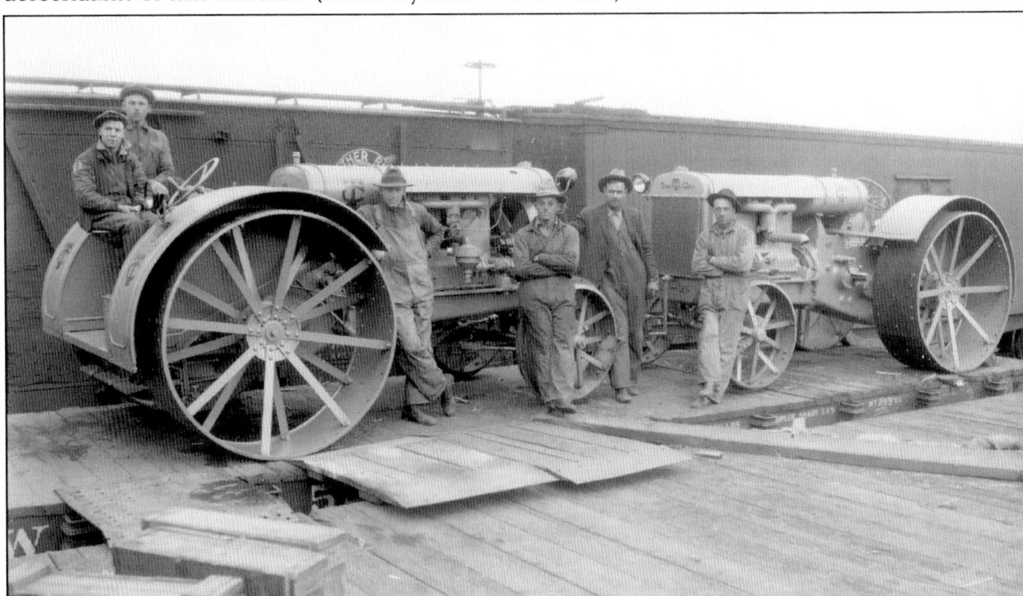

In 1908, a consortium of land developers initiated a major agricultural development about 40 miles from Rock Springs. The area that came to be known as Eden Valley soon was importing mechanized equipment like these tractors to till the soil to produce alfalfa hay and other farm products. This photograph was taken in 1921. The area soon began to supply Rock Springs and markets far beyond. (Courtesy New Studio.)

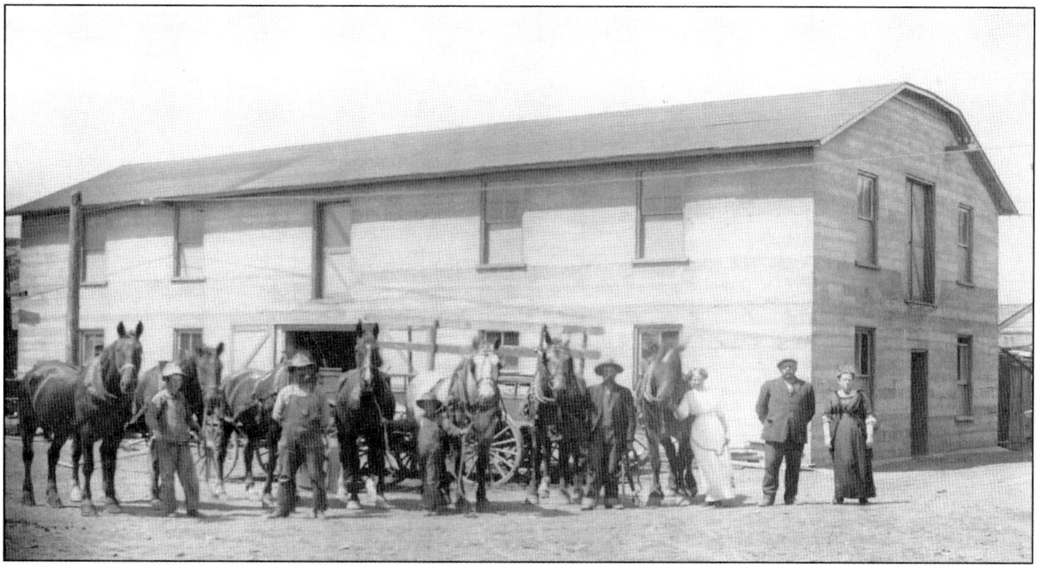

Peter Christian (P. C.) Bunning and his wife, Marianne, stand on the far right in this photograph. P. C. served Rock Springs as mayor from 1924 to 1933. From left to right, the other individuals pictured in front of the Bunning warehouse are Howard Moffit, Chris Moeller, an unidentified child, Guy Moffit, and the eldest Bunning daughter, Myrtle. Mule-drawn freight wagons moved goods from the railroad in Rock Springs to hinterland communities and industrial operations. Today the John Bunning Transfer Company, operated by descendants of P. C., is a well-known regional trucking company. (Courtesy the Bunning family.)

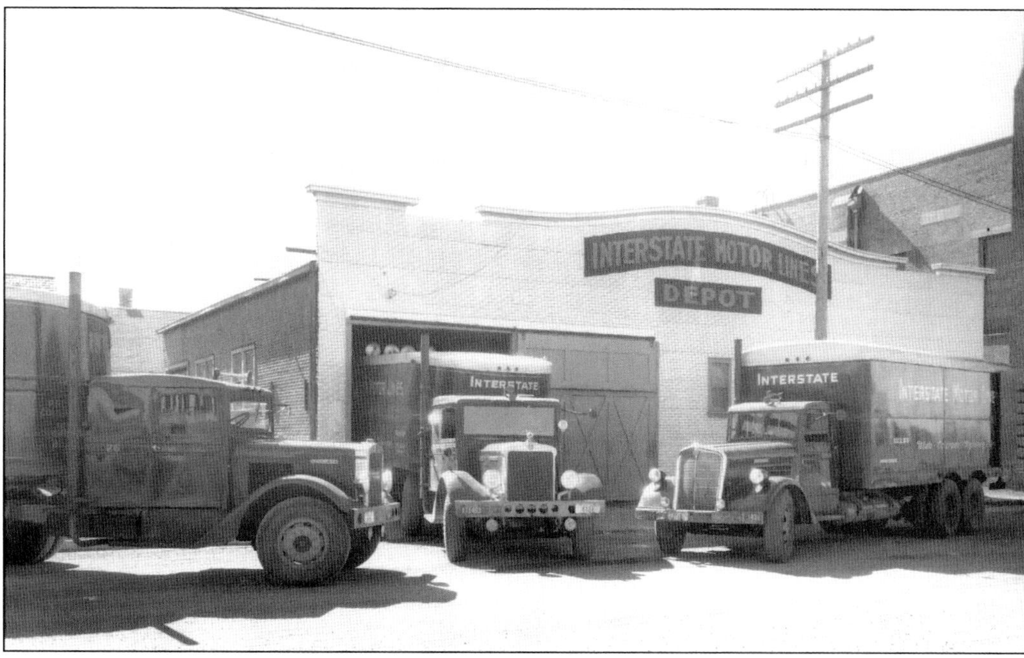

The natural corridor across the Rocky Mountains facilitated by the Great Divide Basin allowed transportation operations to become an important enterprise in the area. By the 1930s, several trucking companies had headquarters in Rock Springs, including Interstate Motor Line, Inc., shown here. (Courtesy New Studio.)

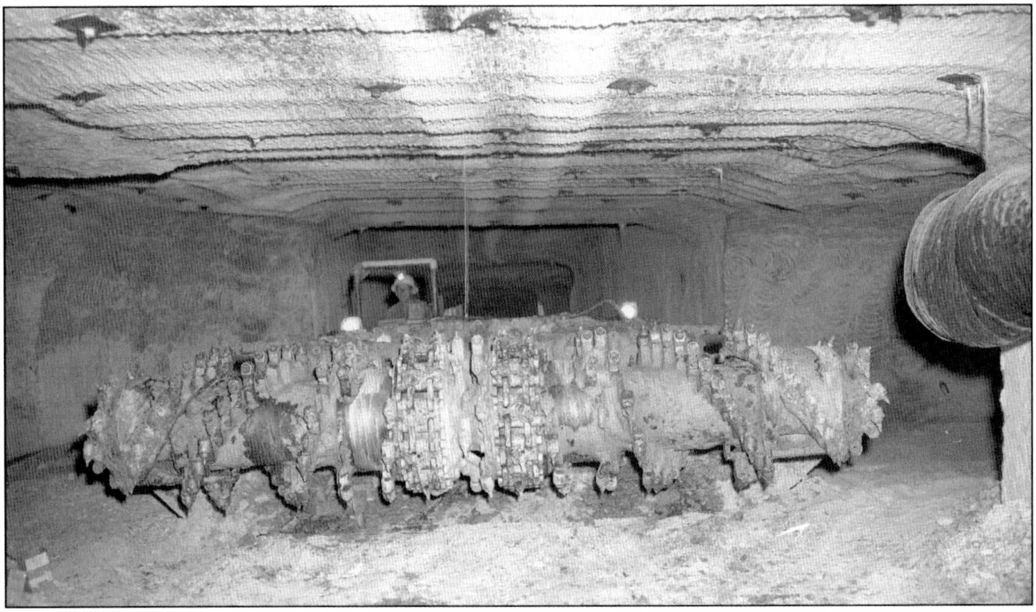

Just when the need for coal began to wane in the wake of conversion of railroad locomotives to burn diesel fuel instead of coal, a new mineral source brought much-needed jobs to Rock Springs. Trona, a calcium carbonate mineral that developed as a result of evaporation of the ancient lake beds that once occurred in this area, began to be commercially developed in the early 1950s. Trona ore is mined using equipment such as this continuous miner. (Courtesy New Studio.)

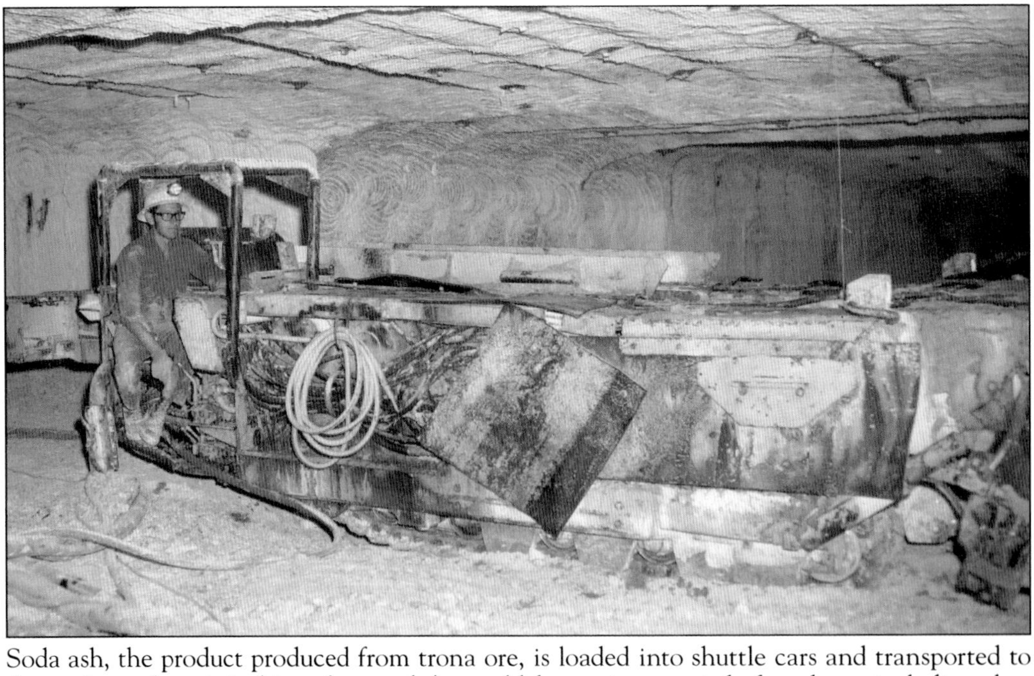

Soda ash, the product produced from trona ore, is loaded into shuttle cars and transported to the surface, where it is shipped around the world for use in a myriad of products, including glass and detergents. Eventually several trona mines would come to operate in the basin west of Rock Springs, providing over 1,000 jobs, many taken by coal miners who lost their jobs when railroads converted from coal to diesel. (Courtesy New Studio.)

Three

Everyday Life
A Diverse Community

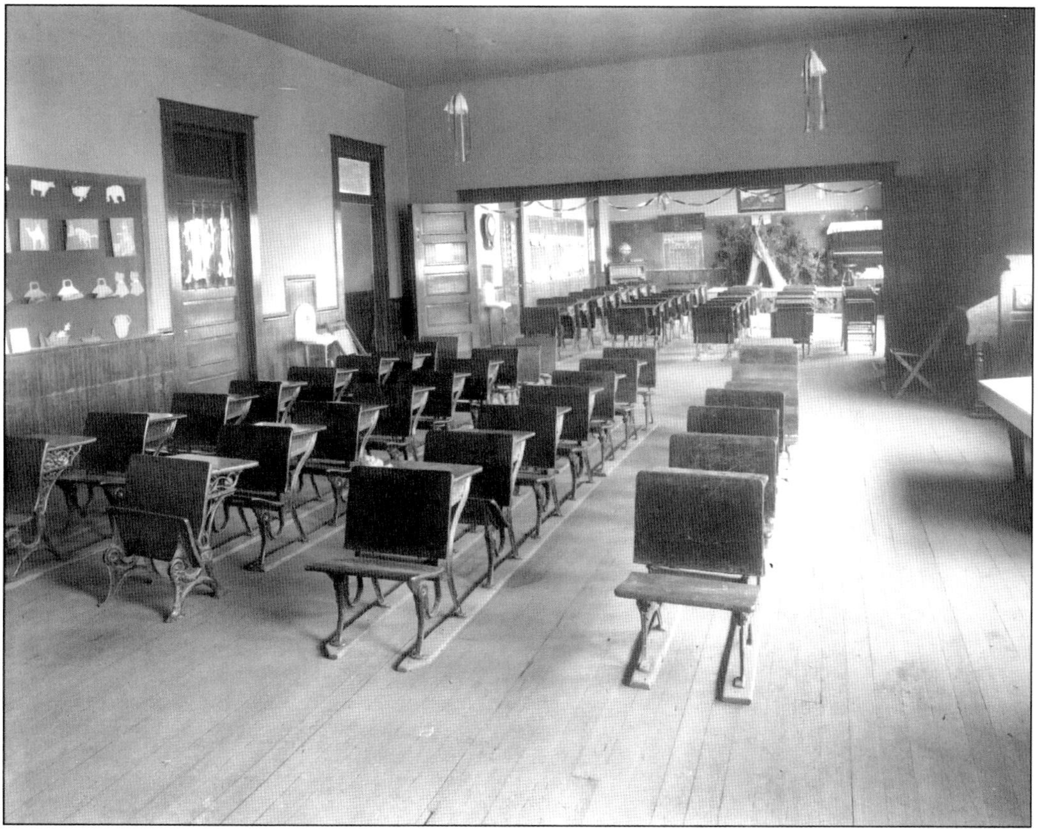

This is a Washington Elementary School third-grade classroom in 1912. The adjoining classroom at the rear has its own piano. Bolted to two planks, the desks form perfectly straight rows and, without children, offer an unimpeded view of the interior of the schoolrooms. Bathroom facilities were located outside, one outhouse for the girls and one for the boys. (Courtesy New Studio.)

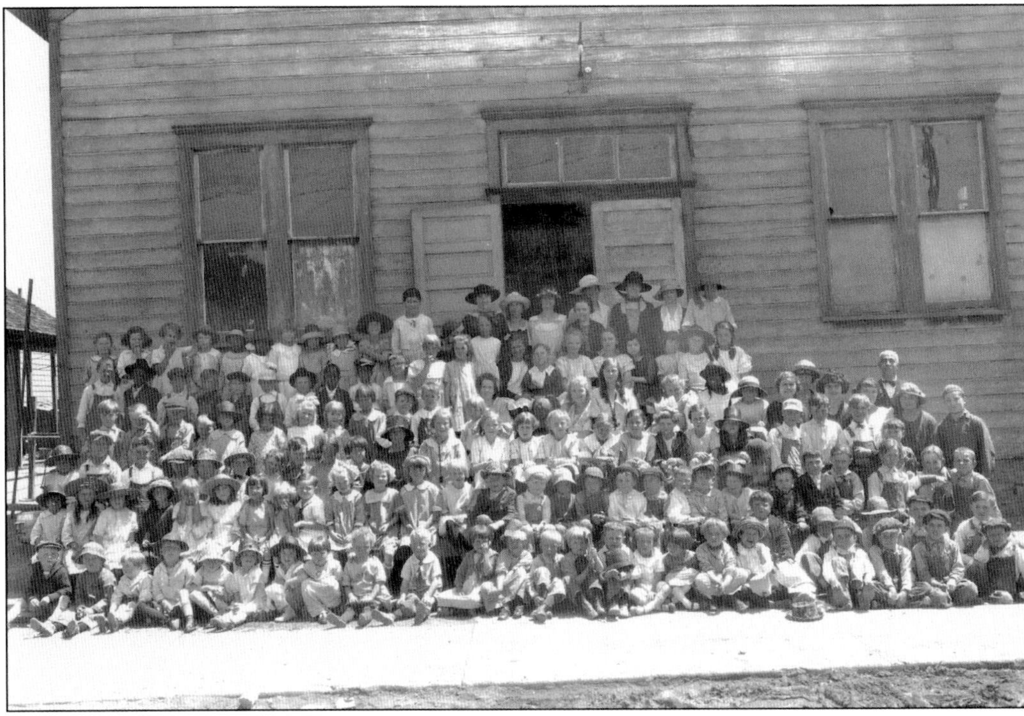

Public school classes in the early days were held in a variety of buildings, including Finn Hall, an ethnic lodge owned by the Finnish people in Rock Springs, shown in this 1923 photograph. (Courtesy New Studio.)

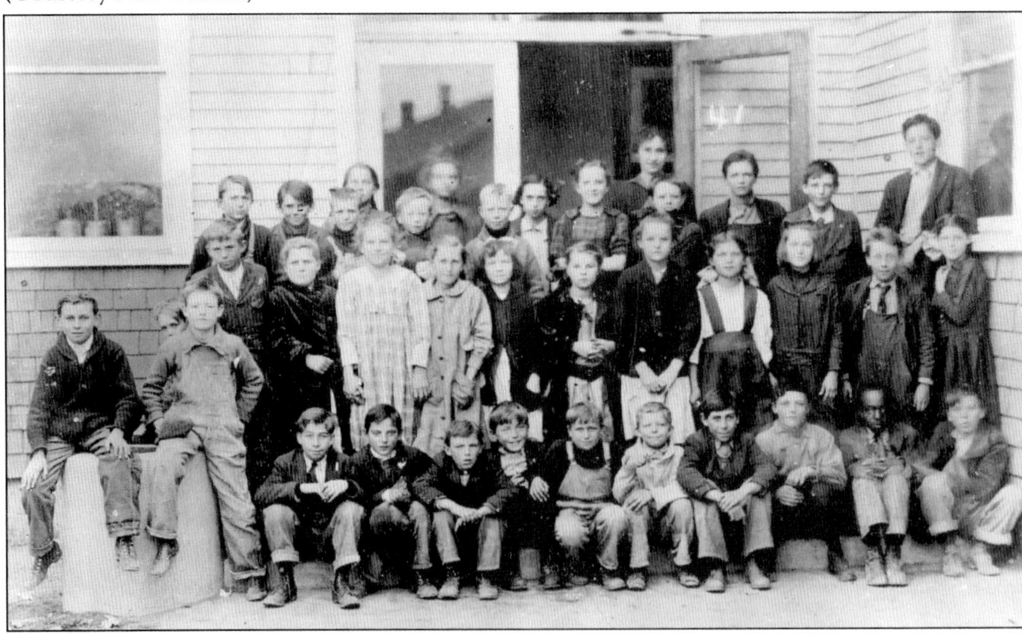

Letitia Smith was the teacher for these fifth-grade schoolchildren at Washington Elementary School. Washington Elementary School was located on Bridger Avenue across from the original Camp Pilot Butte. The barracks had been converted to housing for miners and their families. (Courtesy New Studio.)

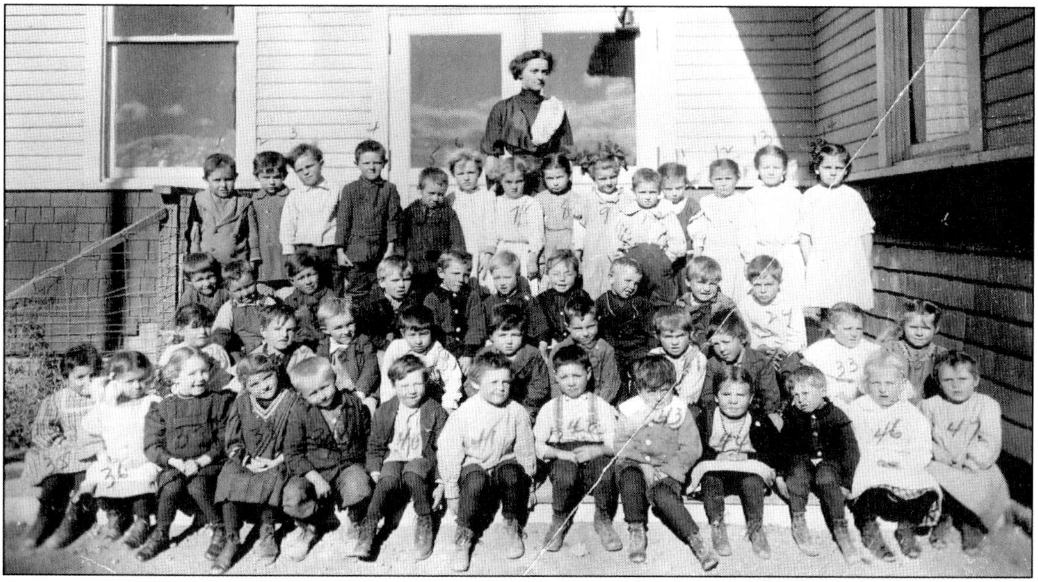

Squinting children had their photograph taken with their third-grade teacher, Miss Lungreen. Familiar Rock Springs surnames included Kershisnik, Subic, McTee, Anselmi, Korfanta, Metelko, Menghini, and Bertagnolli. These names remain familiar in Rock Springs today. (Courtesy New Studio.)

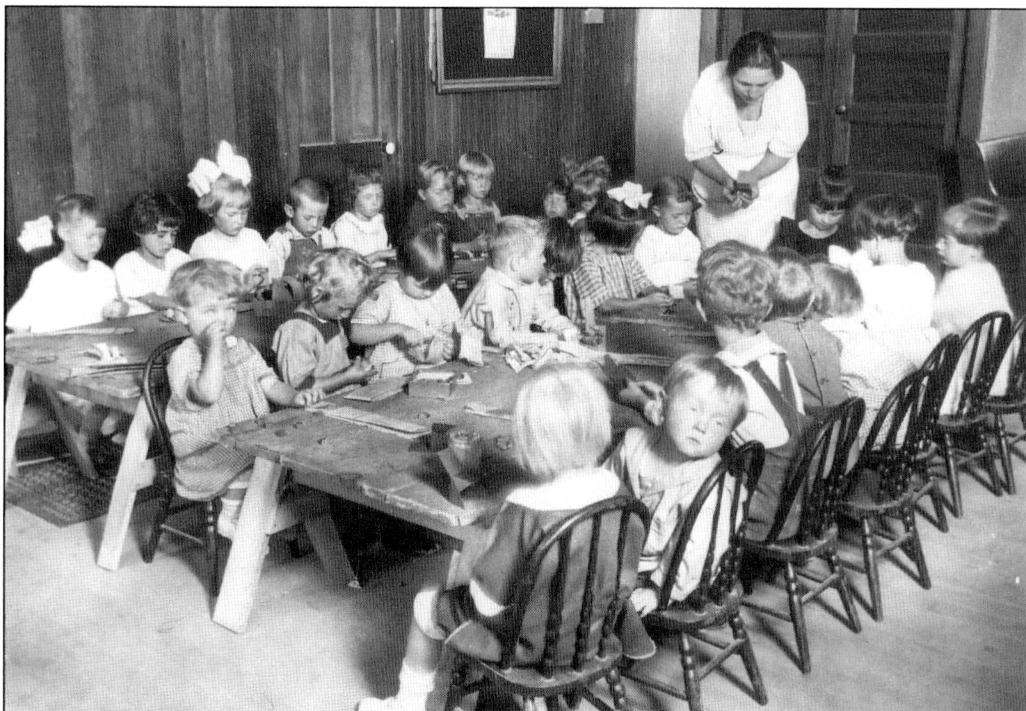

The First Baptist Church was the setting for a school. Pictured in 1922, these children were busy crafting with paper. While most of the children were attentive, one youngster looked straight at the camera, unaware of the social faux pas she was committing—picking her nose. The church schooled only the younger children in the community. (Courtesy New Studio.)

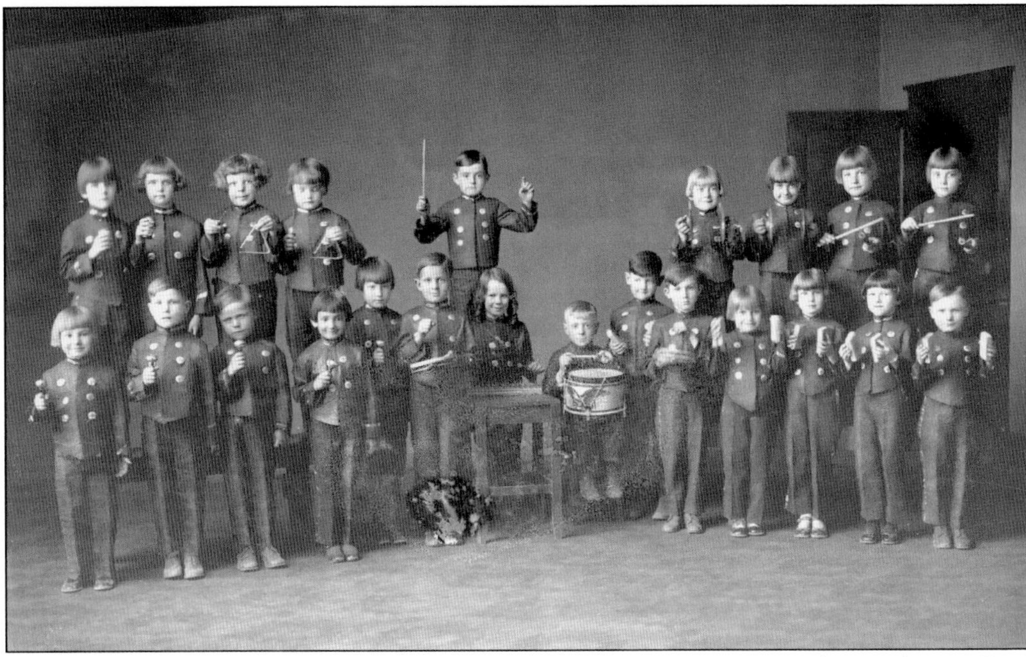

This well-appointed youth band used a variety of instruments to entertain their audience. Band instruments and band uniforms were handed down to younger siblings so they could be reused. Thriftiness was a quality valued in the early 1900s. Some of the instruments and uniforms are displayed at the Rock Springs Historical Museum. (Courtesy New Studio.)

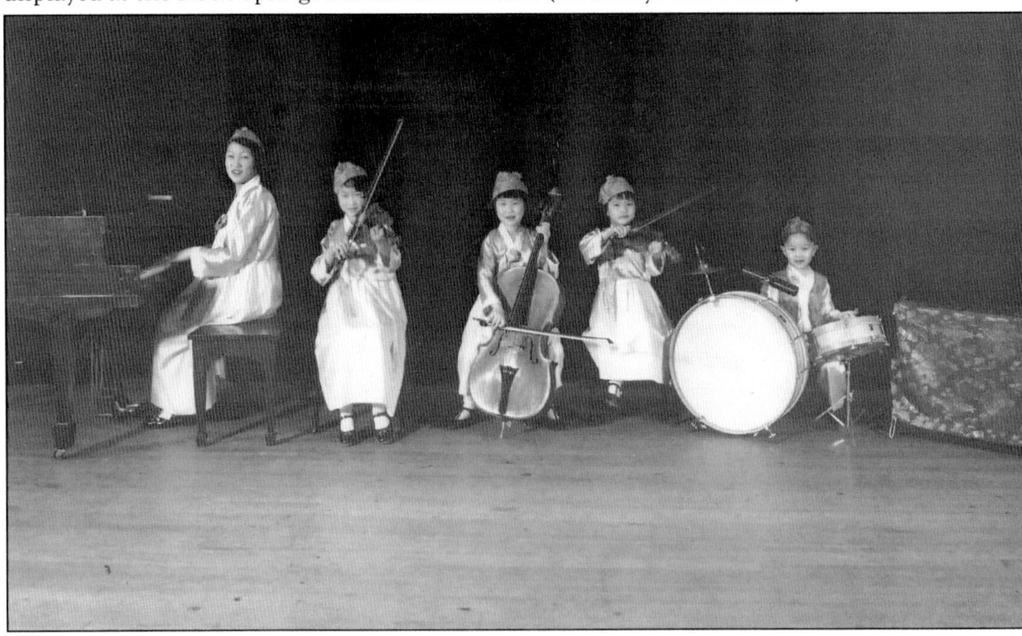

The Sinn family was replete with musicians. Sarah Sinn was the pianist, Nora played violin, Sadie played cello, Nellie played the violin, and Harry was the six-year-old drummer. Shortly after this photograph was taken in 1934, four-year-old Harriet joined the group as an acrobat, comic, singer, and dancer. The group often performed for events in the Rock Springs area and later joined the West Coast vaudeville circuit. (Courtesy New Studio.)

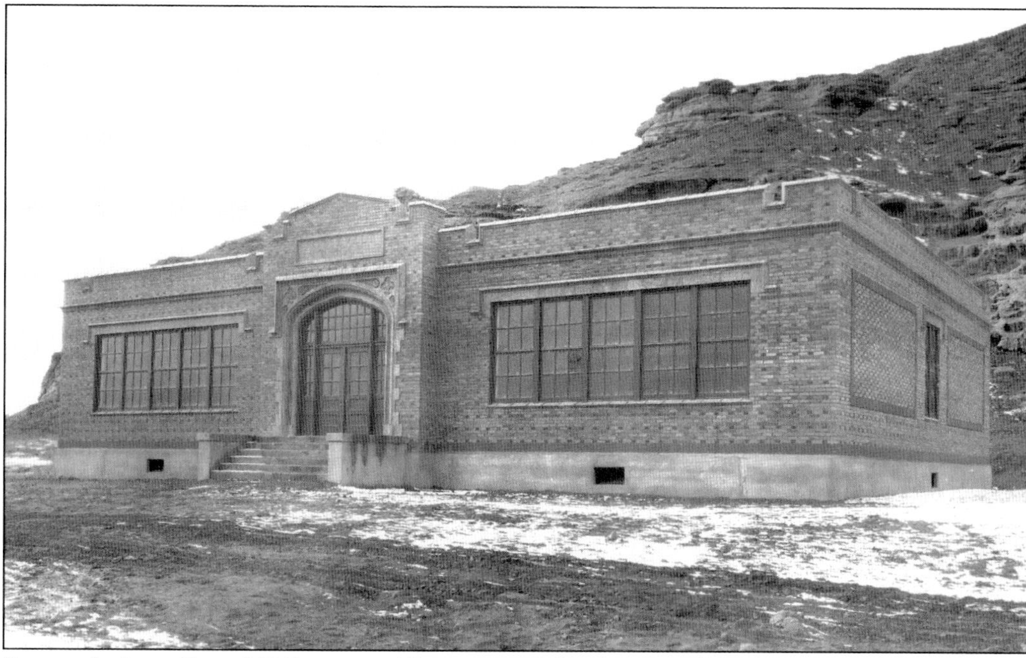

Roosevelt, Lowell, and Yellowstone Elementary Schools were all built in the 1920s. Roosevelt students helped move into the new four-room brick school pictured here by carrying books and other small items. Earlier schools were held in a variety of different places, including the city hall, fraternal lodges, above saloons and restaurants, and in private homes. (Courtesy New Studio.)

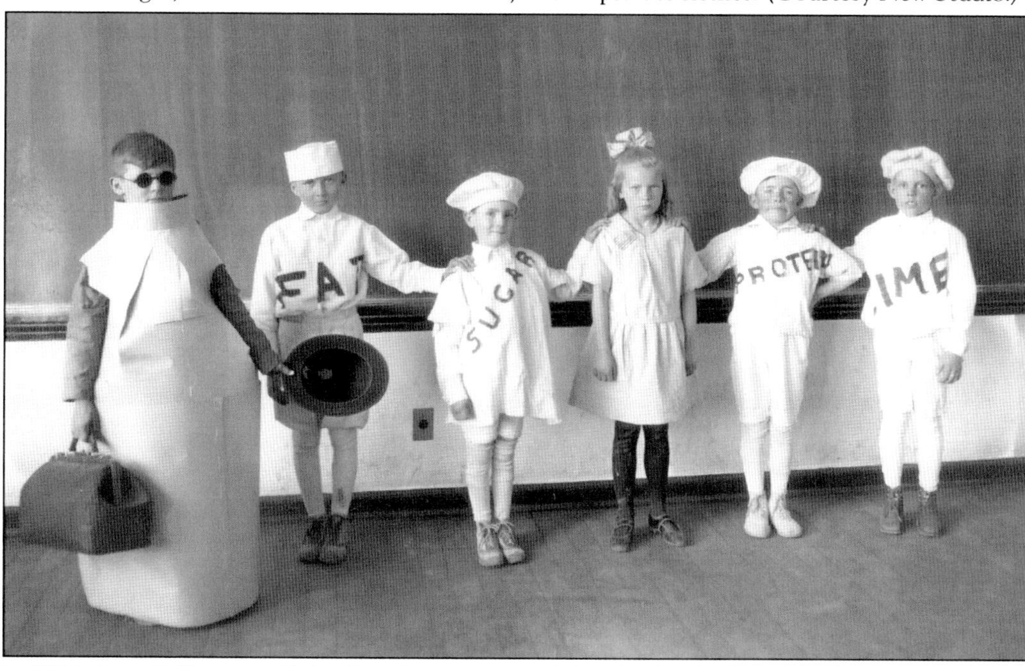

In 1924, these Yellowstone School students presented the play Dr. Milk Bottle. Dr. Milk Bottle and his associates Fat, Sugar, Protein, and Lime were educating the schoolgirl about the importance of nutrition. Important health lessons learned in school were often brought home and helped families in their daily life. (Courtesy New Studio.)

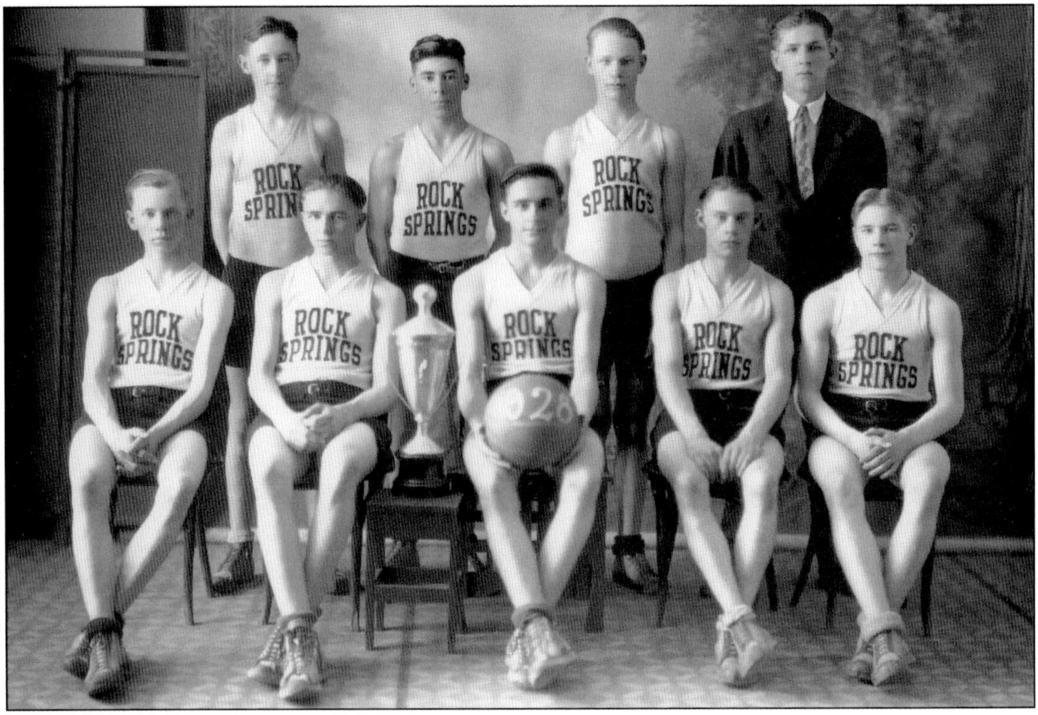

The 1928 Rock Springs High School basketball team won the state championship and posed for this photograph. The economy of the United States was faltering, and sport was a great way for the players and fans to momentarily forget their troubles. (Courtesy New Studio.)

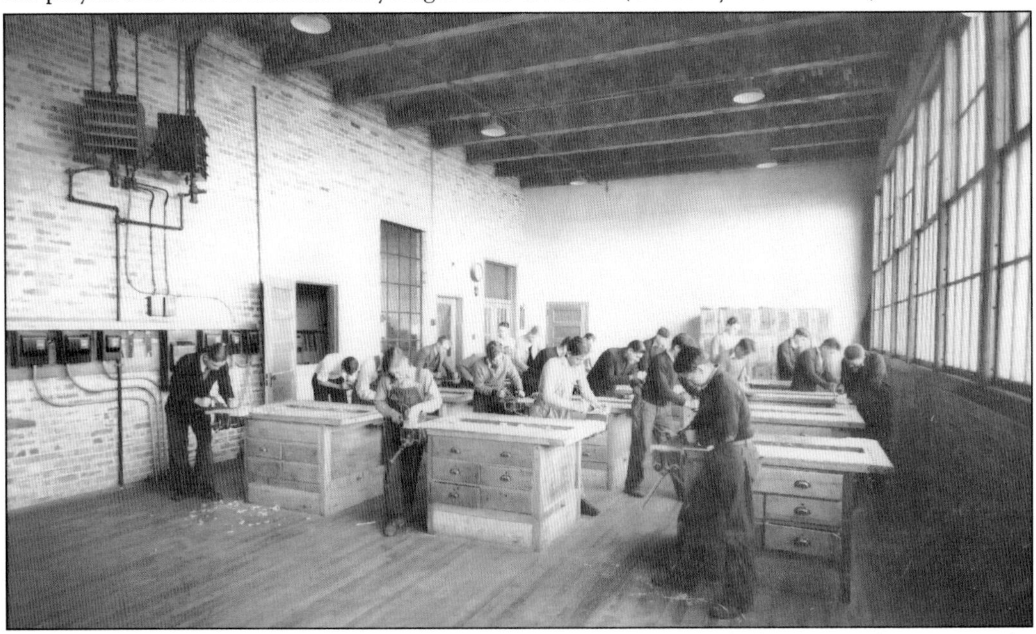

This 1932 high school wood shop class taught young men valuable skills they might use to make their livelihood. In the depths of the Depression, Rock Springs was suffering with the rest of the nation, and having special skills could mean the difference between getting a job and joining the swollen ranks of the unemployed. (Courtesy New Studio.)

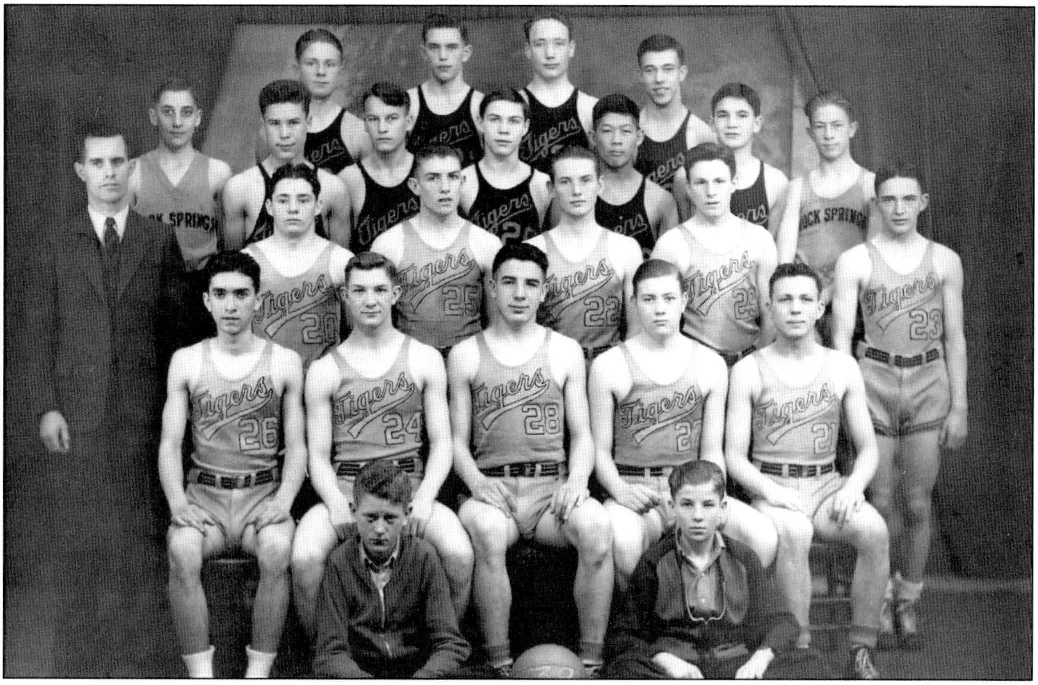

High school student athletes were a source of pride for the Rock Springs community. Upon graduation, many of the young men on this 1939 basketball team enlisted in the military to serve their country. World War II would forever change their lives. (Courtesy New Studio.)

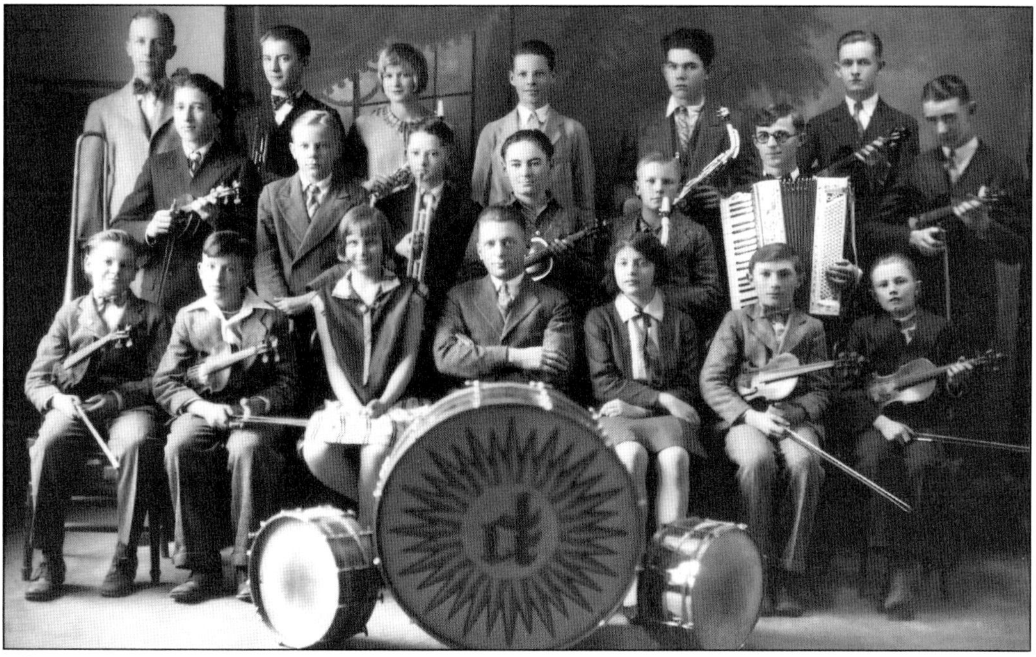

John Brueggeman's Orchestra from Rock Springs High School was photographed here in 1928. Music crossed the cultural barrier; audiences and musicians alike could communicate without using language. Brueggeman (center) also had an orchestra that played at the Rialto Theater. (Courtesy New Studio.)

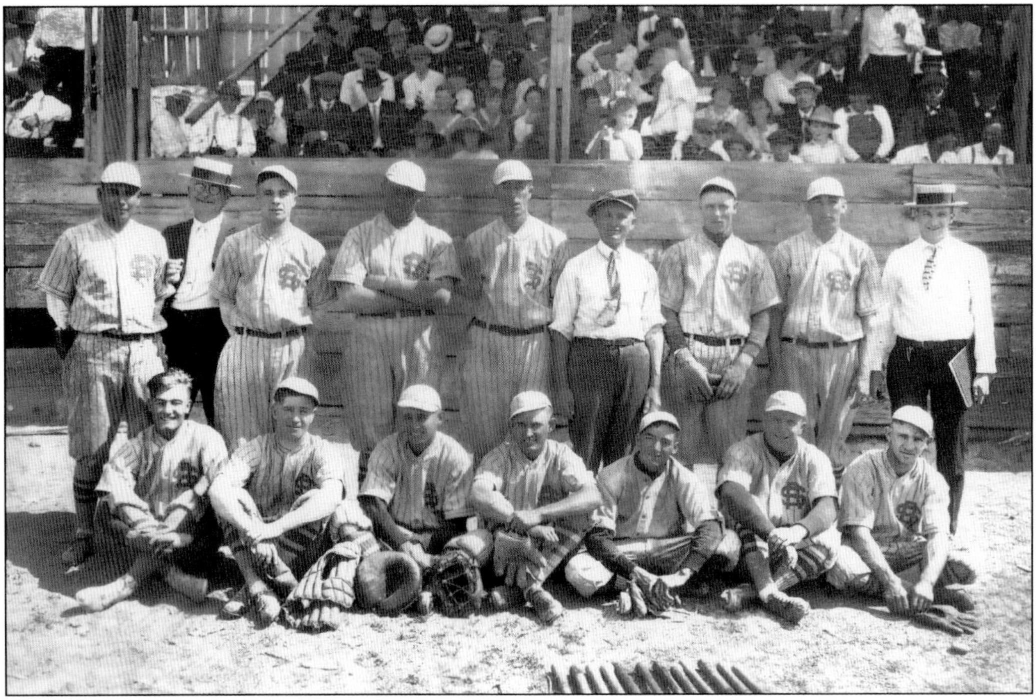

In 1922, this Rock Springs baseball team posed for their photograph at Gilpin Field. Unlike today, the only people wearing ball caps were the team members. Most everyone else pictured here wore hats and caps that were popular in the 1920s. (Courtesy New Studio.)

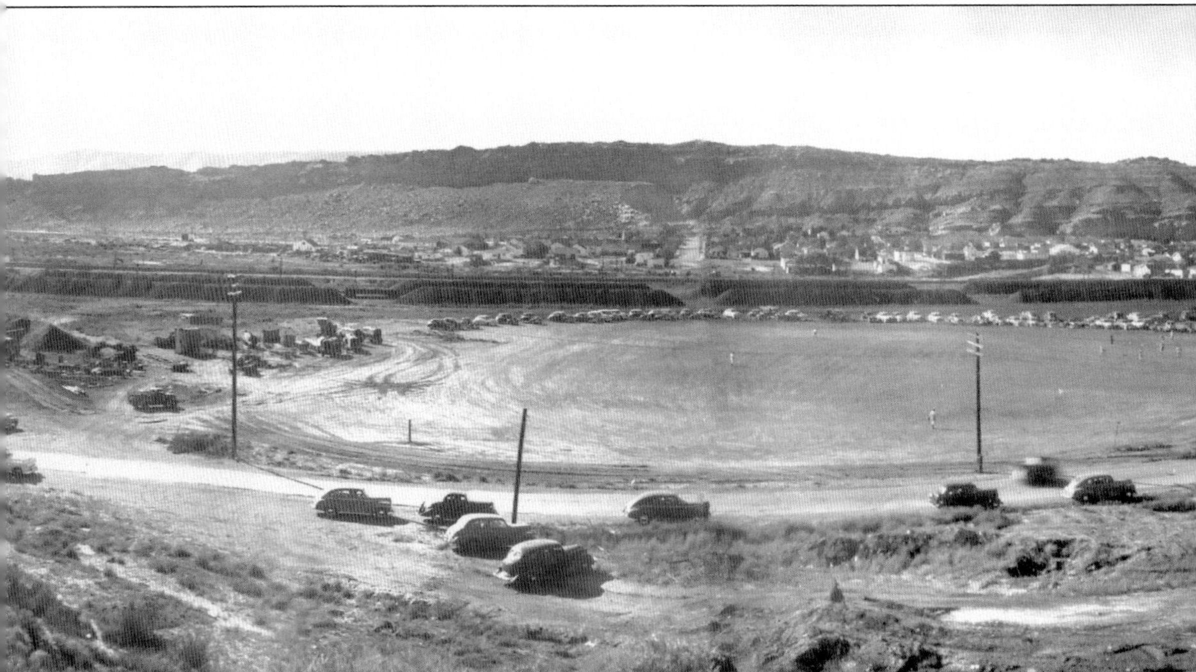

The Twilight League baseball games held at Gilpin Field were a source of great pleasure for Rock Springs residents. It was not unusual for line drives to knock out the windshields of cars parked

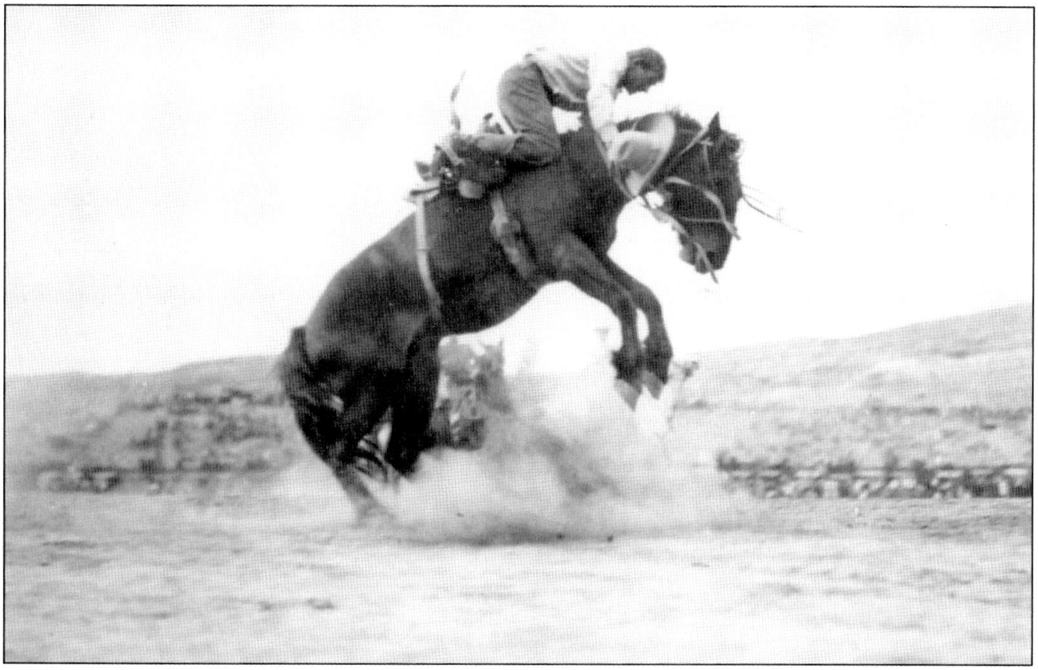

Rodeos were also held at Gilpin Field. Many rodeo events were based on activities practiced by cowboys on cattle ranches. Rough stock, like this bucking horse, would be led to the center of the arena with a gunny sack under his halter and over his eyes. The animal was saddled then mounted, and when the blindfold was removed, the bucking began. (Courtesy New Studio.)

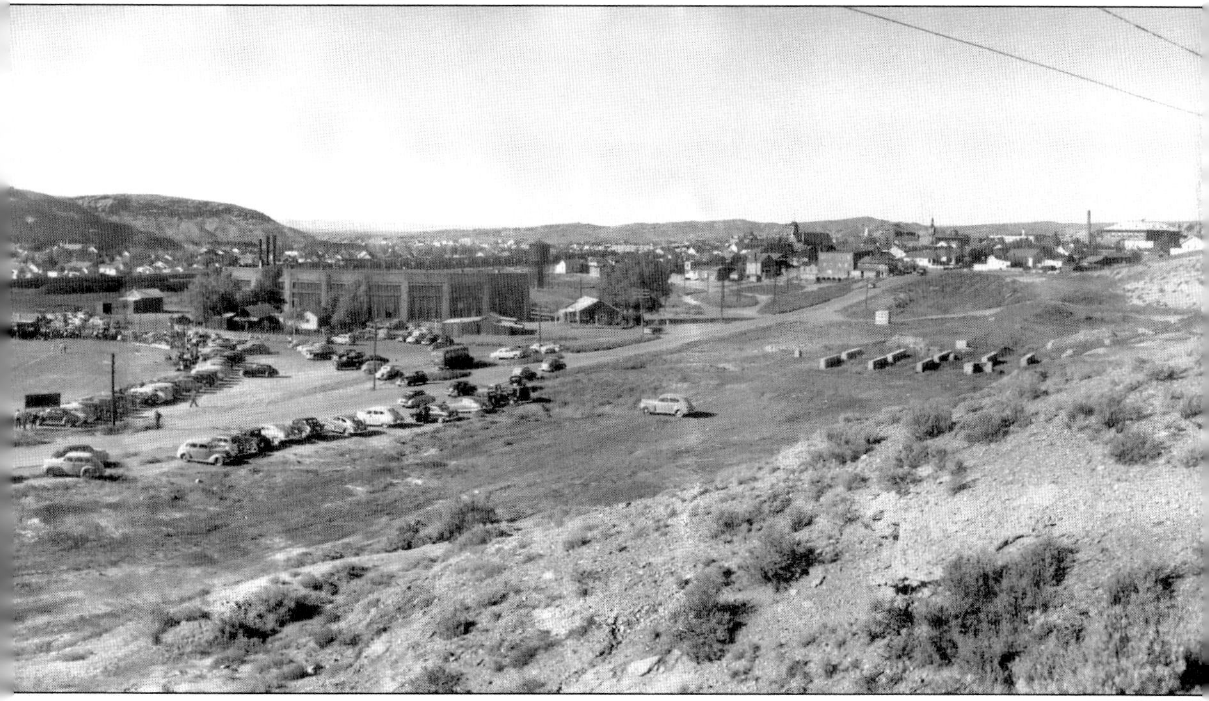

along the third baseline. Baseball great Satchel Page pitched at Gilpin Field and impressed onlookers with his athletic prowess. (Courtesy New Studio.)

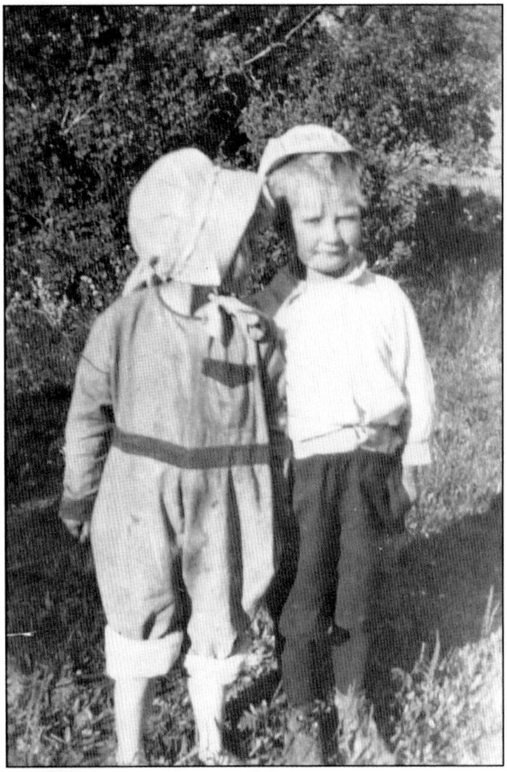

July 24, Pioneer Day, is an important Latter-day Saints holiday celebrating the arrival of the Mormons to the Salt Lake Valley in 1847. These cousins, Hannah Young and Robert Fletcher, were enjoying each other's company during a big Mormon gathering at Kent Ranch just south of Rock Springs. All the families would picnic, play games, hold sack races, and visit. (Courtesy the Fletcher family.)

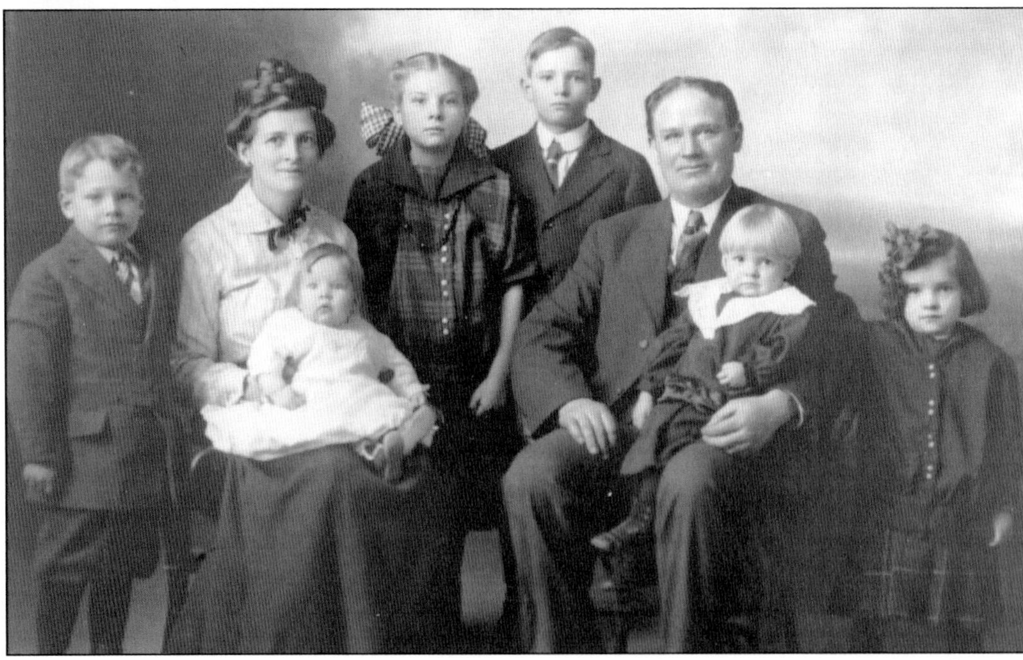

Robert and Elizabeth Fletcher and their children pose for a studio portrait in 1915. Baby Robert sits on his mother's lap while the elder Robert holds his youngest daughter, Vera. The other children are (from left to right) George, Katherine, Samuel, and Jessie. Families could send their photograph to distant relatives and assure them that they were doing well. (Courtesy the Fletcher family.)

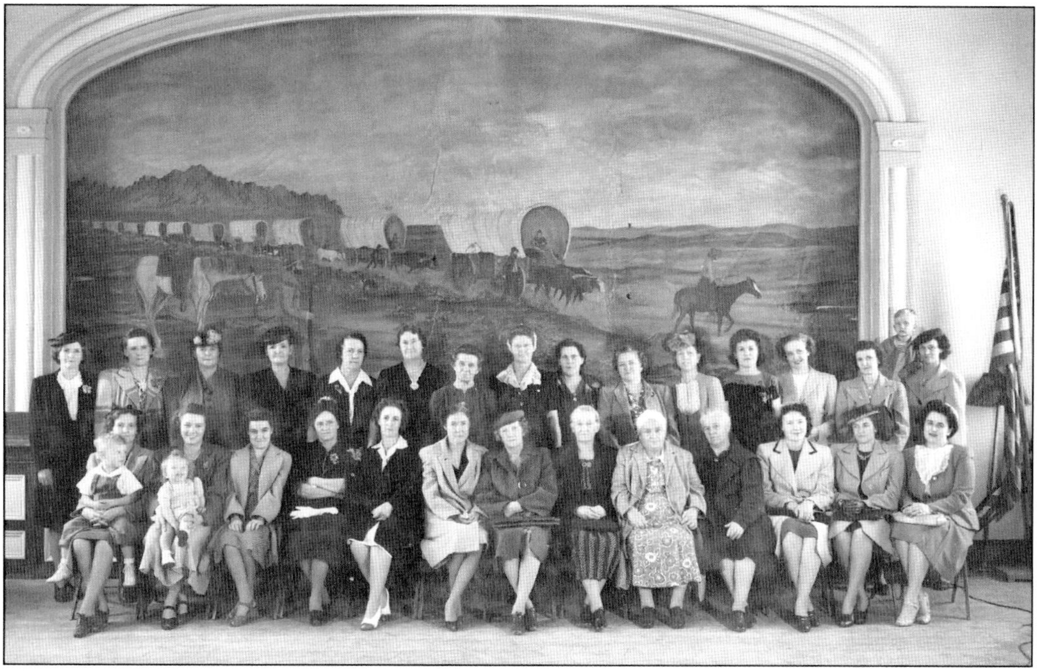

The Mormon Relief Society ladies pictured here are, from left to right, (first row) Phelps, King, Soulsby, Field, Hatch, Phillips, Phillips, James, Robinson, Robinson, Thomas, Rawlings, and Rouse; (second row) Spicer, Smith, Landeen, Syme, Sellers, Armstrong, Bluhm, Overy, Flor, Yakse, Phillips, Botero, Shedden, and two unidentified. (Courtesy New Studio.)

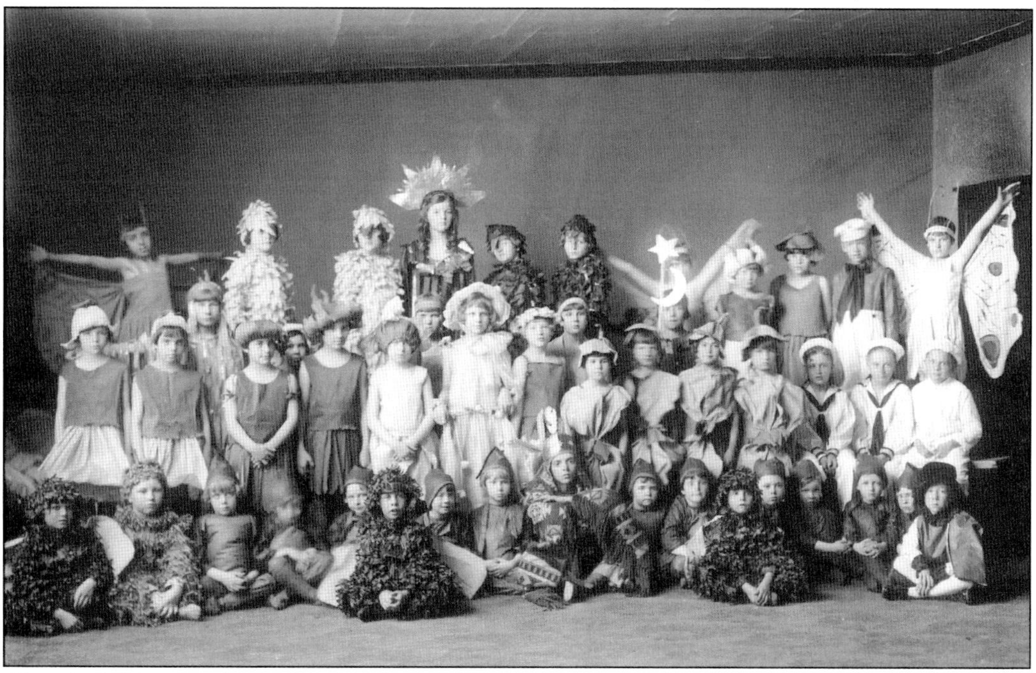

Church children in this undated photograph wore costumes representing butterflies, birds, flowers, sailors, and more. This spring pageant was held for a number of years, and other photographs show different children wearing the same costumes. (Courtesy New Studio.)

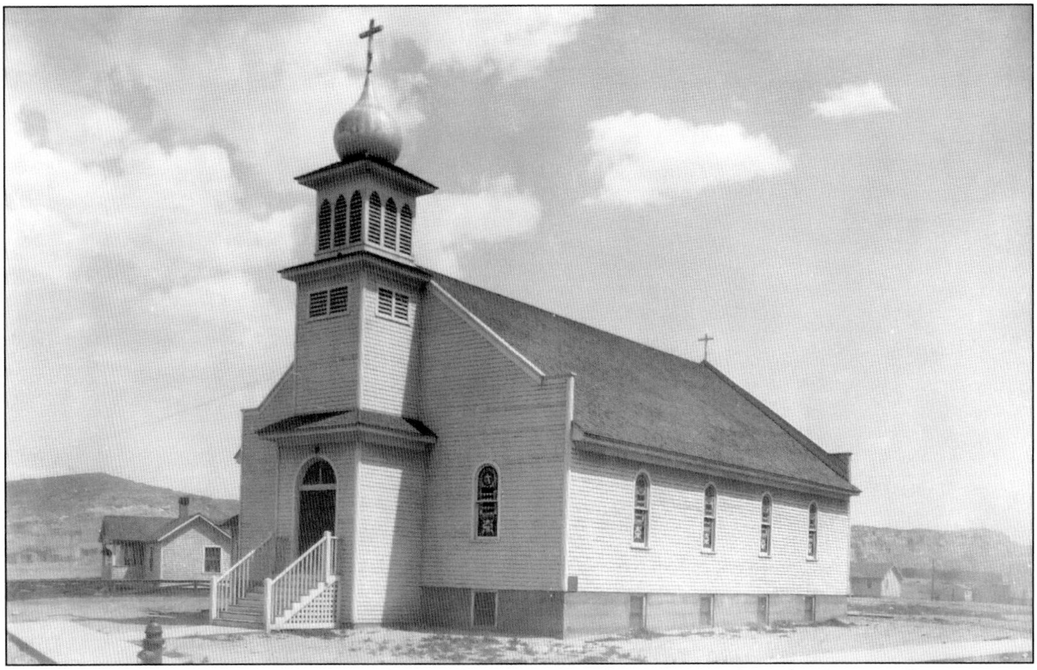

The Trinity Greek Orthodox Church was first organized in 1925 and, with 100 members, met in the Episcopal Church of the Holy Communion. In 1927, the church bought this building located at the corner of Pilot Butte and N Streets. The building, now used by the Trinity Orthodox Church, originally had an "onion dome" cupola typical of Eastern Orthodox churches. The reason for the change to the cross is a matter of debate. Some maintain the change was to better fit the Greek tradition, while others believe the onion dome was blown off in a windstorm; obviously both circumstances could be true. (Courtesy New Studio.)

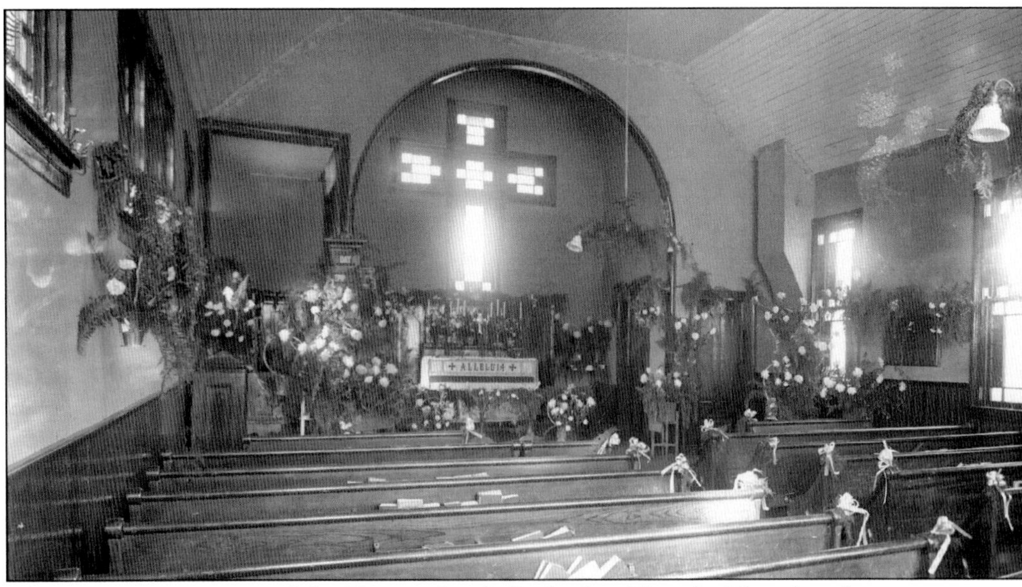

This is an interior view of the Trinity Greek Orthodox Church. This church remains a vital institution in Rock Springs and is attended by many people of Slavic and other Eastern European ethnicities as well as by Americans of Greek heritage. (Courtesy New Studio.)

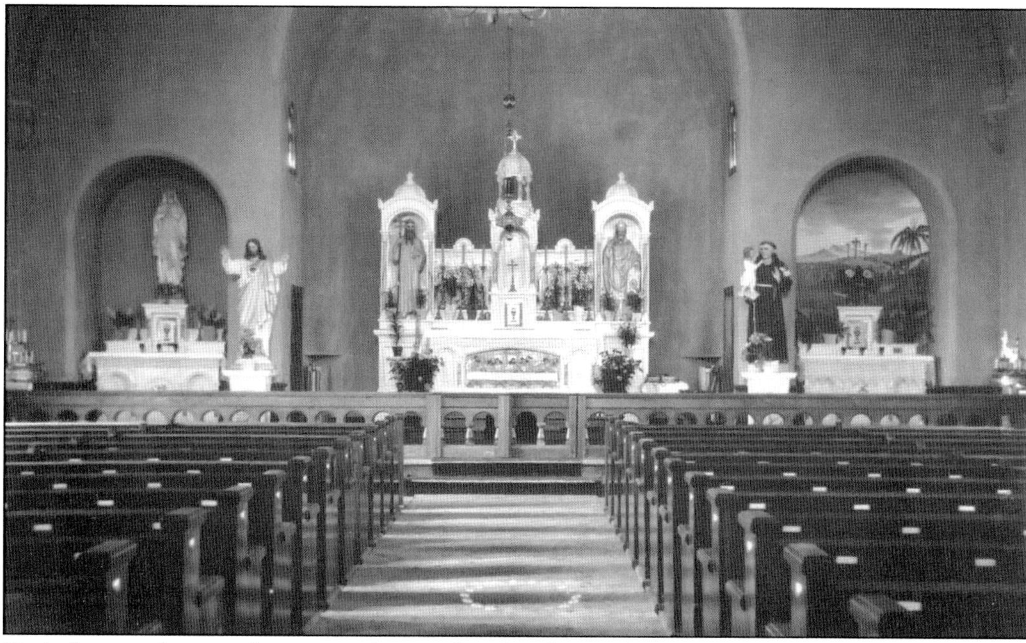

Catholic parishioners living on the north side of town had to make a dangerous crossing of multiple train tracks to attend church. In 1926, SS. Cyril and Methodius, or North Side as it is commonly known, was finished. This photograph shows the interior of the church. SS. Cyril and Methodius were brothers who translated the Bible from Greek to the Slavic language using Cyrillic characters in the eighth century. (Courtesy New Studio.)

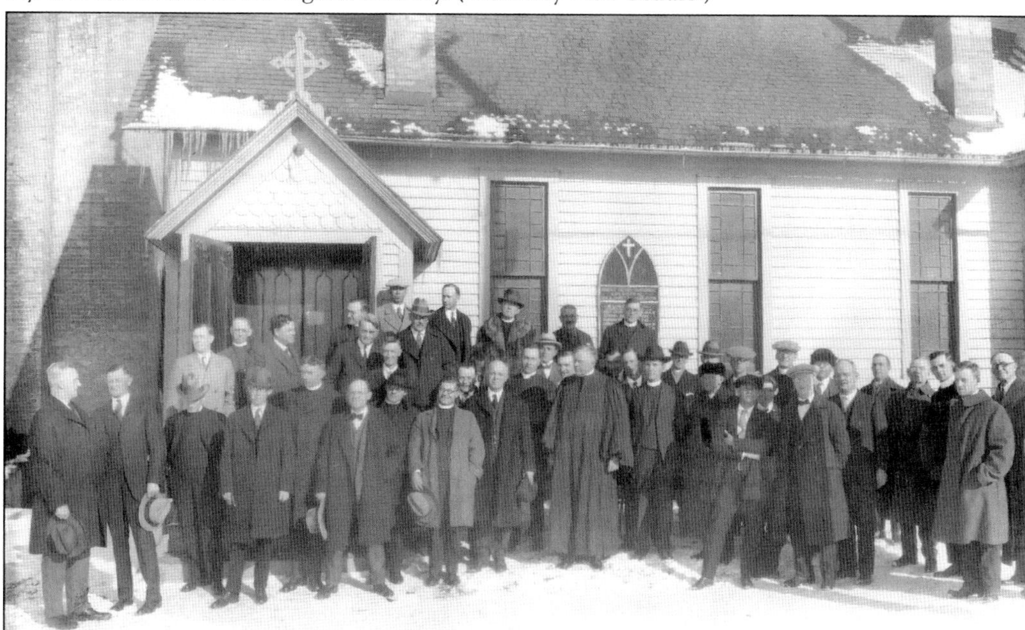

In 1895, services for the Episcopal Church of the Holy Communion were held upstairs in the Fountain Club saloon on South Front Street. A popular saying around town was, "There's spirits above and spirits below." The Episcopal Diocese of Wyoming held its convention in Rock Springs in 1925, and this photograph shows men bundled up for cold weather. (Courtesy New Studio.)

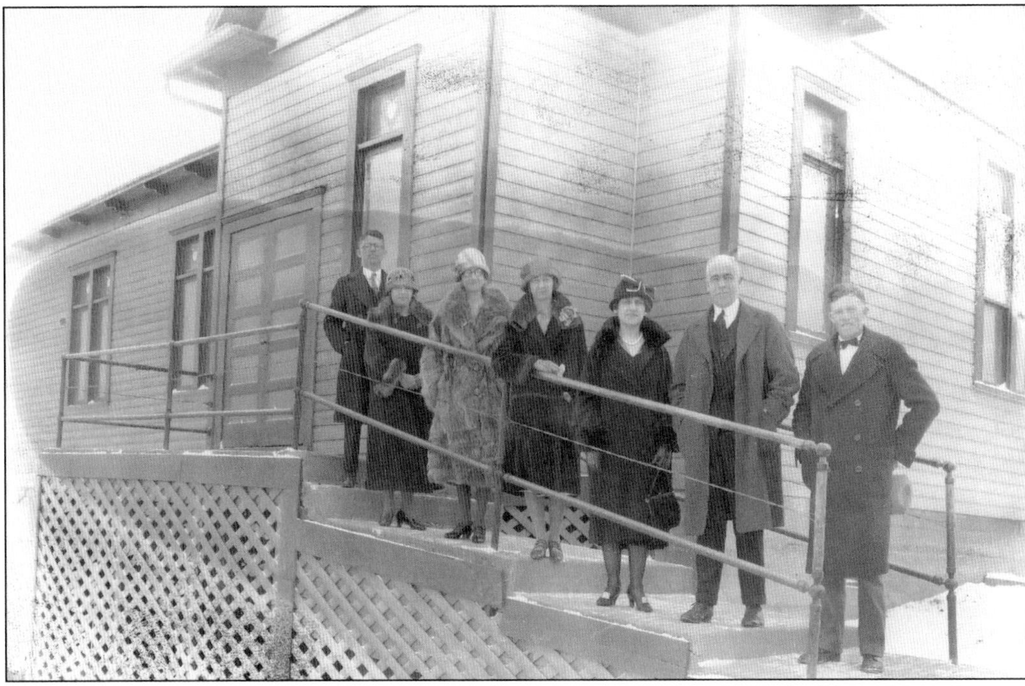

In 1928, Gov. Nellie Tayloe Ross (1876–1977), the first woman governor in the United States, posed with members of the First Baptist Church. Ross, third from the right, was elected to the position after her husband, Gov. William Bradford Ross, died in office. (Courtesy New Studio.)

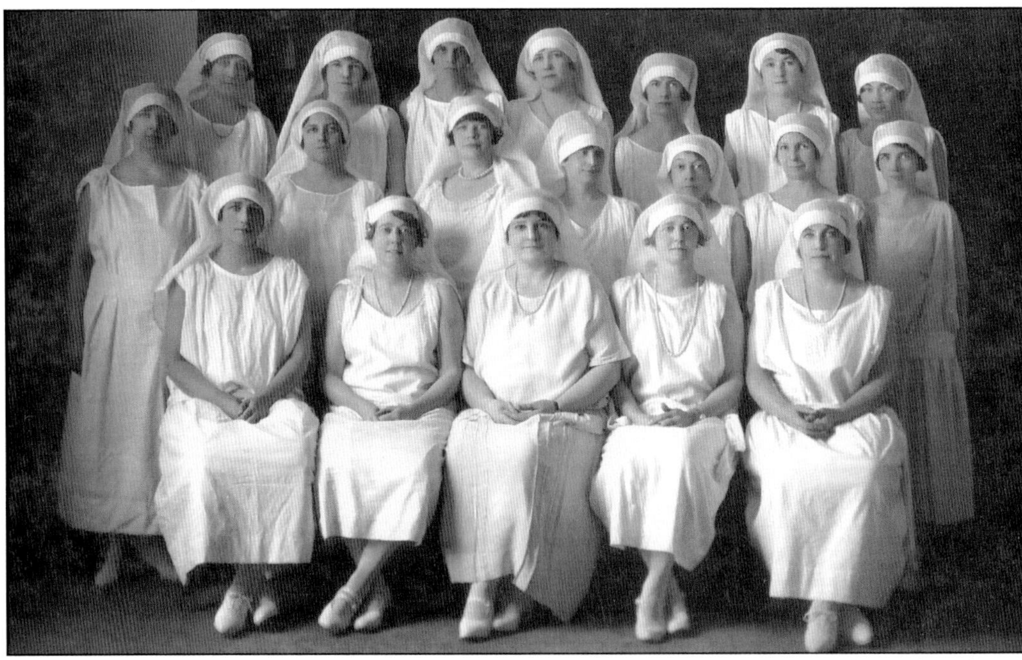

The United Methodist Church choir was composed of angelic-looking women. Their white dresses appear to be uniform, but closer examination reveals that each dress was custom made. In 1891, Methodists held their services in the Odd Fellows Hall. Parishioners soon raised enough money to buy a store building on Broadway Avenue and convert it into their first church. (Courtesy New Studio.)

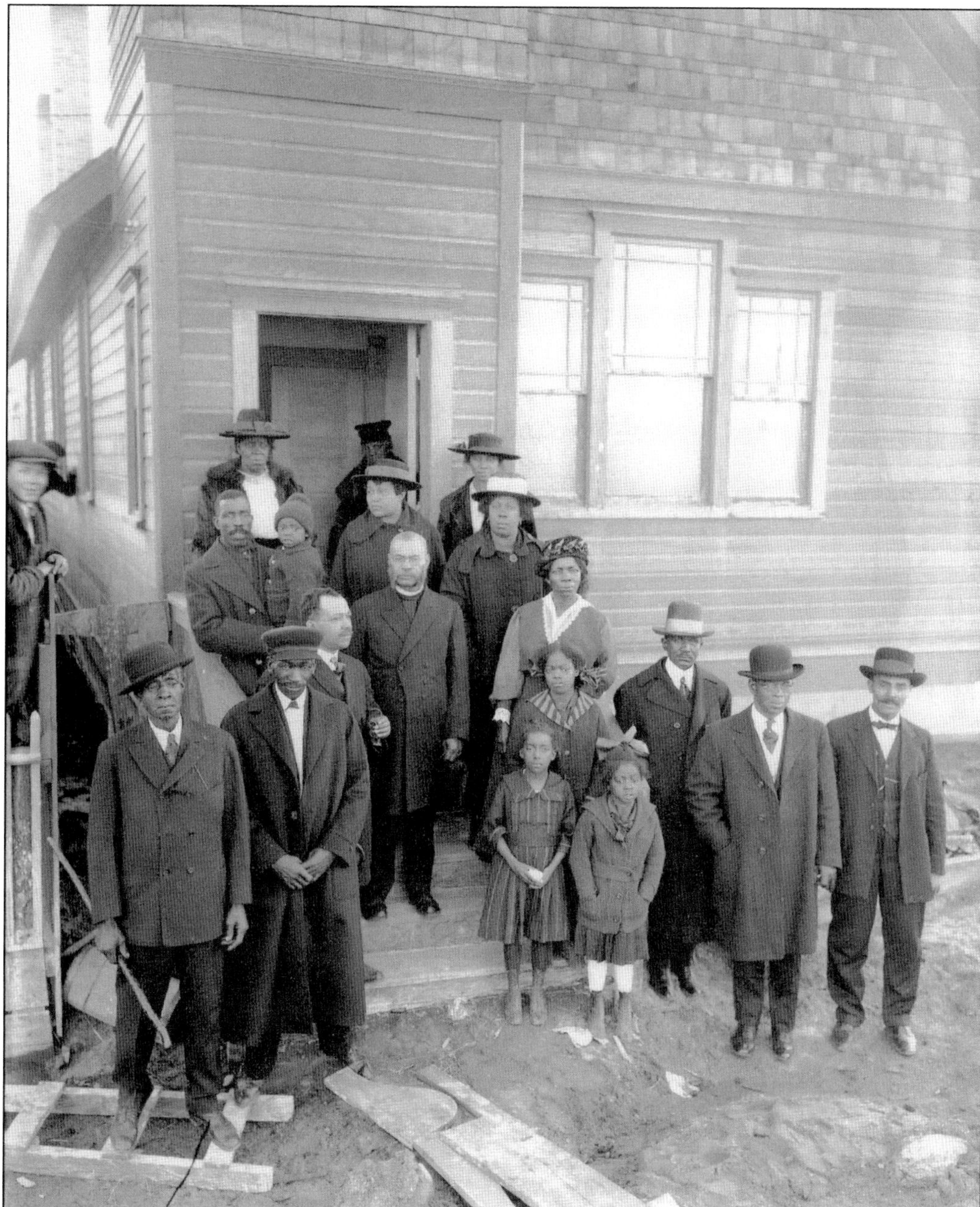

These churchgoers had their photograph taken in front of their church at 327 N Street in 1925. The Baker's Chapel African Methodist Episcopal Church (AME), built in 1923, was named after the first minister, the Reverend William N. Baker. (Courtesy New Studio.)

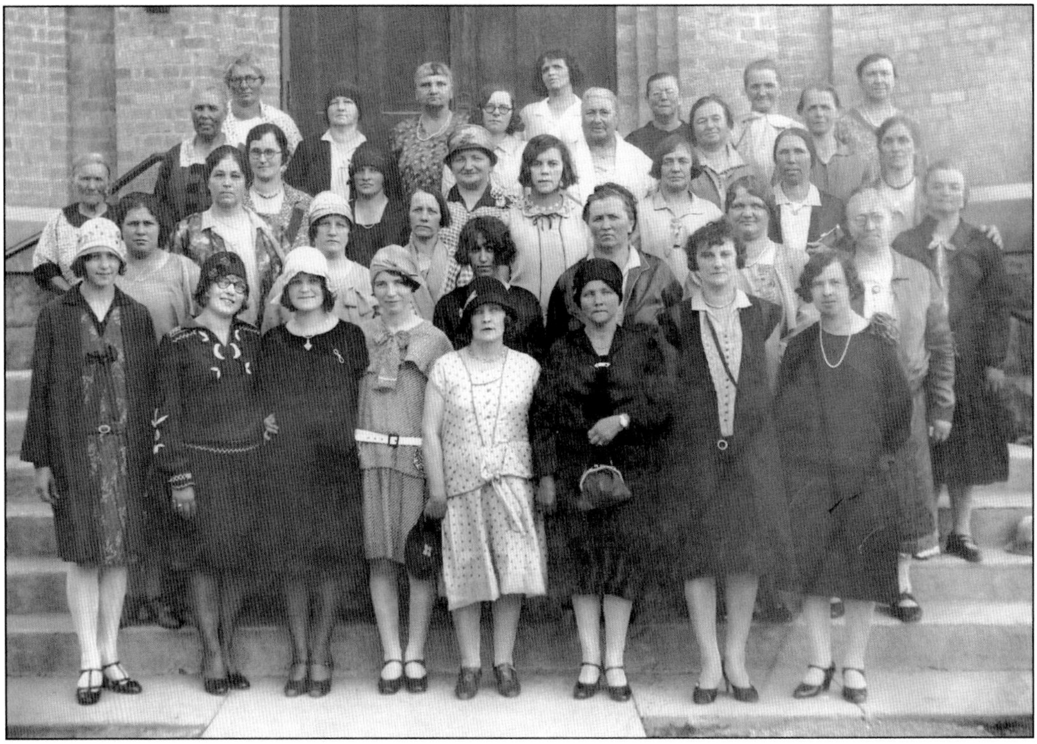

The SS. Cyril and Methodius Altar Society was photographed on the steps of the North Side Catholic Church in 1929. Many Slovenians lived near the mines on the north side of the track, and most of the women in the altar society were of Slovenian descent. (Courtesy New Studio.)

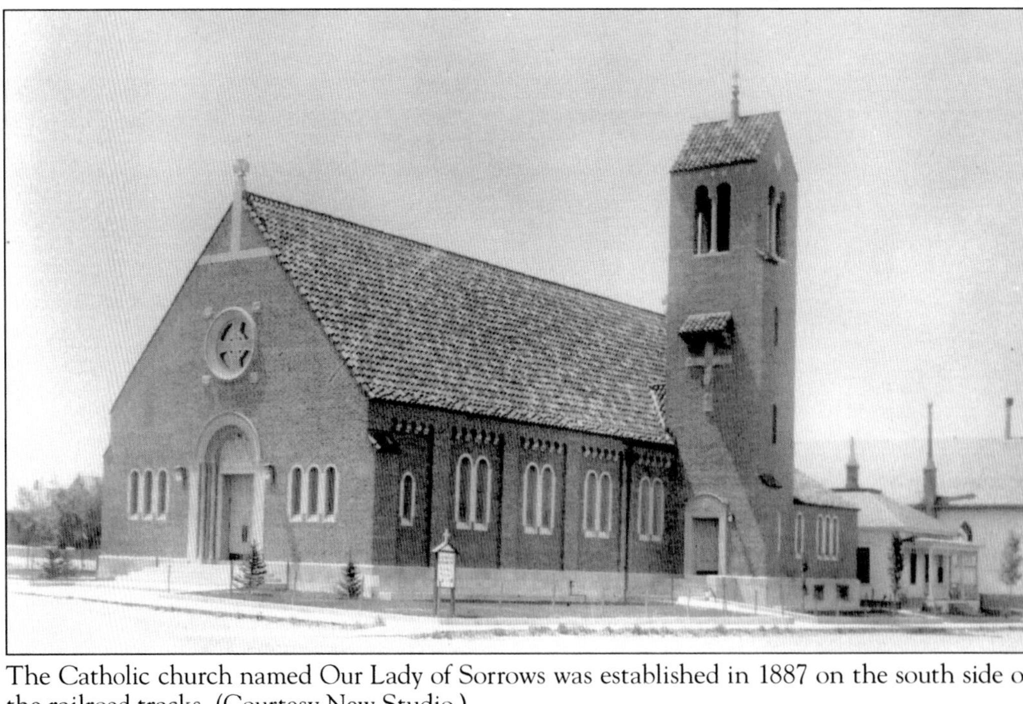

The Catholic church named Our Lady of Sorrows was established in 1887 on the south side of the railroad tracks. (Courtesy New Studio.)

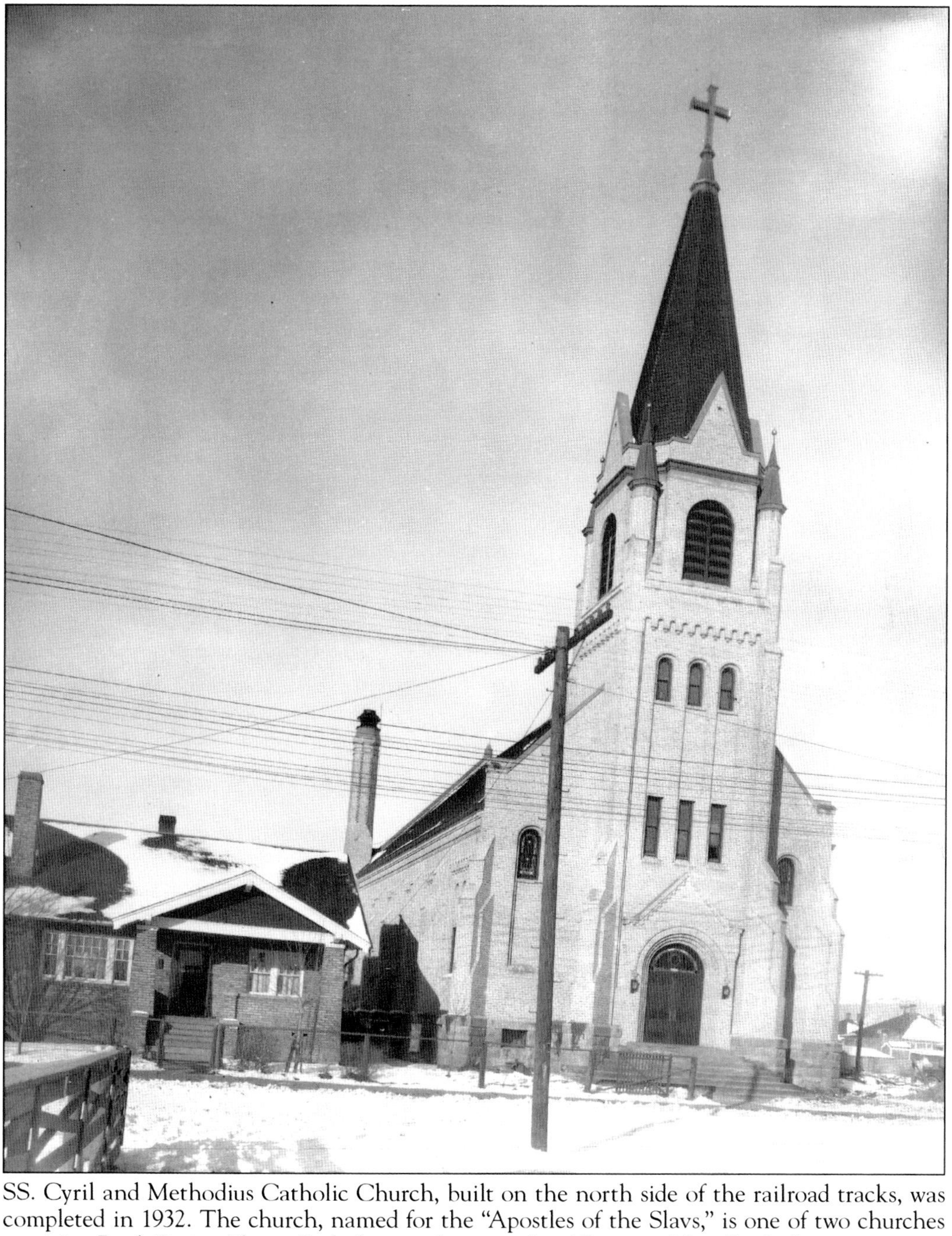

SS. Cyril and Methodius Catholic Church, built on the north side of the railroad tracks, was completed in 1932. The church, named for the "Apostles of the Slavs," is one of two churches servicing Rock Springs' large Catholic population today. (Courtesy New Studio.)

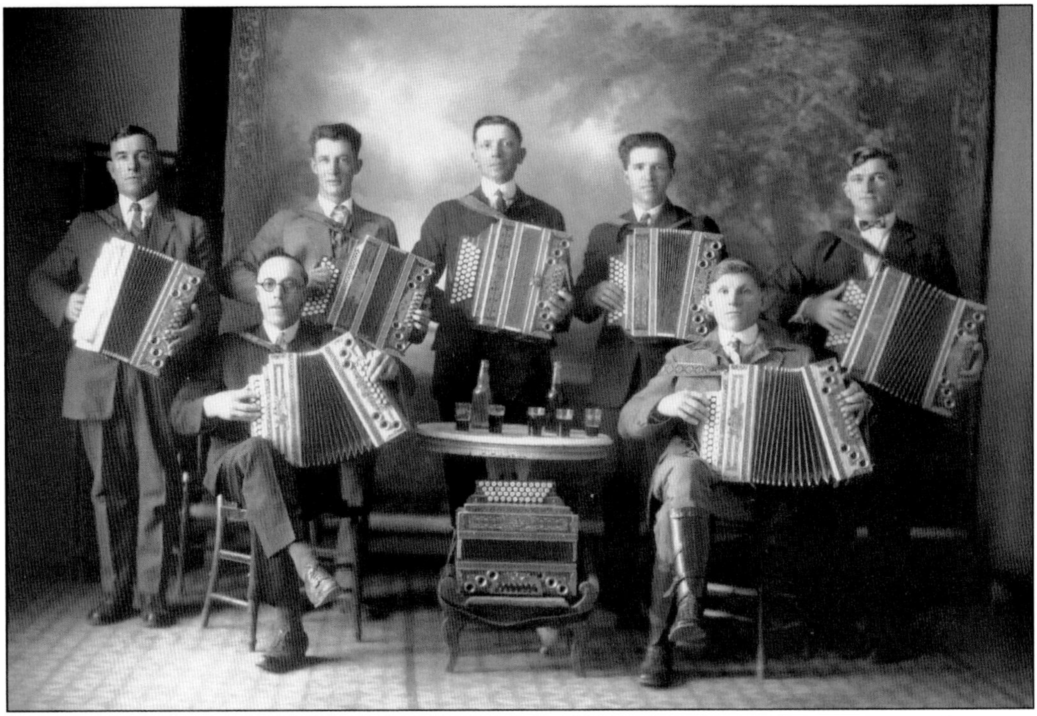

The button accordion used by these musicians, also known as a button box or squeeze box, was extremely popular in Rock Springs as it was ideal for performing the polkas and waltzes so loved by the European immigrants. This photograph was taken in 1927. (Courtesy New Studio.)

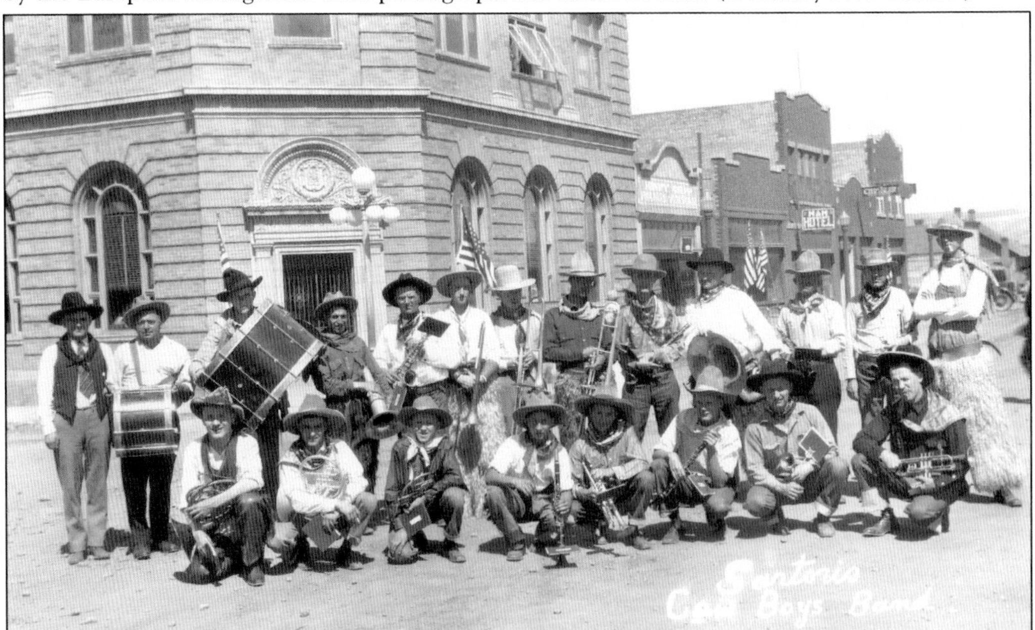

The Sartoris Cowboys Band performed in front of North Side State Bank on North Front Street in September 1927. Instruments included trombone, trumpet, French horn, and drums. (Courtesy New Studio.)

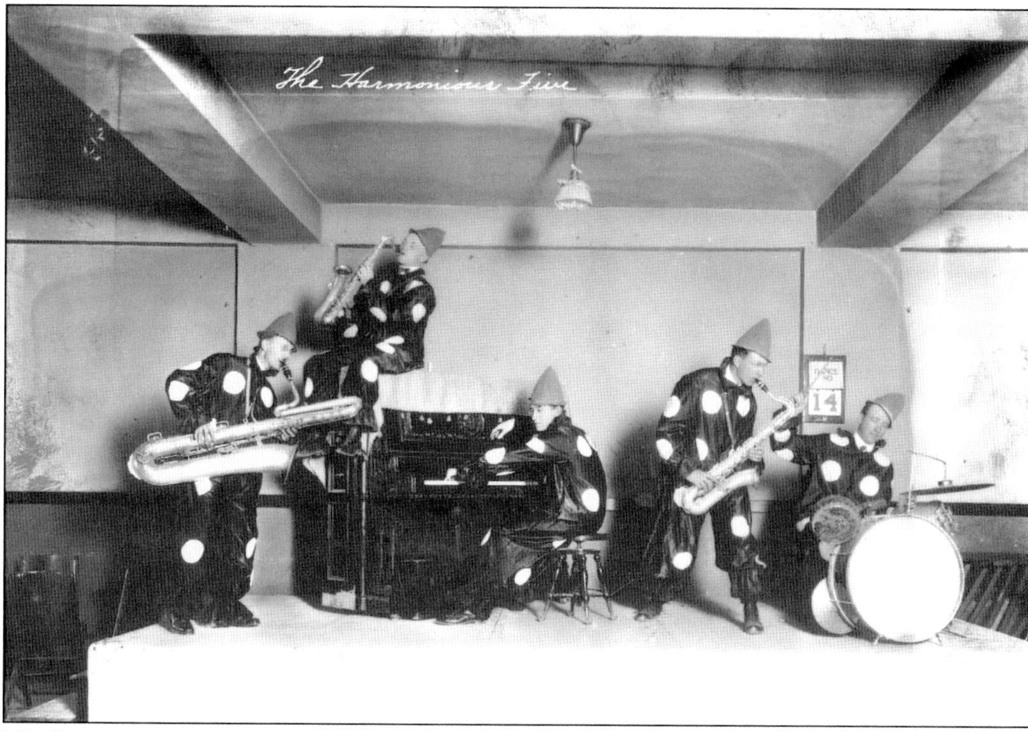

The Harmonious Five played on May Day 1921. Note the dance number posted on the wall. Dance cards could be signed to reserve a special dance with a special person. (Courtesy New Studio.)

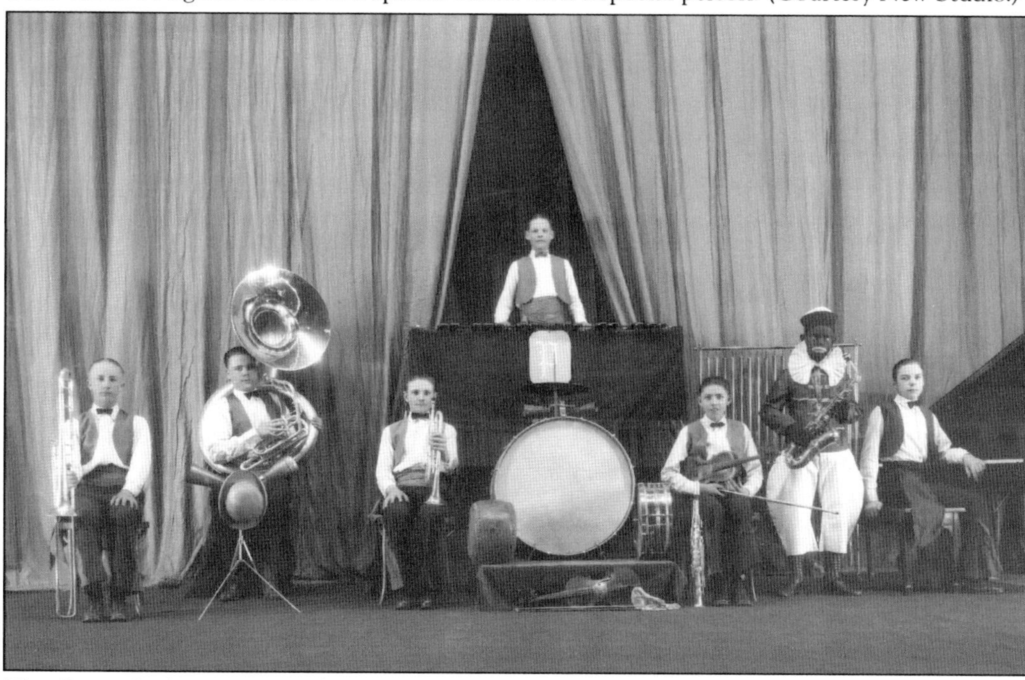

The Cazin Orchestra is seen here playing at the Rialto Theater in 1927. The seven-piece group played popular jazz hits for Rialto patrons. A wide variety of entertainment was featured at the Rialto, the most popular emporium in Rock Springs. (Courtesy New Studio.)

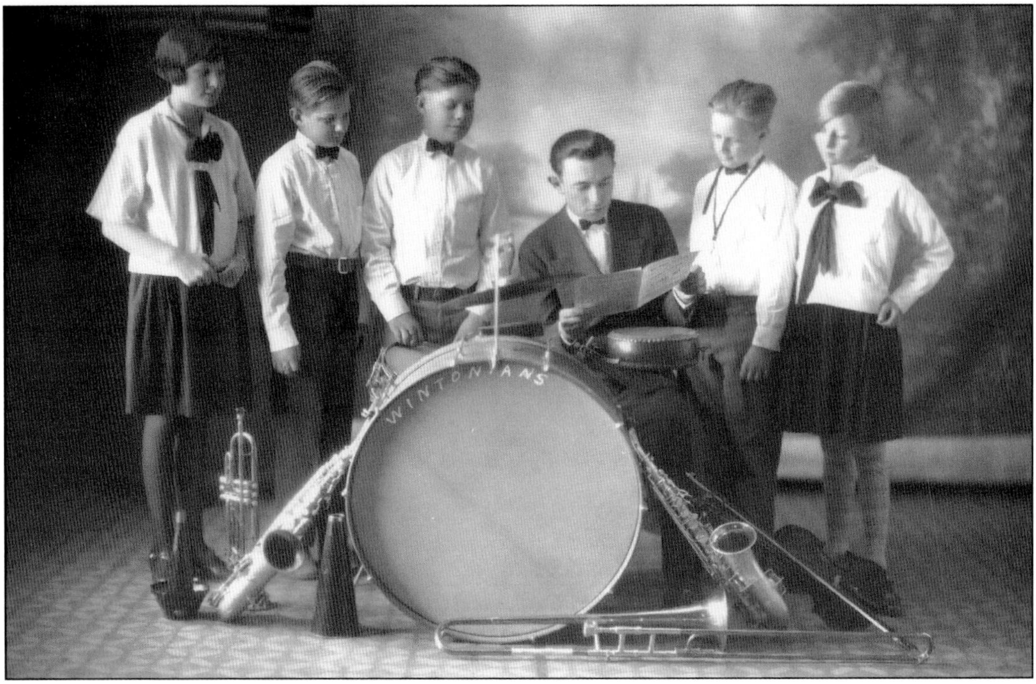

The Wintonians, shown in this 1928 photograph, was an orchestra from the Winton Coal Camp north of Rock Springs. Winton was one of several small communities located at coal mines in the greater Rock Springs area. (Courtesy New Studio.)

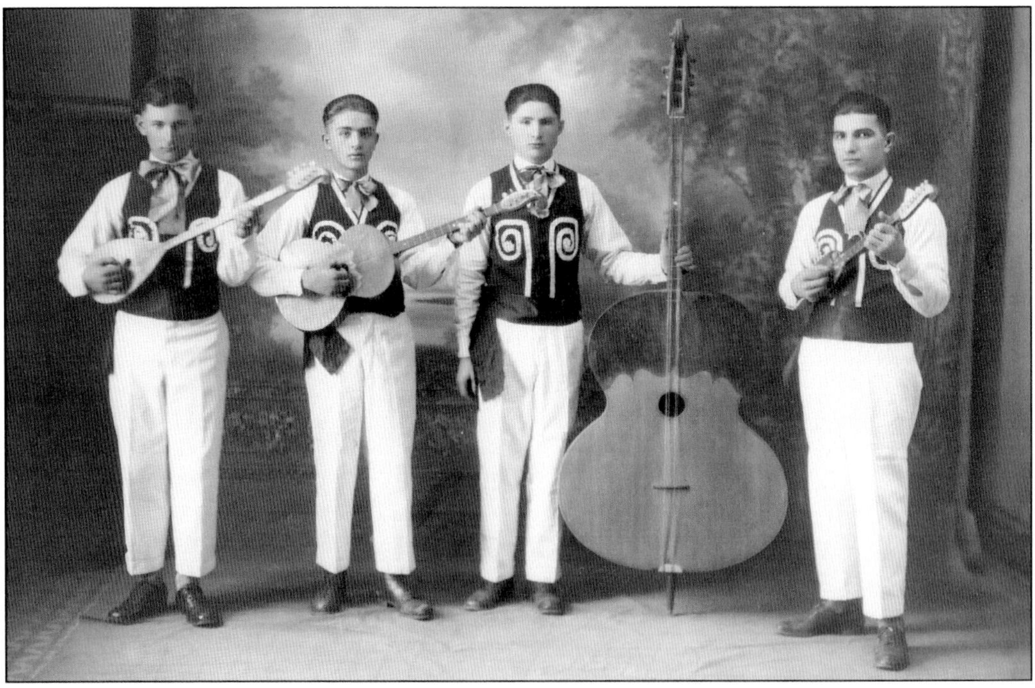

The two musicians on the left are John Zakovich and Emil Zigich. The largest instrument in the band is a burda, and the smallest is a tombrista. Music was a universal language connecting the many ethnically diverse groups in Rock Springs. (Courtesy New Studio.)

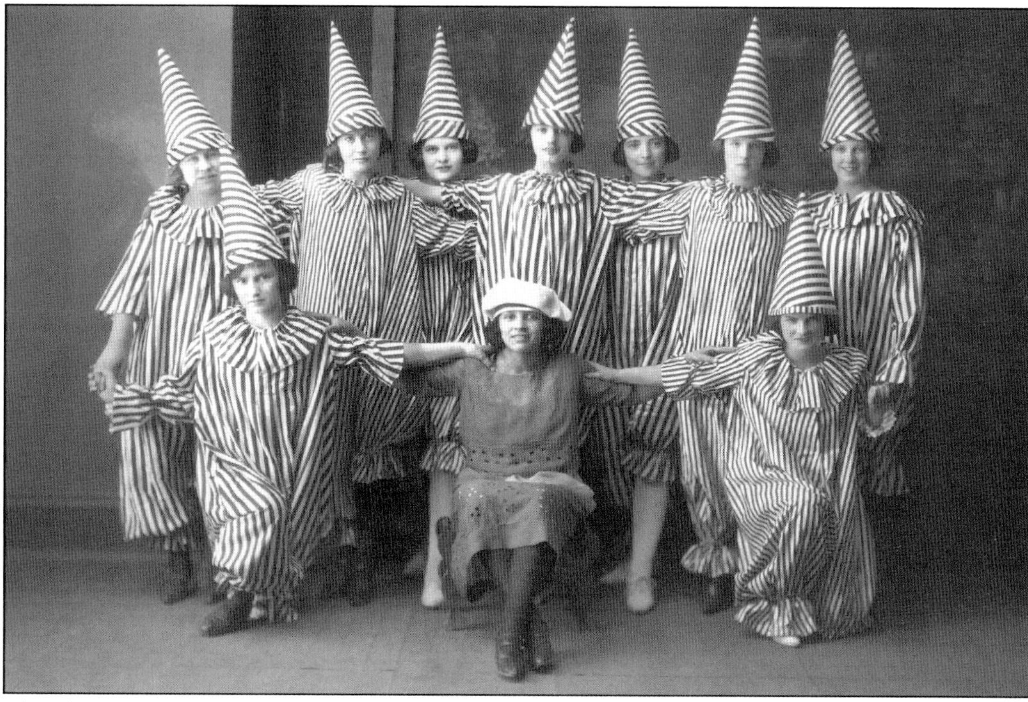

This dance troupe is from Western Amusement Enterprises. Traveling dance troupes performed at either the Rialto Theater on the south side of the railroad tracks or at the Grand Theatre on the north side. This photograph was taken in 1921. (Courtesy New Studio.)

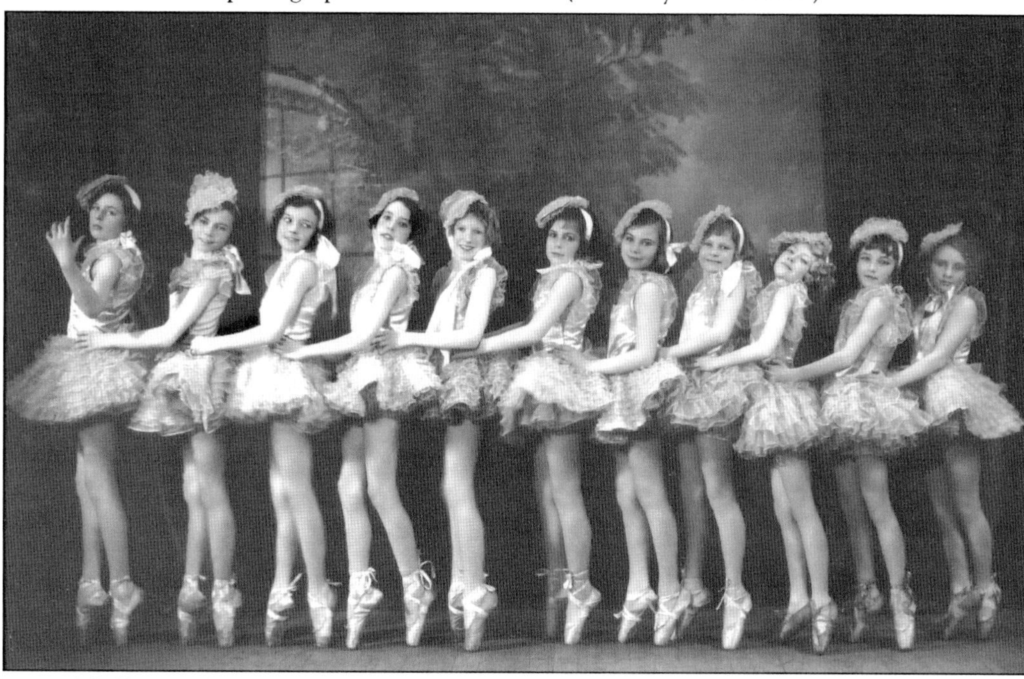

In 1935, ballerinas from the Fegerlhome Dancing Group stop dancing long enough to pose for this photograph. Community pageants afforded local youth an opportunity to exhibit their talents. (Courtesy New Studio.)

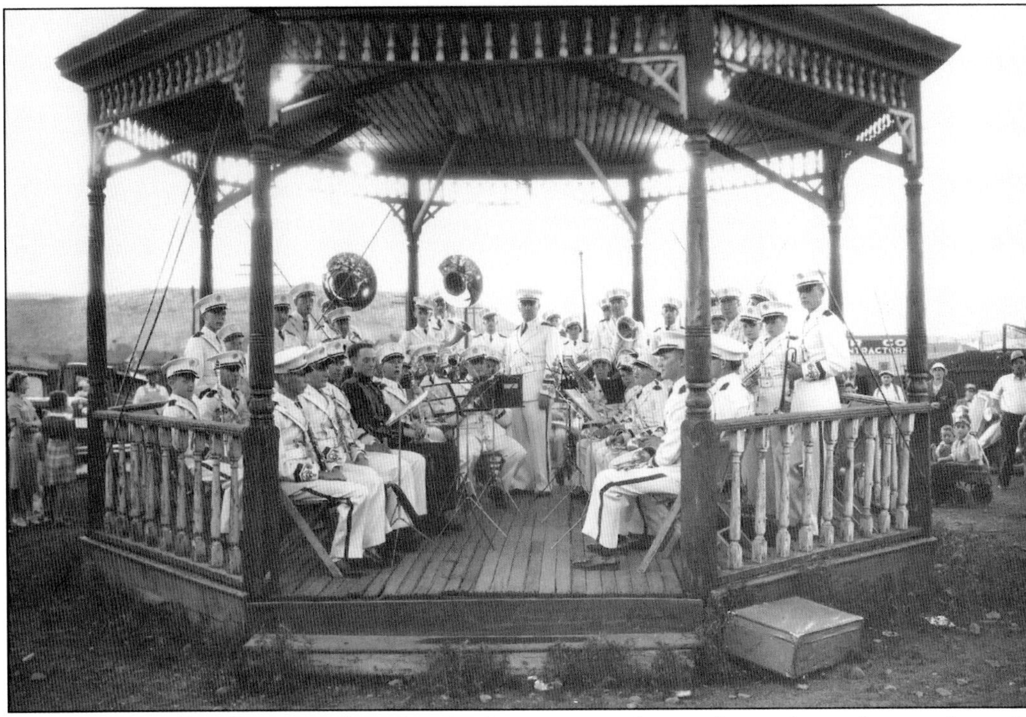

In 1935, the Odd Fellows marching band takes a rest in the gazebo at the park near the train station. Musical entertainment was a popular activity of many of the fraternal orders in early Rock Springs. They were one of several fraternal lodges that performed musical numbers at the gazebo located in the park near the Rock Springs railroad depot. (Courtesy New Studio.)

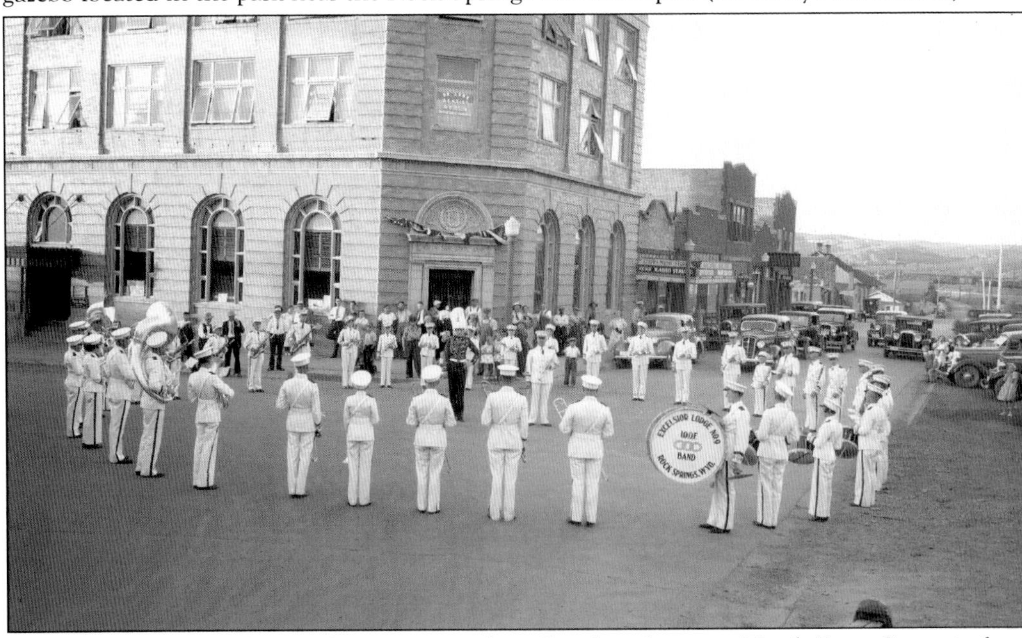

The Odd Fellows Excelsior Lodge No. 9 Marching Band performs on North Front Street in front of the North Side State Bank. The Odd Fellows band included men, women, and children, as seen in this 1935 photograph. (Courtesy New Studio.)

George Griffiths was leader of the band in 1924. Musical bands were a very important part of Rock Springs culture, and almost every ethnic group had a band of some kind. Sometimes bands were organized by a church or fraternal lodge. (Courtesy New Studio.)

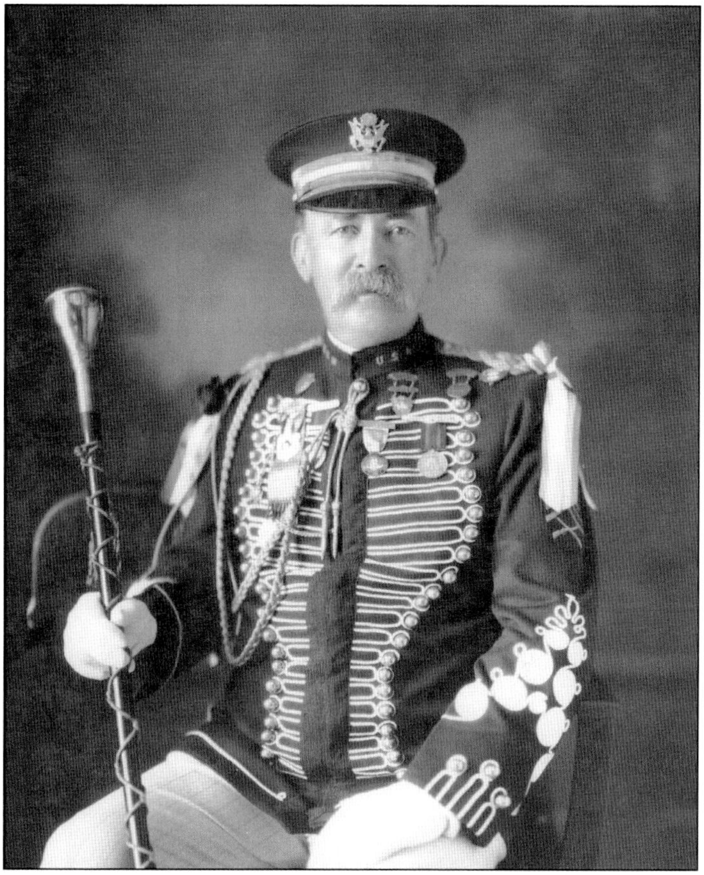

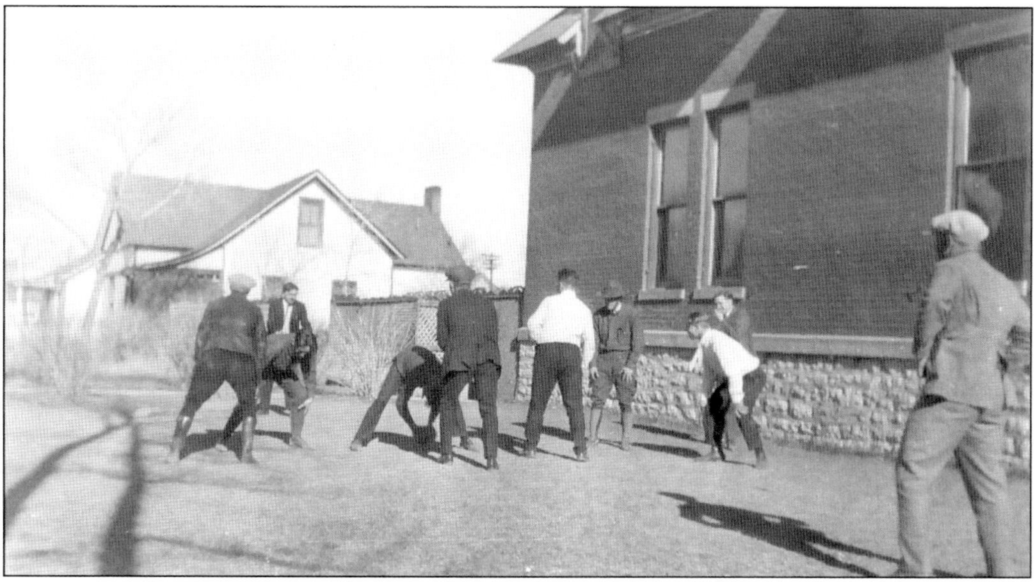

A group of young men play an impromptu game of football next to the old Washington School building. Young people played many street games, including hide and seek, kick the can, run sheepie run, and mumble peg. (Courtesy the Spence family.)

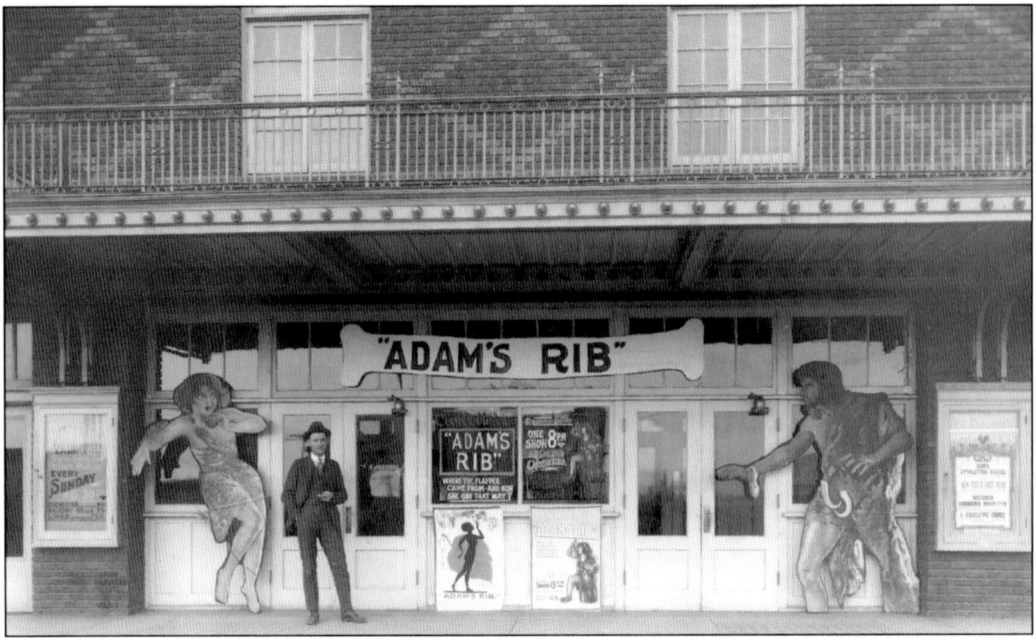

Thomas Berta stood in front of the Rialto Theater when this photograph was taken in May 1923. The theater opened in February 1921 and closed April 1959. In addition to showing films, the Rialto was an excellent venue for performances, community events, vaudeville, orchestra, bands, and a variety of entertainment. (Courtesy New Studio.)

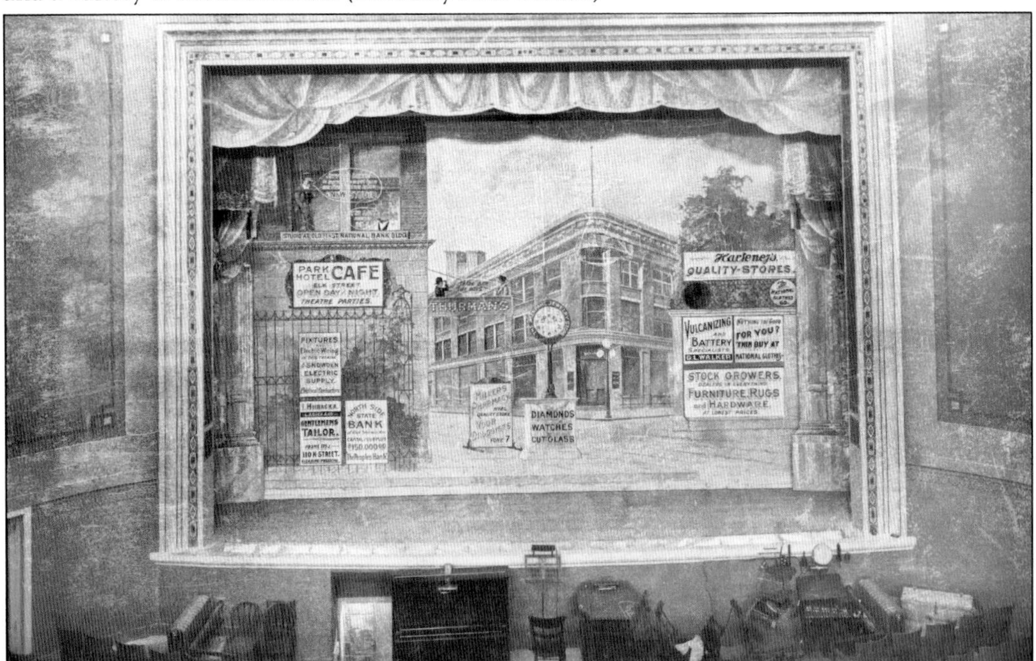

This painted scene at the Rialto depicts several of the most important buildings in town. The Rock Springs National Bank, Stock Growers Mercantile, and the Park Hotel are represented in this rendering. Advertisements for local business helped make up this scene and perhaps enticed theater patrons to buy a product or utilize a service. (Courtesy New Studio.)

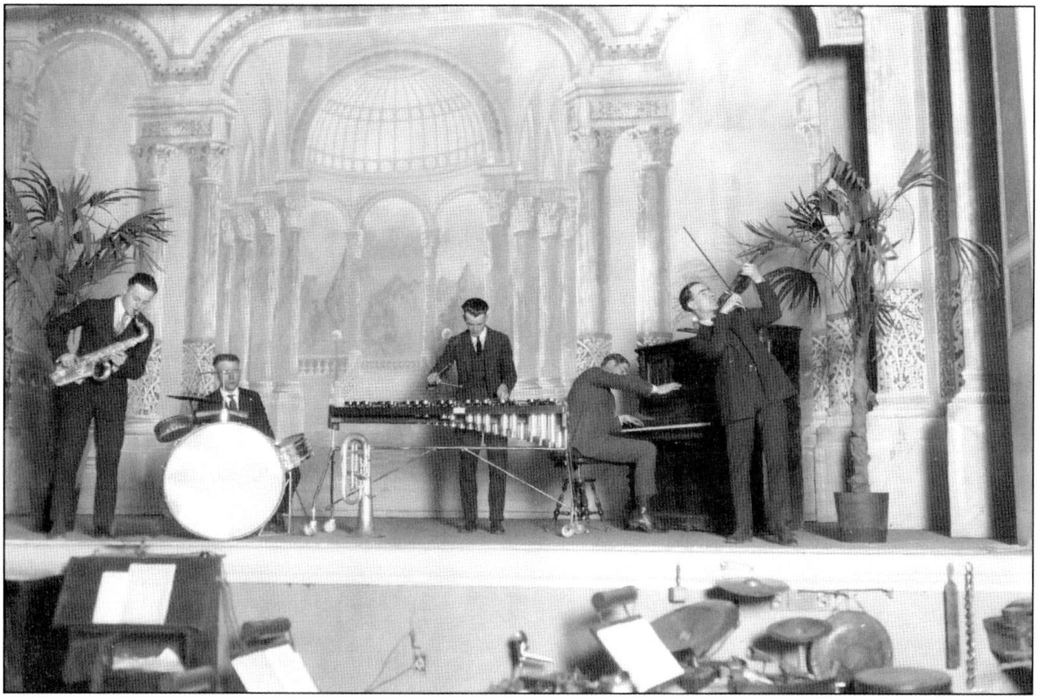

The Burt Chapman band shown in this 1922 photograph performed in Rock Springs. Jazz bands were a sign of the times during the Roaring Twenties. Many traveling bands like this five-piece group played at the Rialto Theater. (Courtesy New Studio.)

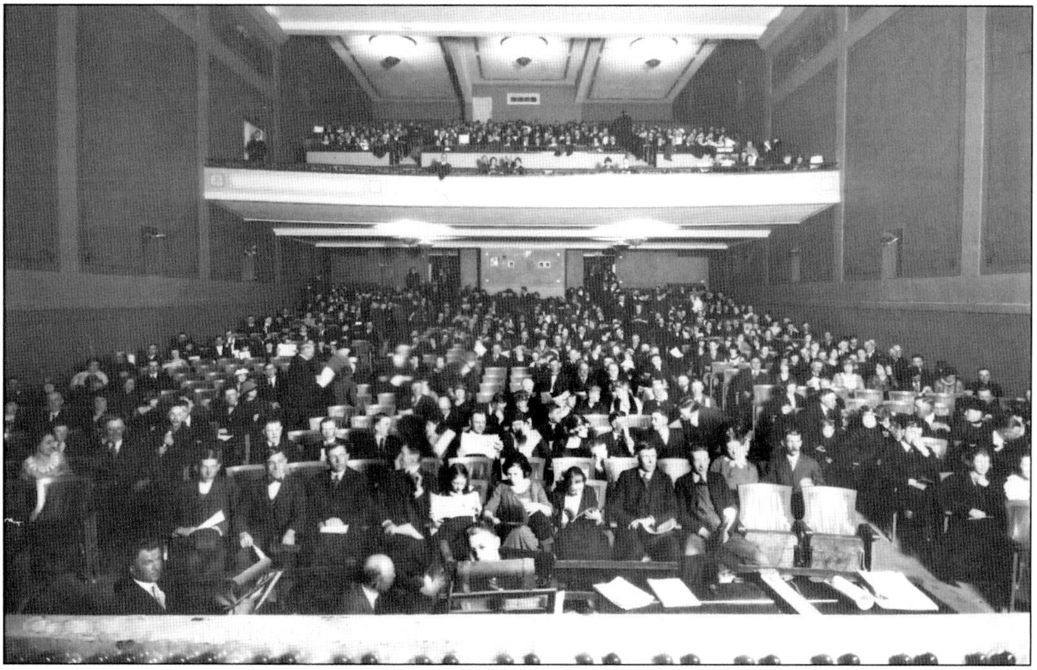

The interior of the Rialto Theater is shown in a photograph taken in 1921. This large, well-dressed audience was attending an orchestral performance. The Rialto was located on South Front Street and was the only theater in Rock Springs with a balcony. (Courtesy New Studio.)

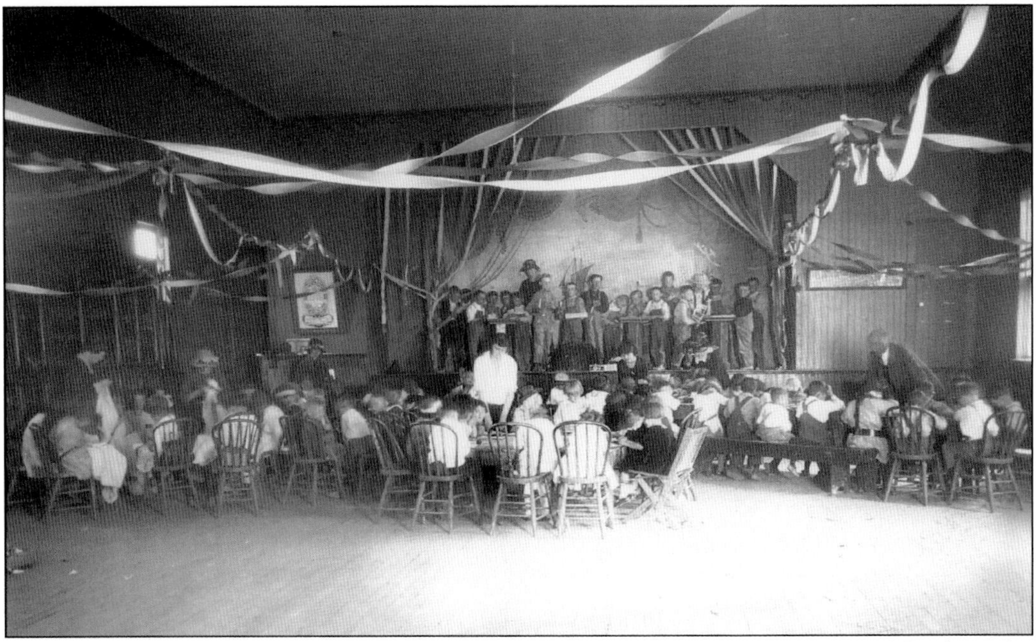

The Finn Hall, where this party is being held, introduced Finnish traditions and foods to the people of Rock Springs as well as providing a taste of the old country for the large population of Finlanders. (Courtesy New Studio.)

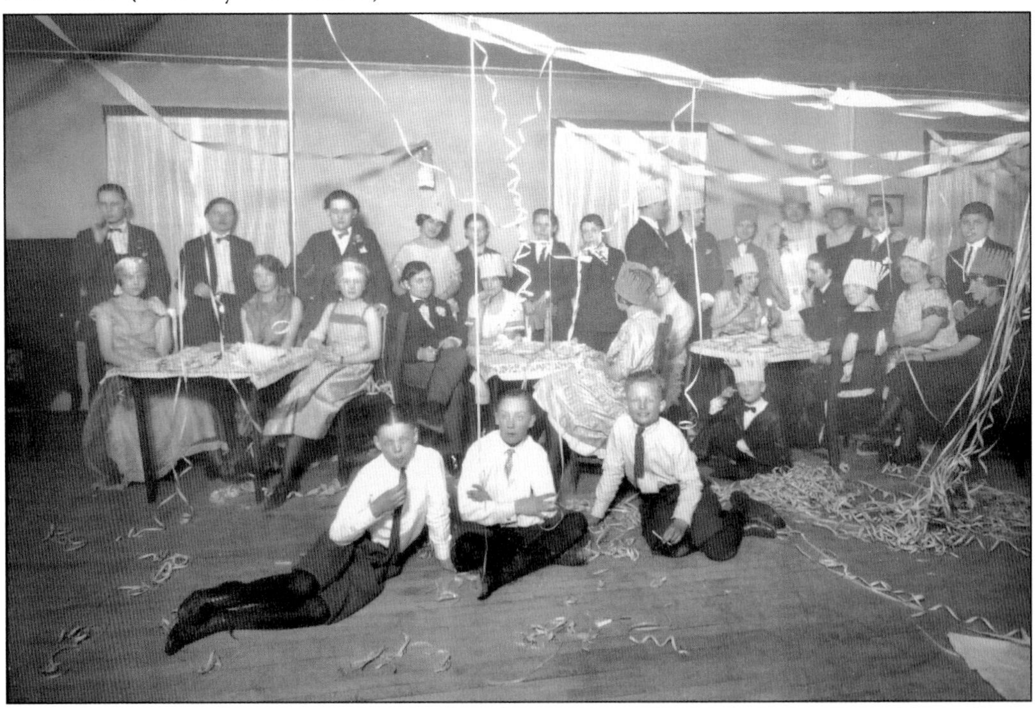

Kids find a way of having fun no matter what the occasion. The special occasion celebrated here has been lost to history, but in any case, folks can always find a reason to party in Rock Springs. This group is shown here meeting for a party at the Union Pacific Club in 1924. (Courtesy New Studio.)

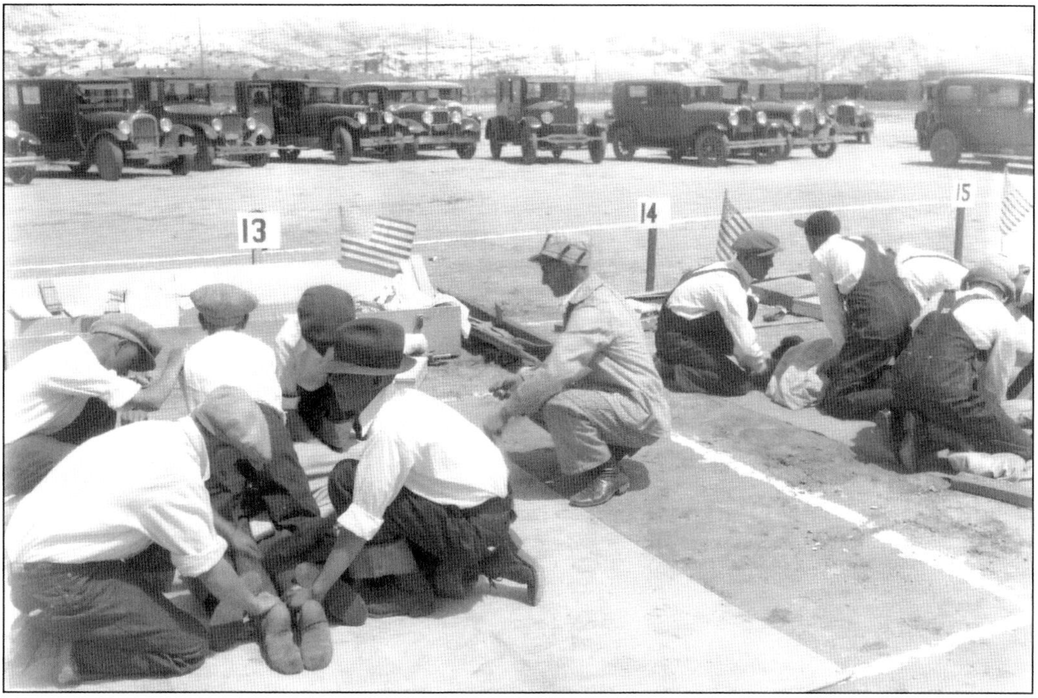

Youth organizations like this Boy Scout group, participating in a first aid competition, help young people learn important skills. The competition was part of an annual event celebrating the mining company agreeing to allow workers to work an eight-hour day. The photograph was taken in 1928. (Courtesy New Studio.)

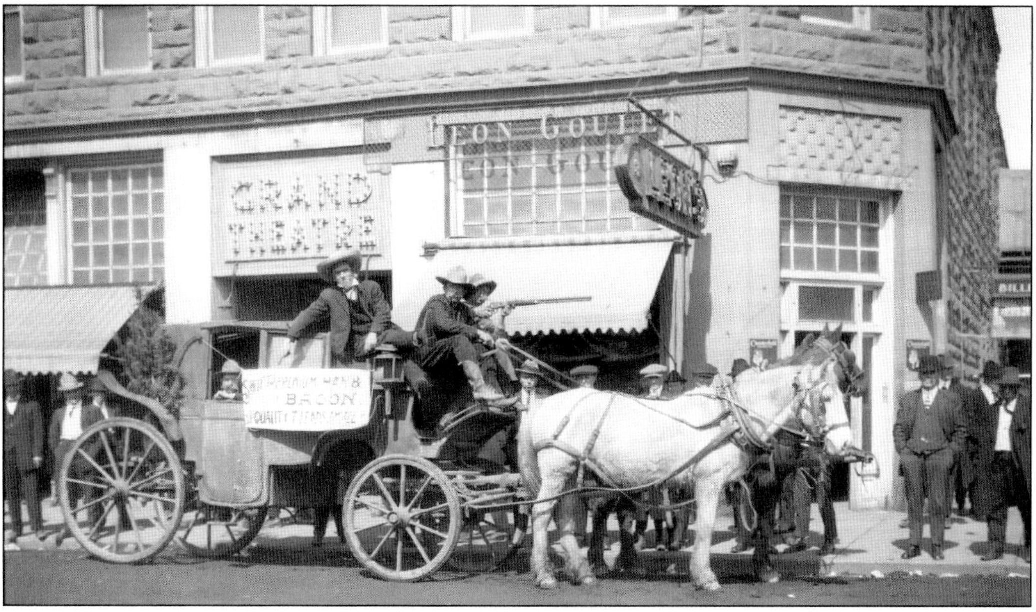

In 1923, this horse-drawn coach stopped in front of the Grand Theatre on North Front Street. "Quality Leads 'Em All" is the slogan used by Swift Premium Ham and Bacon to promote their product. At the Grand Theatre, admission was a nickel for children under 12 and a quarter for adults. (Courtesy New Studio.)

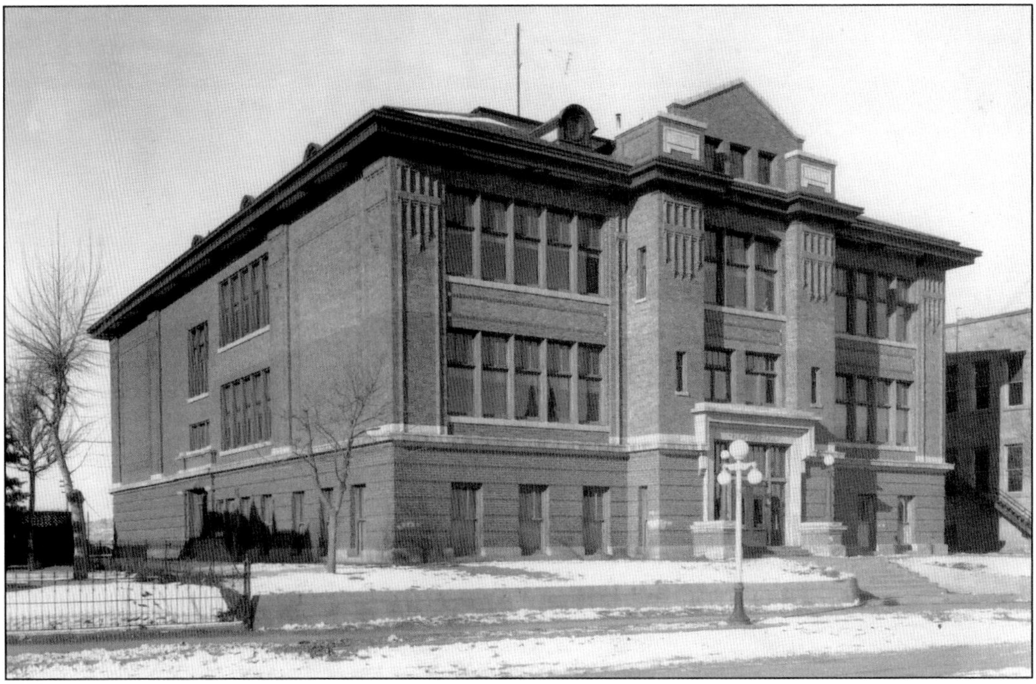

This versatile building served first as the Rock Springs High School; later the building became Rock Springs Junior High, then it was repurposed to house the District Education Building. Its last incarnation was Vista Bible Church. This stately building was recently razed, and Rock Springs National Bank was built on the site. (Courtesy New Studio.)

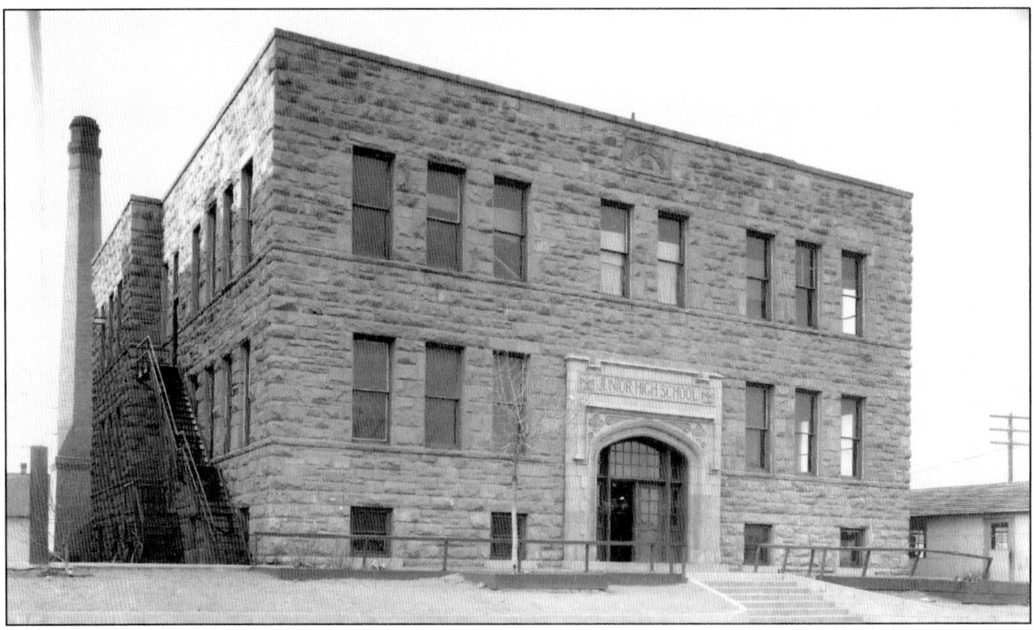

This old rock building was the junior high located next to Rock Springs High School. It was torn down in the early 1930s, and the stones were reused to form a wall around the new high school located in the Number One Hill area. That school now serves as East Junior High, and the stone wall has been removed, replaced by a chain-link fence. (Courtesy New Studio.)

Four

BRICKS AND MORTAR

SCENES AROUND TOWN

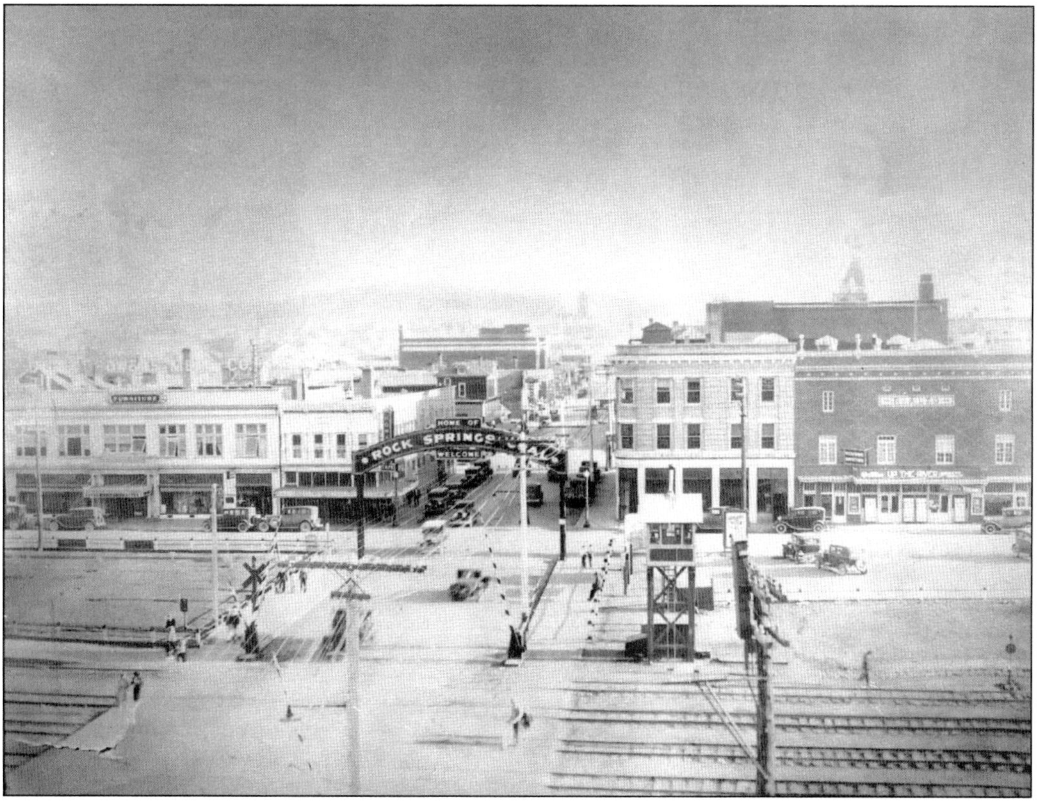

This view of Rock Springs is looking across South Front Street and south on C Street in 1930. This major city street was bottlenecked as travelers had to cross eight sets of track of the Union Pacific Railroad main line. The Rock Springs Coal sign welcomed travelers on the Lincoln Highway, the first transcontinental highway, which was established in 1913. (Courtesy New Studio.)

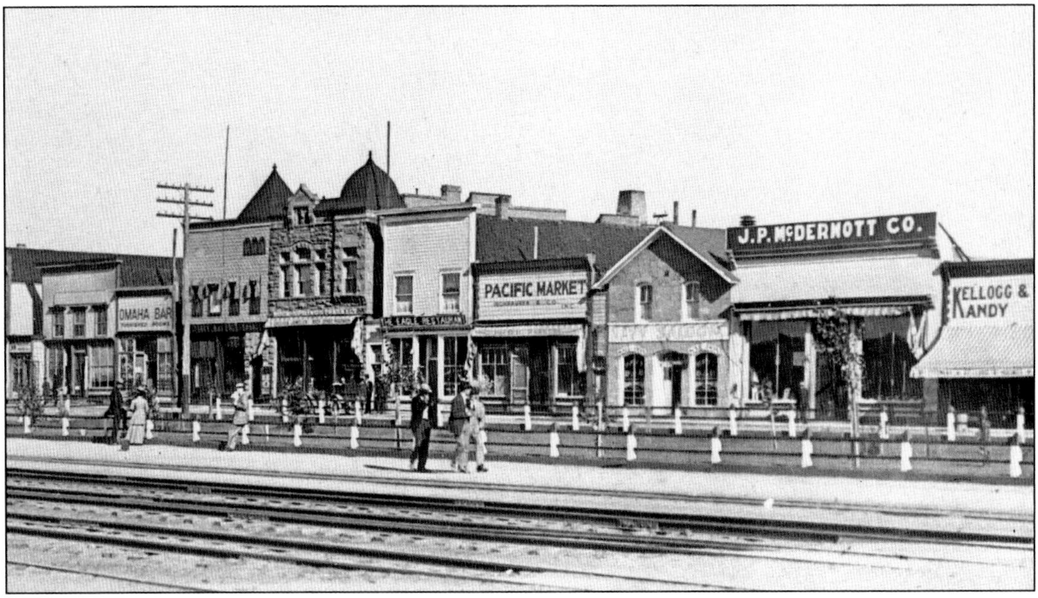

Many of the buildings along South Front Street are still standing, including the First National Bank (the stone building left of center) with the date "1892" carved in stone above the right window. The building is one of the most architecturally interesting buildings in town. But, alas, the stone face is a facade in front of a quite ordinary brick building. The butcher shop at Otto Schnauber's Pacific Market in the center of the photograph is said to have been the workplace where Robert LeRoy Parker picked up the moniker "Butch Cassidy." (Courtesy New Studio.)

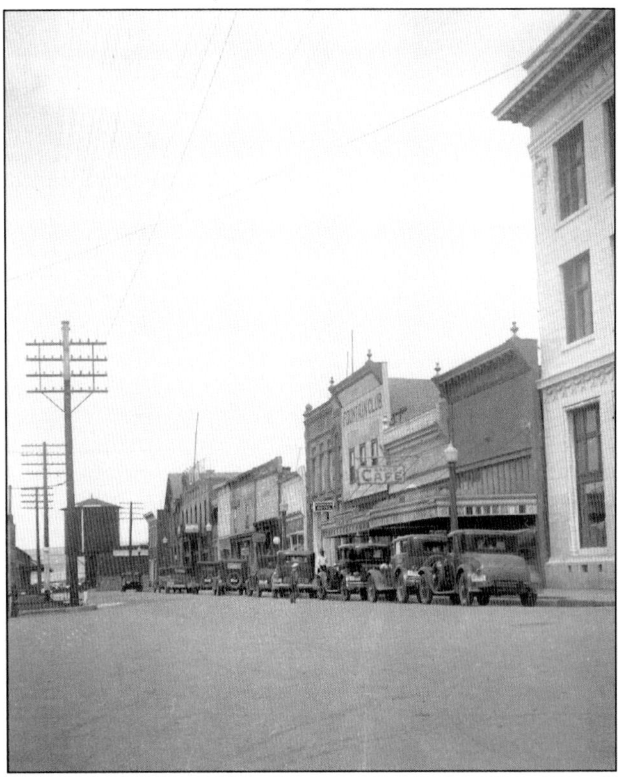

This is a 1920s view along South Front Street. The Fountain Club, near the center next to the Grand Café, was the meeting place and dance hall for several civic organizations. The Fountain Club was a favorite gathering place for the large Tyrolean population in Rock Springs. The impressive, newly built First Security Bank building is shown at the right. (Courtesy New Studio.)

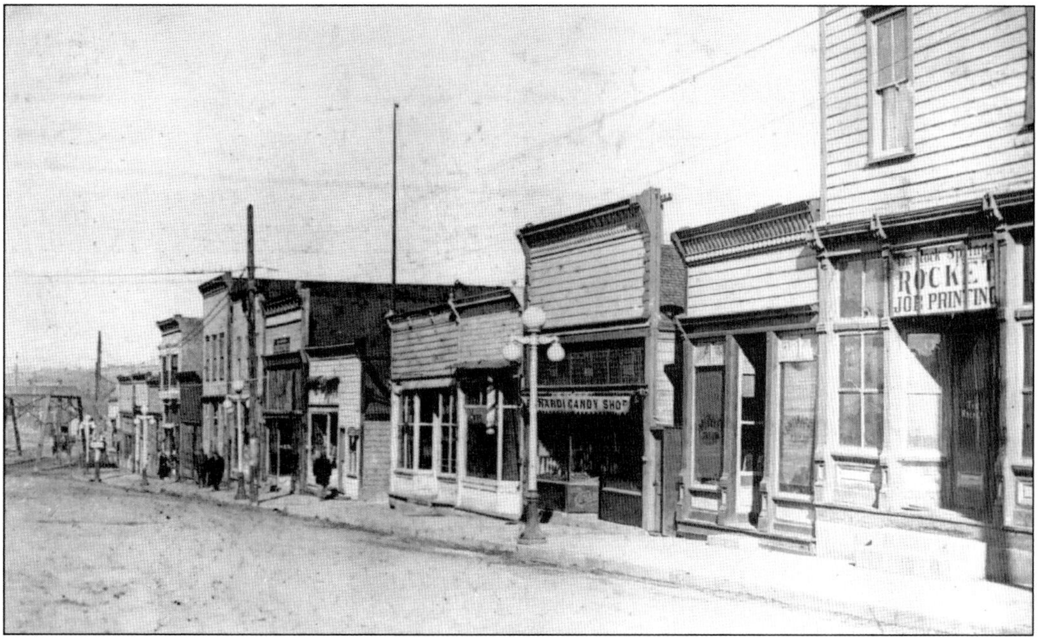

The Rock Springs Rocket newspaper office also did job printing, as shown here in an 1890s view of K Street. The original route of Bitter Creek was at the north end of this street where the bridge can be seen. After many years of flooding episodes, the whole creek was rerouted several blocks to the north by Mayor Peter Christian "P. C." Bunning in the mid-1920s. K Street was long recognized to be a "tough" part of town. (Courtesy New Studio.)

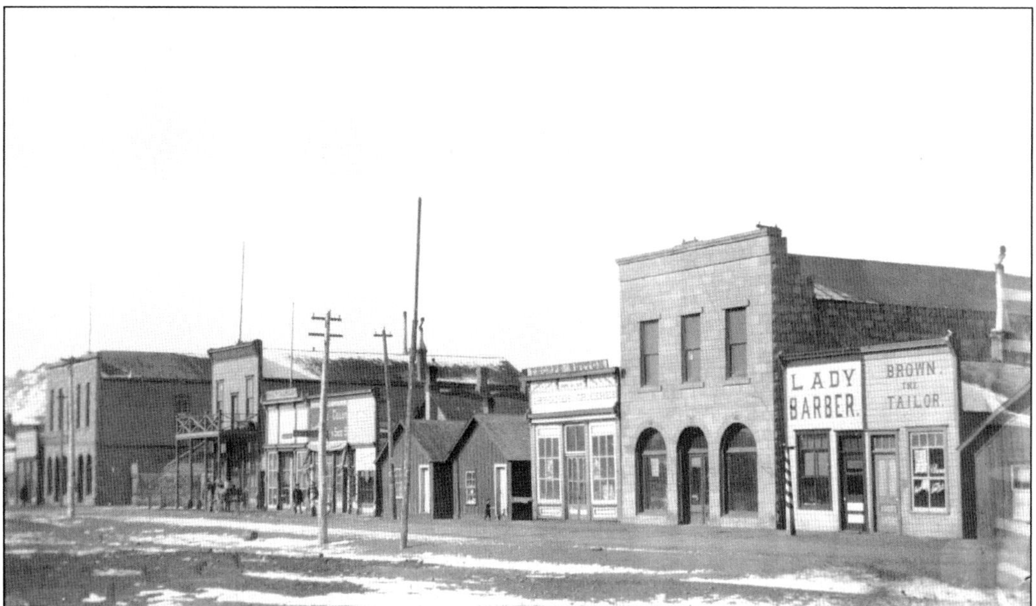

This 1890s-era photograph of North Front Street shows a seemingly less affluent part of town than South Front Street at about the same time. The Edgar Opera House was in the stone building next to the Lady Barber. Thorpe and Sutton Dry Goods and Brown the Tailor were also on the north side of the tracks. (Courtesy New Studio.)

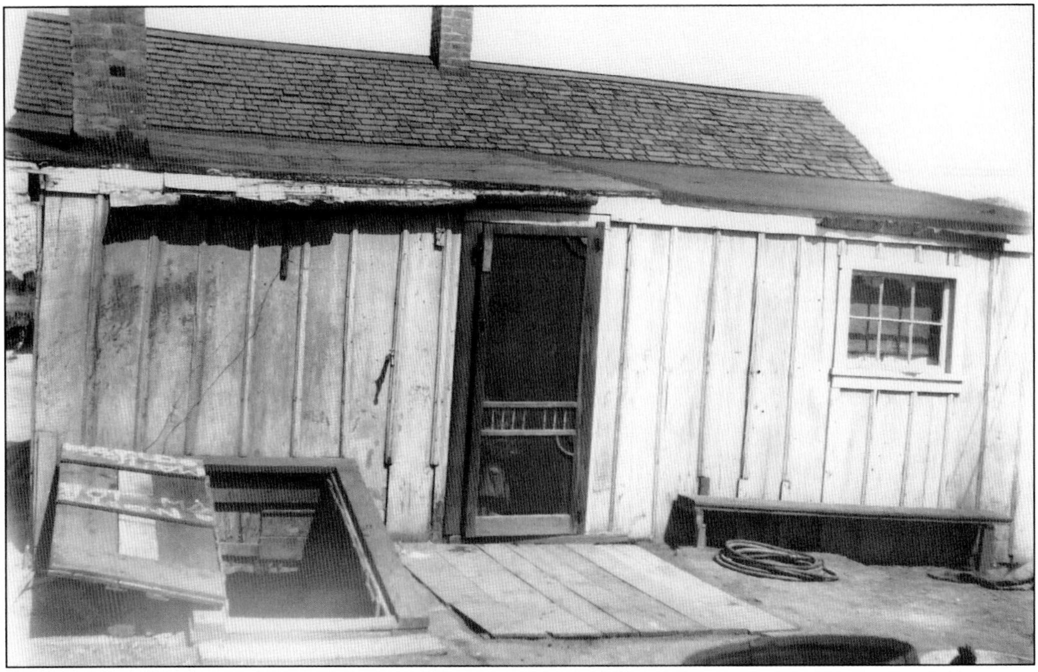

This miner's family residence indicates the sparseness of life of the working class in Rock Springs. The doorway to the coal cellar is open to the left of the main door of this two-room company-built house, which may have housed a family of five or more. A few of these "little Bohemian houses" are still around town being used as garages or outbuildings or as part of houses that have been made by combining several structures together. (Courtesy New Studio.)

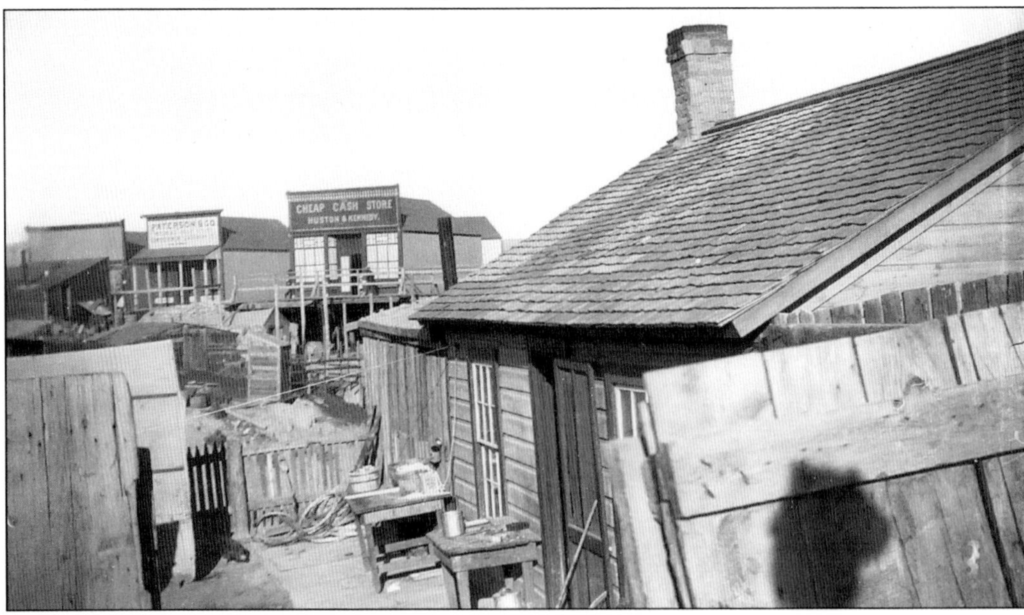

A mine company official named David G. Thomas liked to write little poems about Rock Springs. In one, he describes how Bitter Creek was soiled by all manner of filth until spring snowmelt "freed the town of foul disease" each year. Many residents in the early days lived in dugouts carved into the stream channel, as seen in this 1896 photograph. (Courtesy New Studio.)

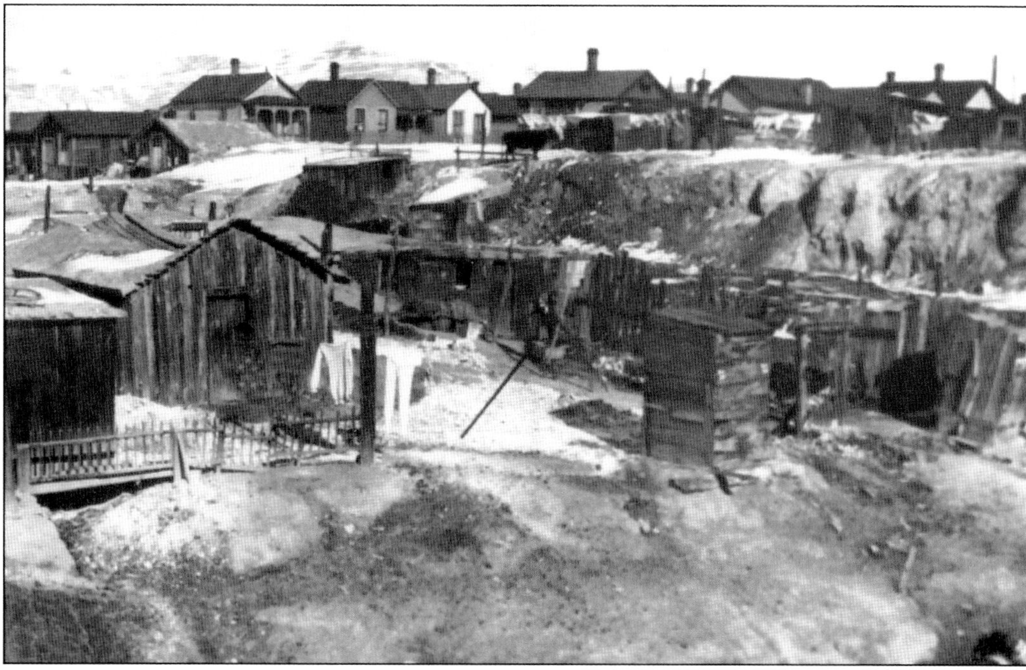

As workers became a little more prosperous and as the mining companies began to provide housing, like those seen above the stream channel, many of the dugouts and shanties became outbuildings. Some people still lived in shacks. Congressman Teno Roncalio would later remark how the economic well-being of the community could be discerned by looking at the laundry hung out to dry. (Courtesy New Studio.)

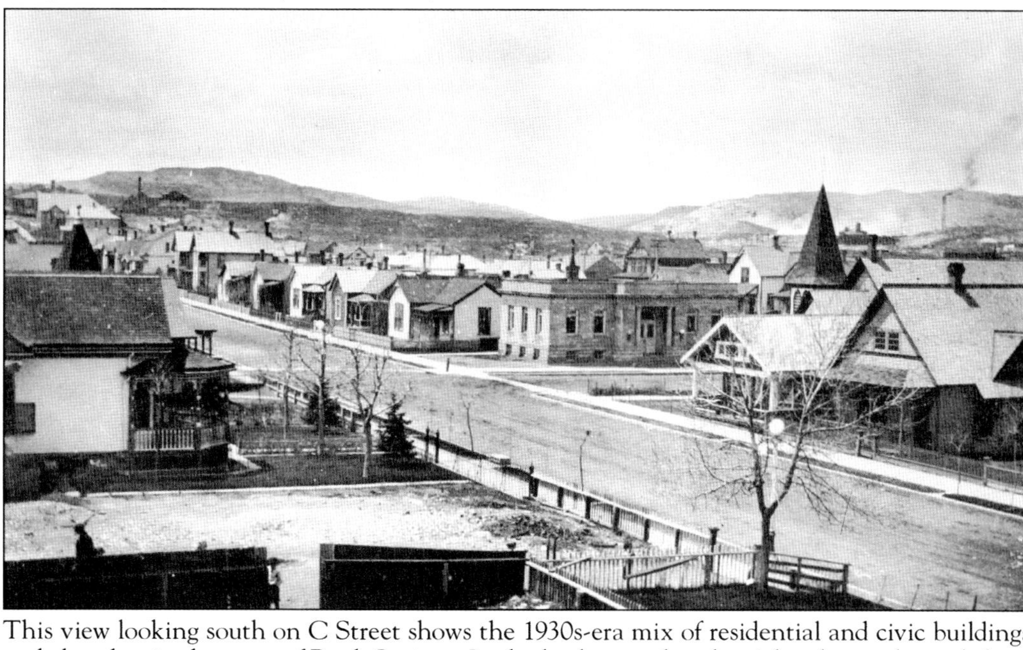

This view looking south on C Street shows the 1930s-era mix of residential and civic buildings and churches in that part of Rock Springs. In the background at the right, the smokestack from a coal mining operation can be seen, and to the left is the first location of Sweetwater County Memorial Hospital. (Courtesy New Studio.)

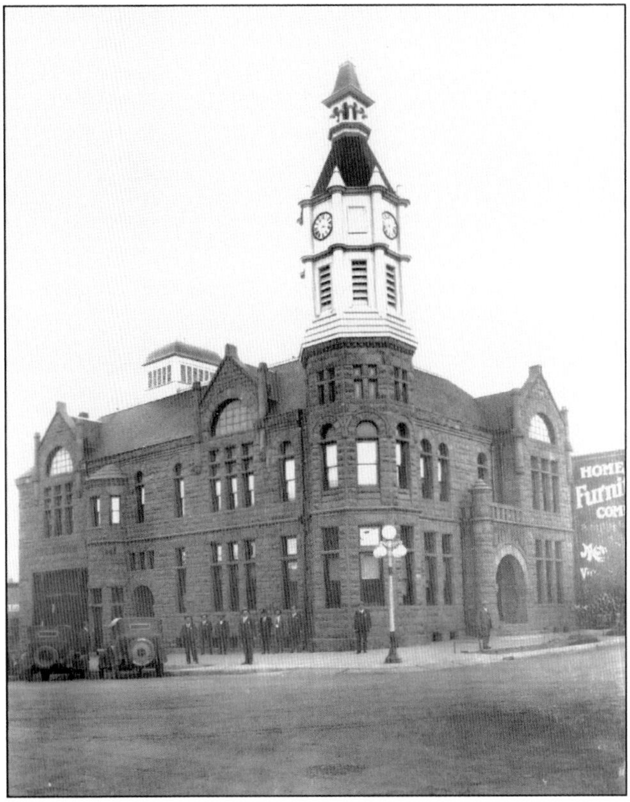

The Rock Springs City Hall is pictured in 1928. The Romanesque-style monumental building was designed by architect Martin D. Kern and inspired by Henry Hobsen Richard's work. Hewn from local sandstone, it was constructed at a cost of $28,000 in 1894, but the cost increased substantially when it was discovered that the foundation had to be augmented because of undermining of the area. (Courtesy New Studio.)

The Rock Springs National Bank, shown here in about 1923, was one of the most prominent buildings, and likely the richest bank, in town. It was located at 518 South Front Street and operated at this location from 1911 until 1970. This bank has long been owned by the Hay family, who were among the first settlers in Rock Springs. (Courtesy New Studio.)

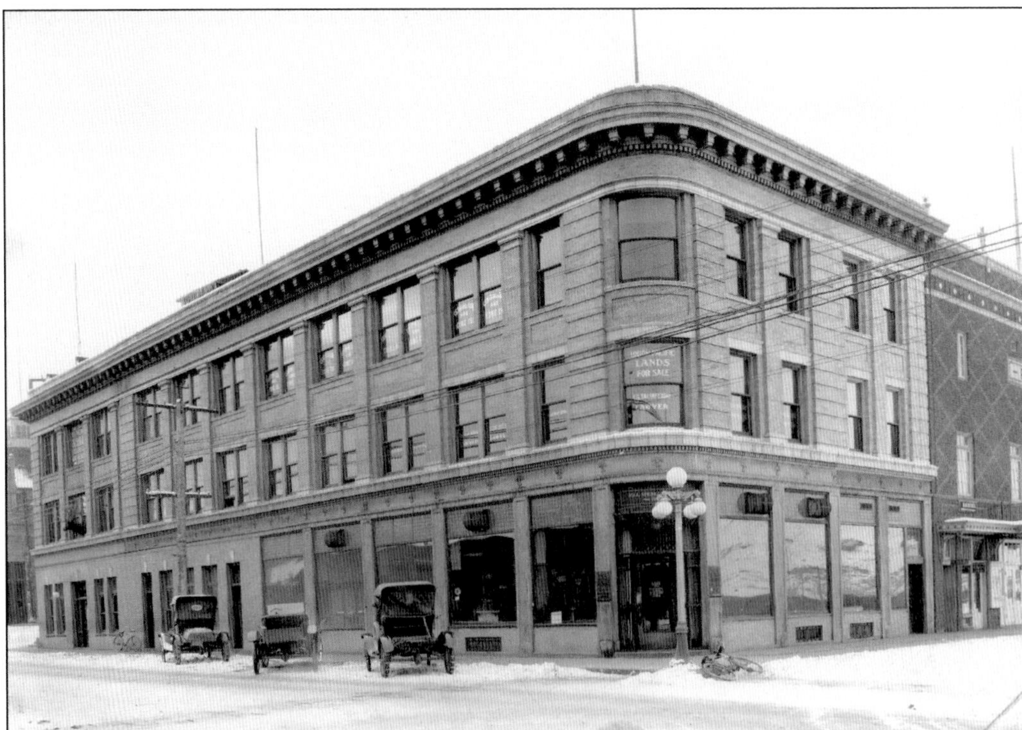

Here is a 1920 view of the newly constructed First National Bank, which later became part of the First Security Bank system. This ornate terra-cotta building stood on what came to be called Bank Court. The building still stands on Broadway Avenue in Rock Springs. (Courtesy New Studio.)

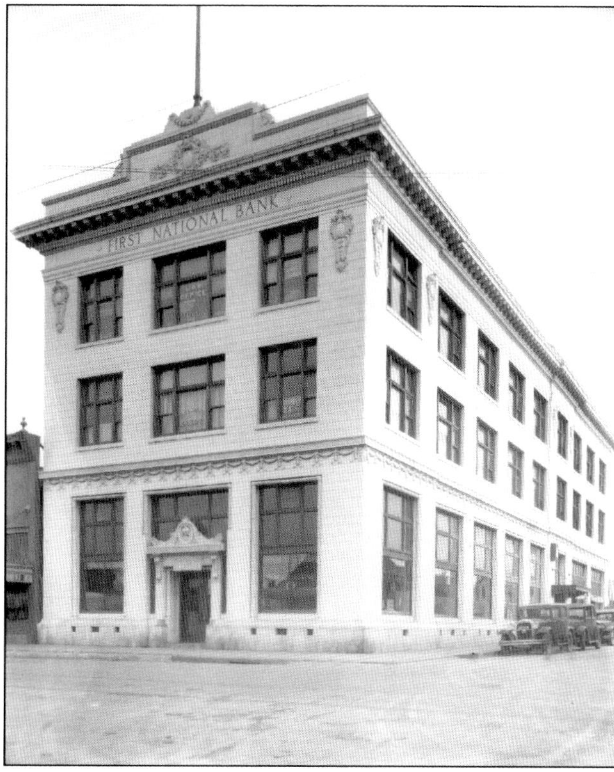

North Side State Bank, shown here in the early 1950s, was a prominent office building on North Front Street. The bank was founded by a group of businessmen, including Peter Christian Bunning, who held stock certificate No. 1. This building was torn down in the early 1990s. (Courtesy New Studio.)

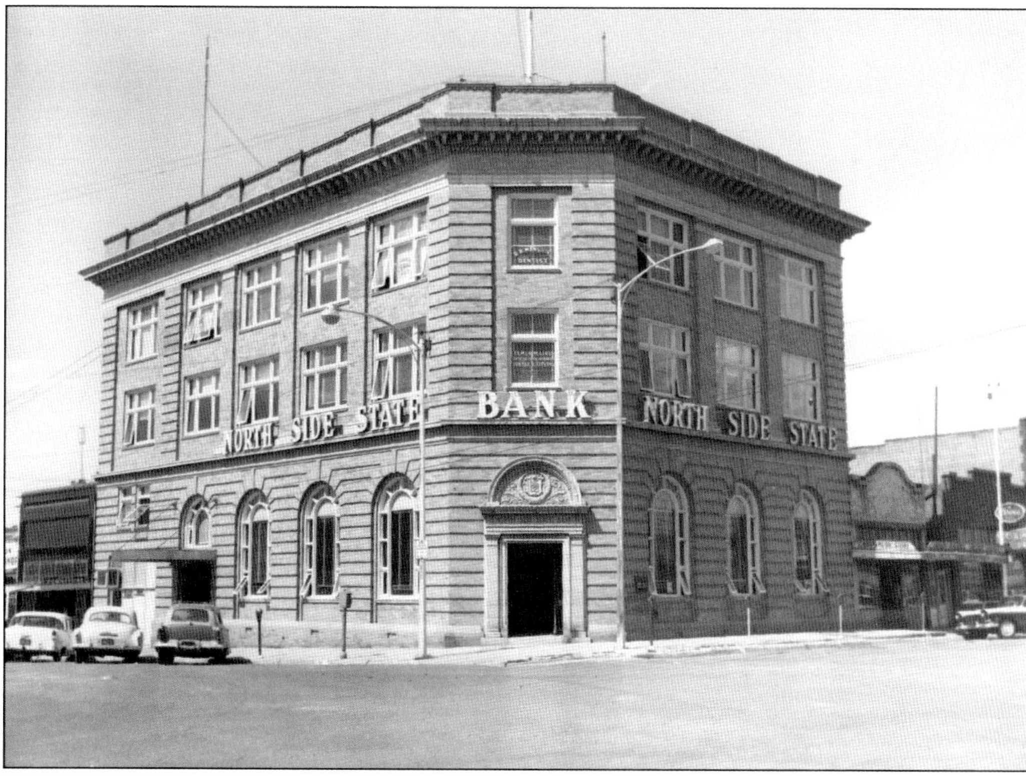

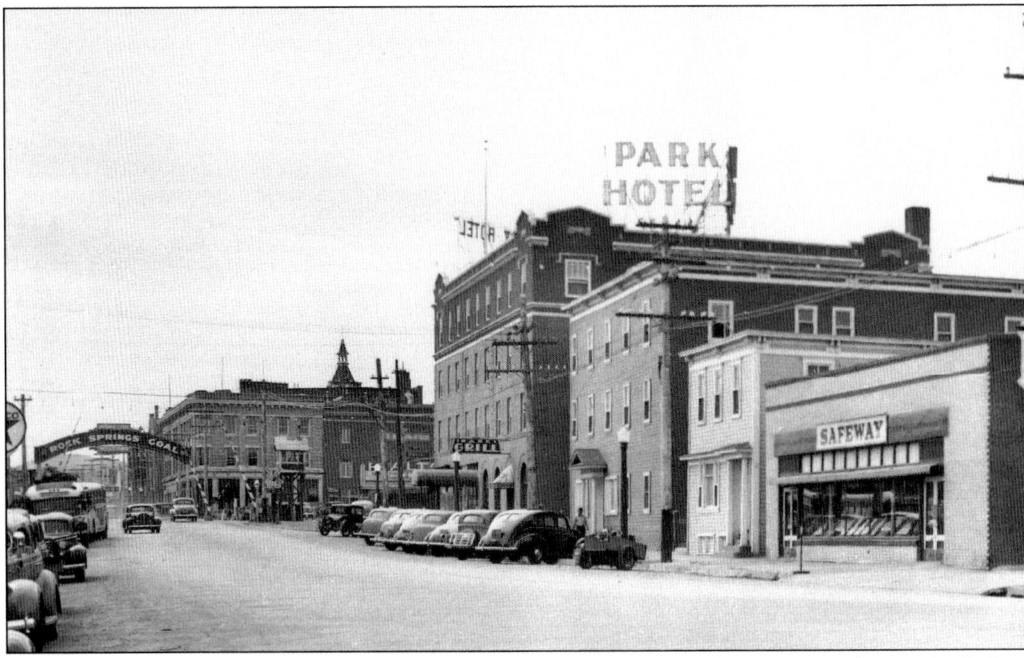

This view is looking south on C Street. The Park Hotel opened in 1914 and was the hub of western Wyoming commercial activity until the late 1950s. The first Safeway Store was also on this block. (Courtesy New Studio.)

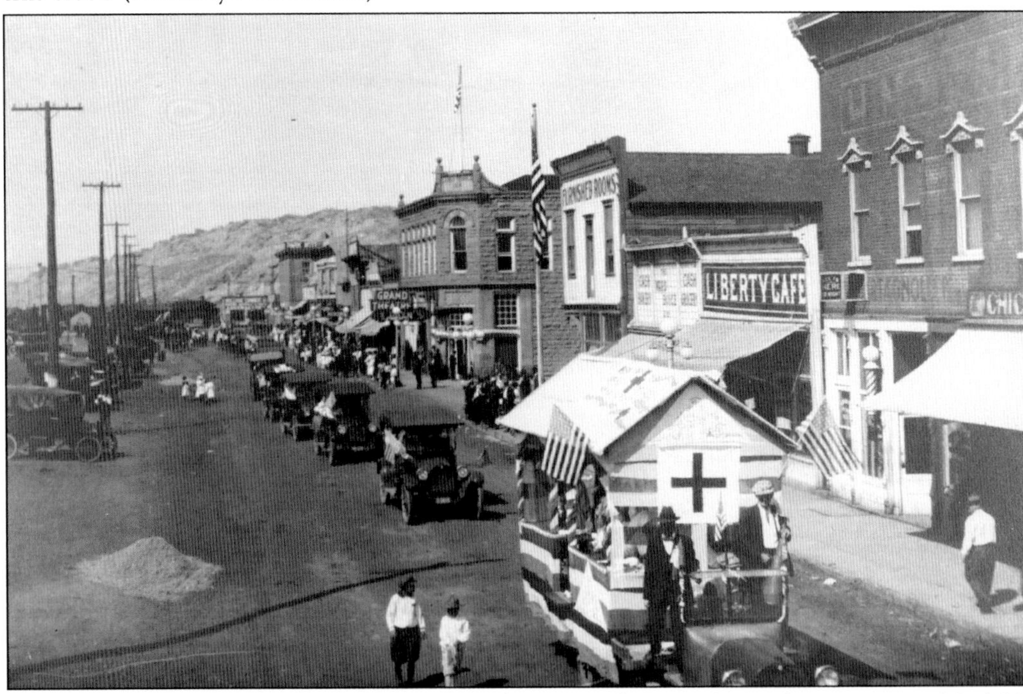

Rock Springs loves a parade. This 1920s parade on North Front Street features many Model T Fords, including one decorated with Red Cross emblems. Businesses on North Front Street at the time included the Chicago Meat Market, Liberty Café, and the Grand Theatre. (Courtesy the Chadey family.)

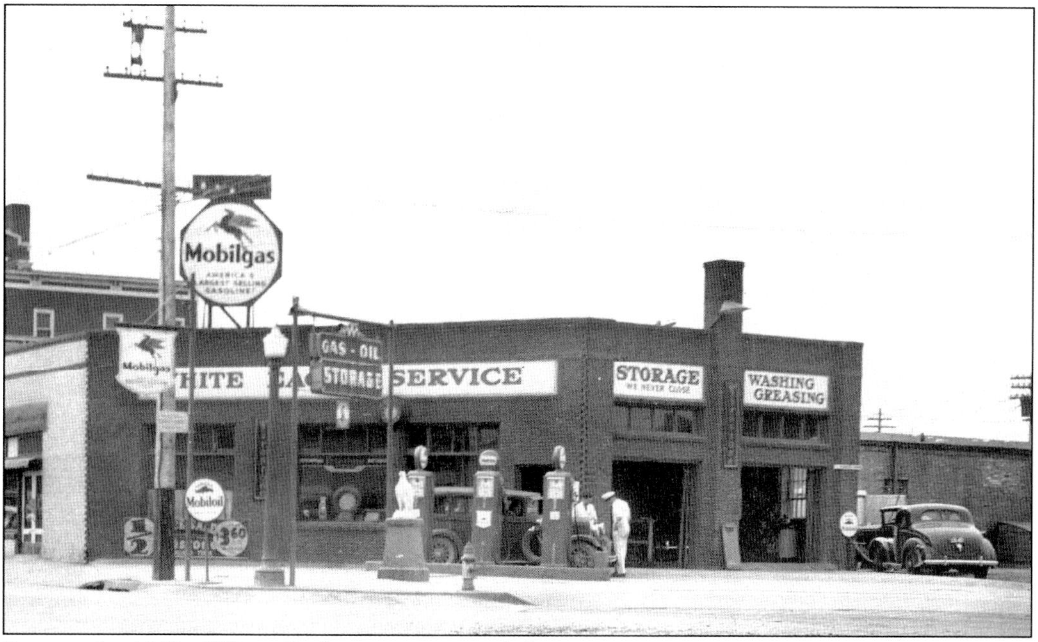

During the 1940s, White Eagle Motors was a full-service garage with a tow truck. White Eagle advertised, "We Never Close," which perhaps indicates the importance the family automobile had attained in sparsely populated places like Wyoming. (Courtesy New Studio.)

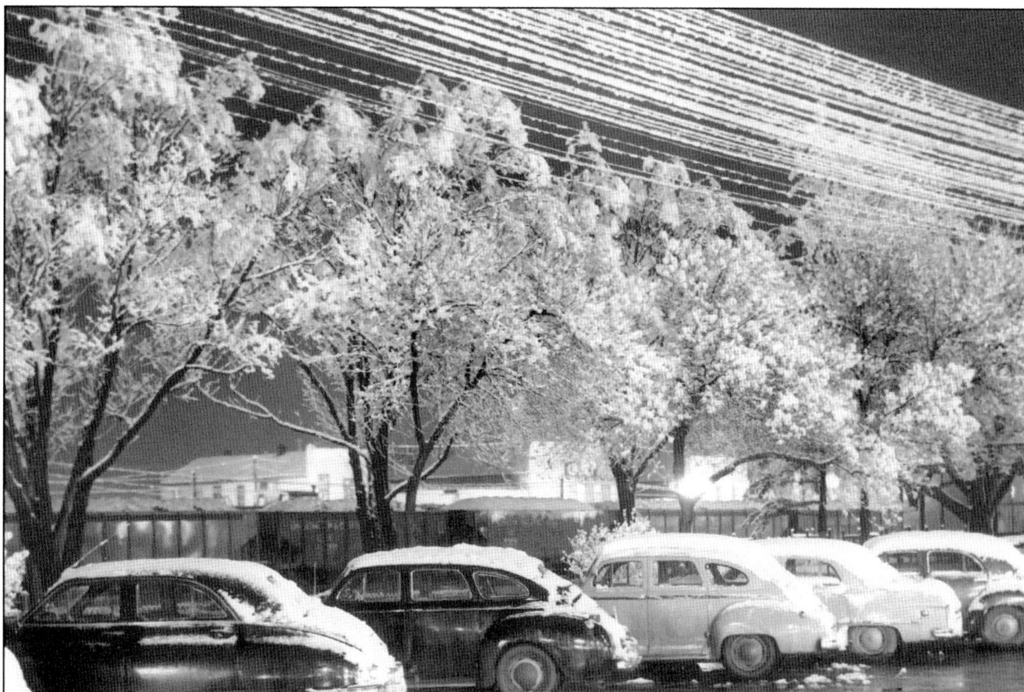

This beautiful picture shows late-1940s automobiles parked along the north side of South Front Street and harkens to the time before electrical power and telephone lines were placed underground. Hoarfrost on the overhead lines creates an artistic impression. (Courtesy New Studio.)

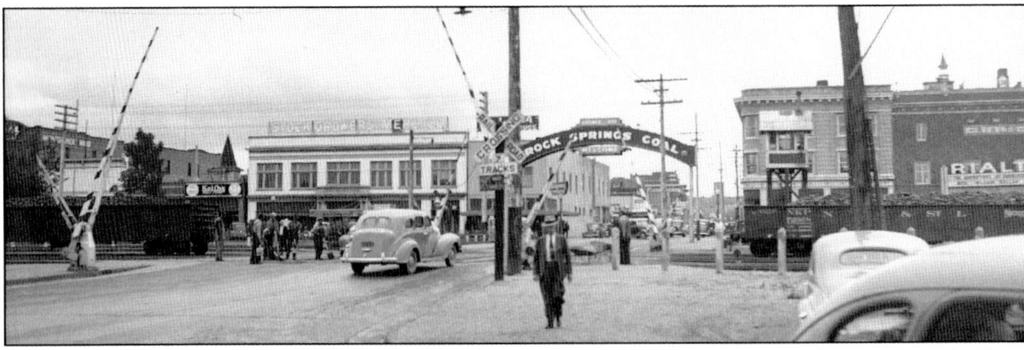

By the late 1940s, the scene at the C Street railroad crossing was decidedly spiffy with shiny new cars. The crossing gate is clearly visible, and the Stock Growers Mercantile had become the most prominent store. Rock Springs National Bank and the Rialto Theater are on the right, or west, side of C Street. Unfortunately, the marquee at the Rialto is not legible, but the theater was advertised as a "complete amusement palace" in the 1920s, featuring silent films and vaudeville shows. (Courtesy New Studio.)

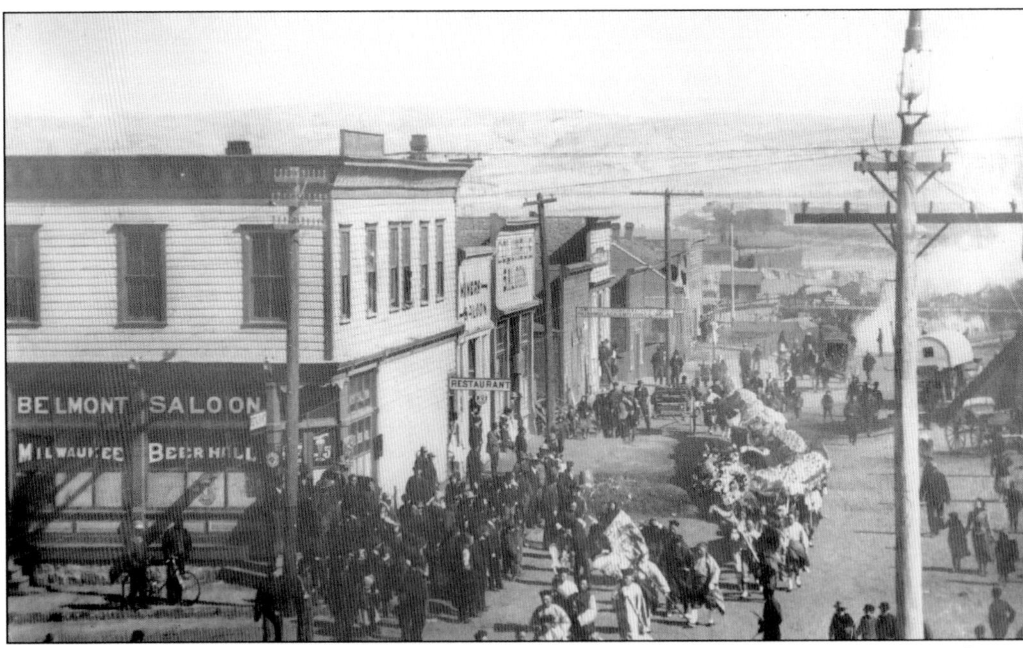

This photograph taken around 1906 records the celebration of the Chinese New Year. The 75-foot silk-and-paper dragon carried by over 50 men paraded up the winding North Front Street. When the Chinese celebrated, they invited the community to attend, and the townspeople were given presents and goodies. (Courtesy SCHM.)

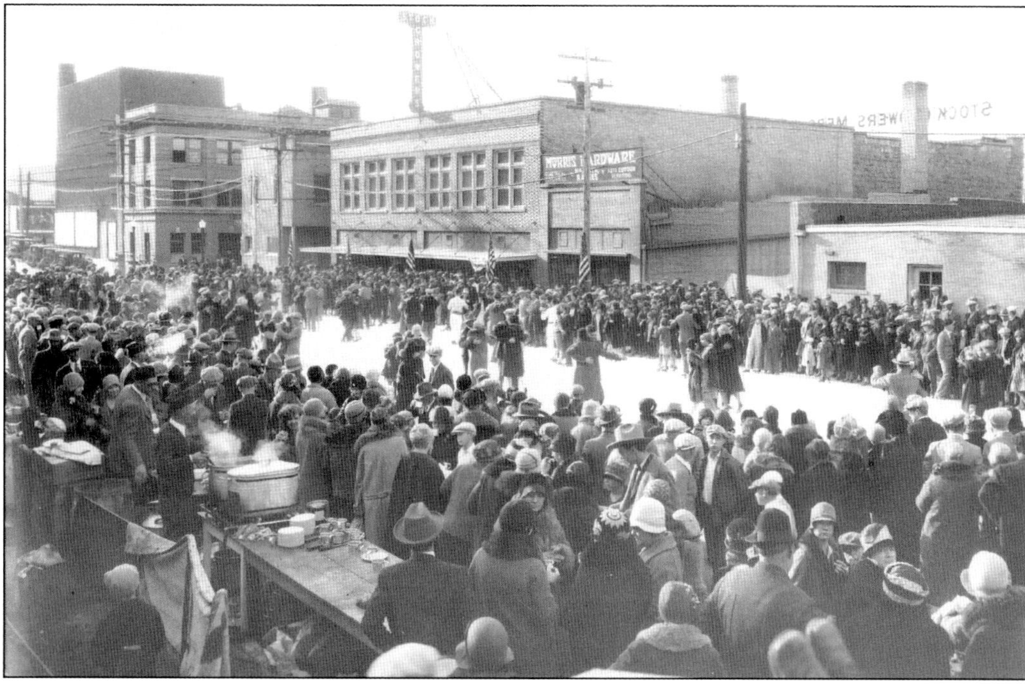

On November 11, 1928, some Rock Springs citizens celebrated Veteran's Day by dancing in the street. The street was closed, and the American Legion catered a meal. Cold weather did not stop people from coming to enjoy the occasion. (Courtesy New Studio.)

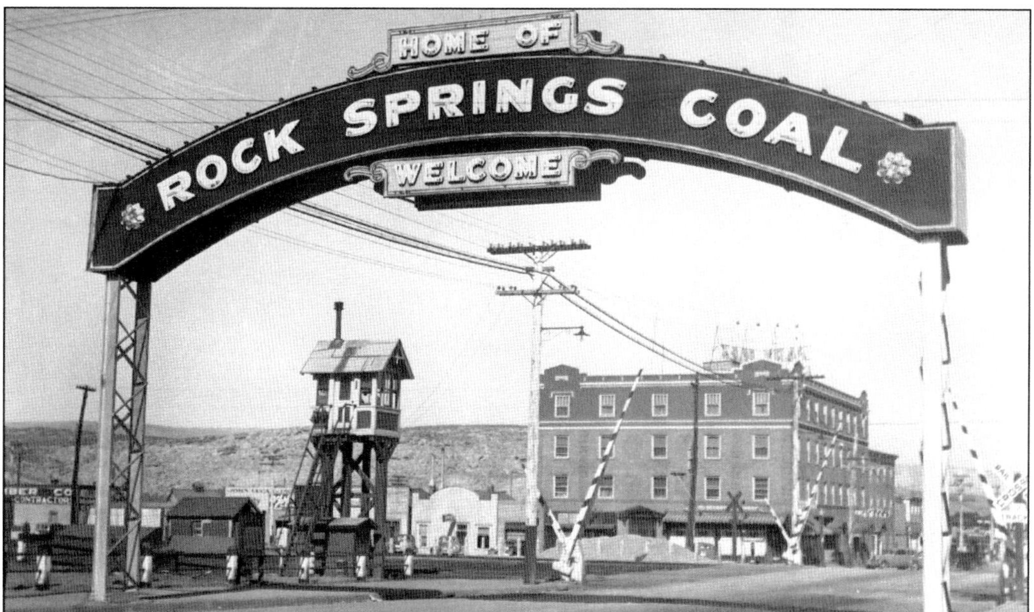

The puzzling lack of order to early Rock Springs caused many to use the "Coal Sign" as a landmark for giving directions. This view is looking northerly from the sign along C Street. The Park Hotel anchors the corner of C Street and North Front Street, and the Union Pacific Railroad yard control tower is visible. All of the buildings west (left of the Park Hotel, including Kellogg Lumber Company) have been torn down. (Courtesy New Studio.)

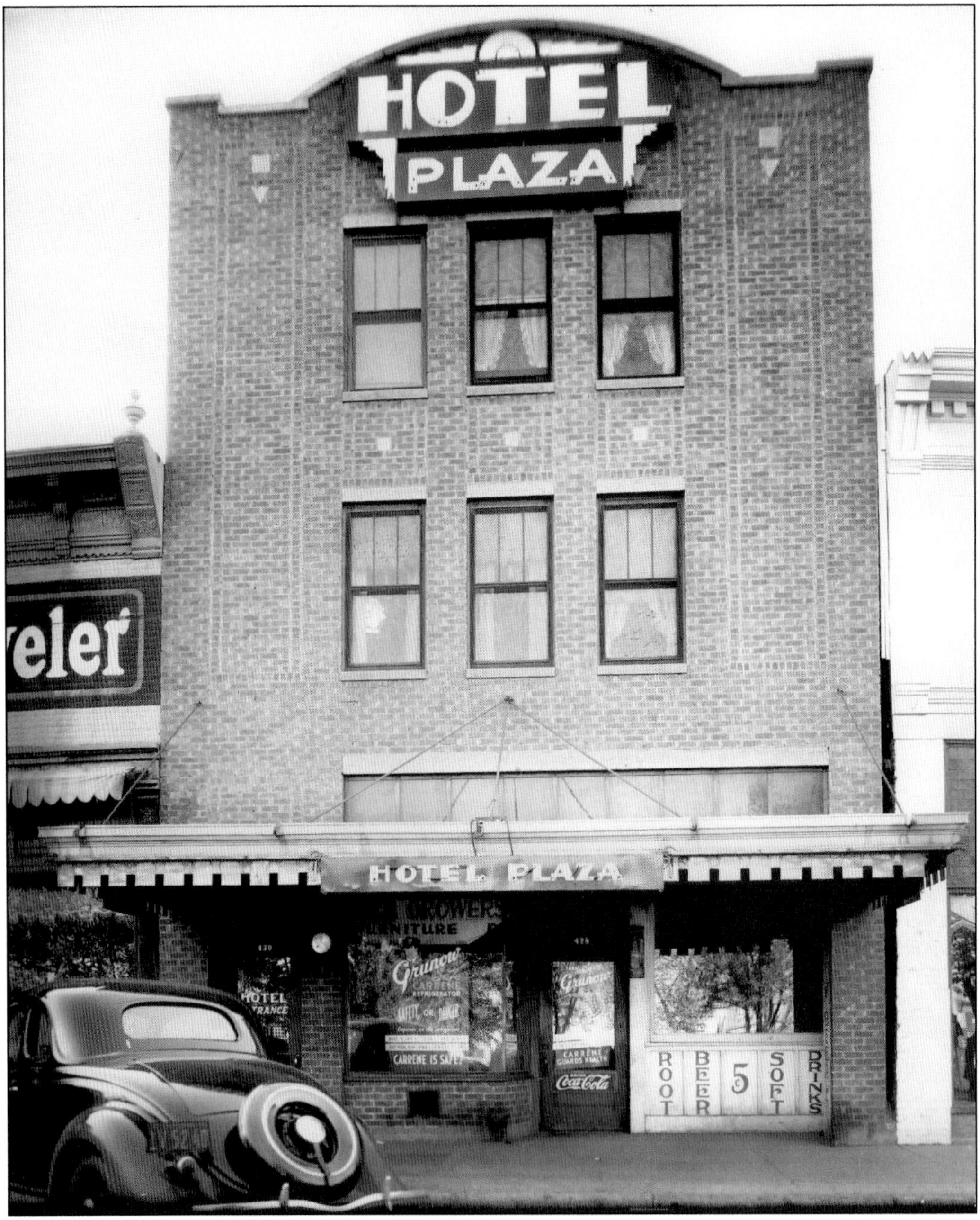

A prominent business, the Plaza Hotel, shown here in 1935, still stands on South Front Street. The hotel offered root beer for 5¢, and the billboard in the window addresses the issue of whether or not the newfangled Grunow refrigerator is safe. (Courtesy New Studio.)

North Front Street by 1939 supported many businesses, including the J. C. Penney Company store and Newberrys five-and-dime store. A sign of the times is evident with the appearance of the New Deal agency Wyoming State Employment Service, affiliated with the U.S. Employment Service. (Courtesy New Studio.)

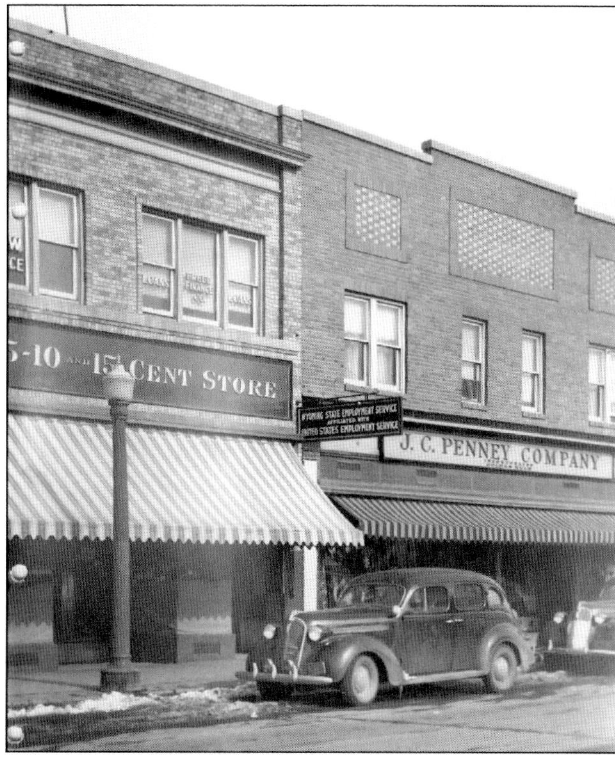

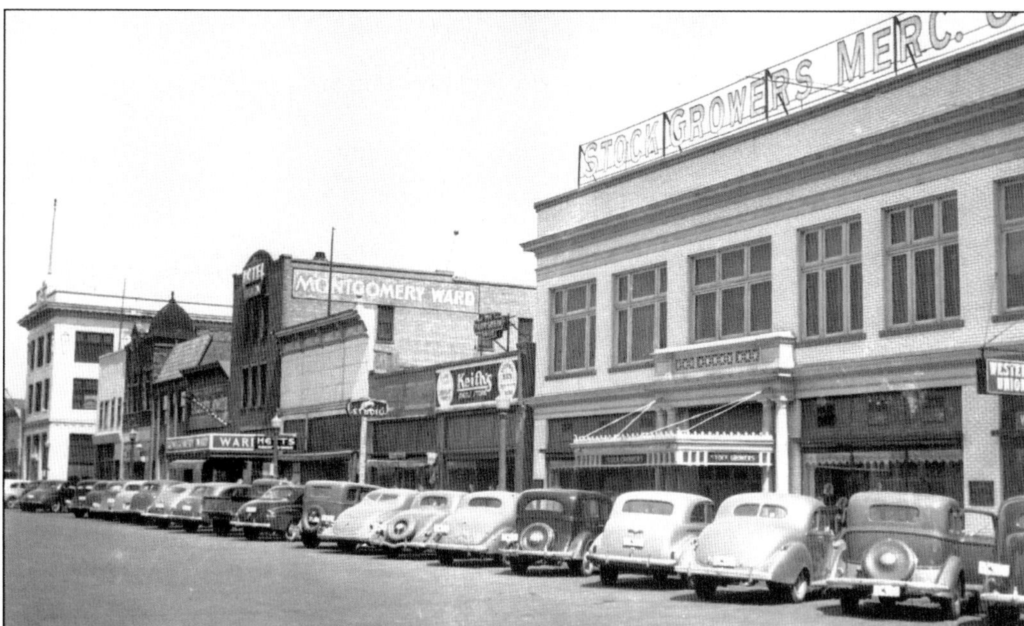

The late 1940s were a prosperous time for Rock Springs as automobiles line South Front Street, where the Stock Growers Mercantile Company and Montgomery Ward department stores drew customers. The New Studio is to the left of Keith's Men's Store. This picture seems not to hint at the impending closure of most of the coal mines in Rock Springs by the mid-1950s, when many residents lost their jobs. (Courtesy New Studio.)

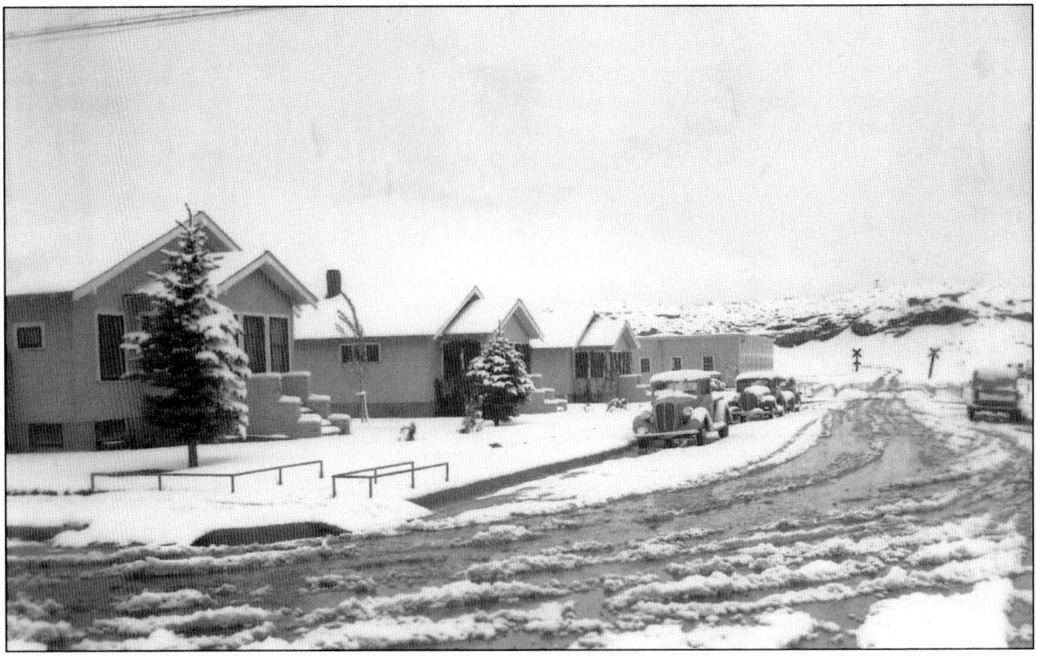

The high desert climate extremes of the region are exemplified by this June 1937 snowstorm. The photograph was taken from the corner of Connecticut Street and D Street looking toward the Mountain Fuel Supply Company Office building. These houses have all been removed because of mine subsidence problems. (Courtesy New Studio.)

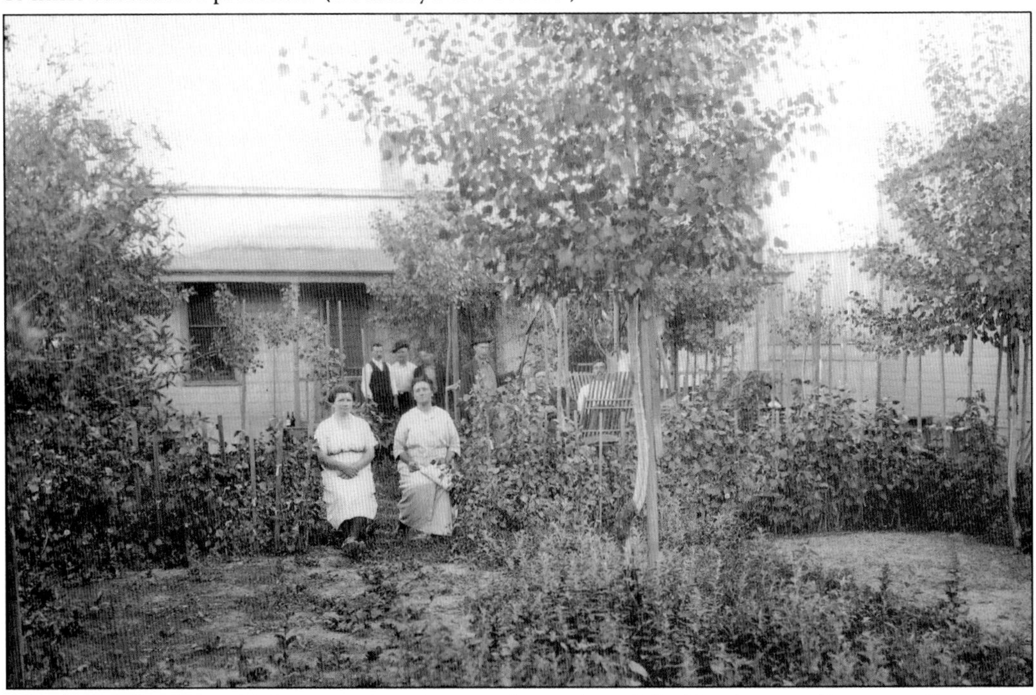

The Anton Frink family's house and gardens are shown here. The Franks were like many Europeans who tried desperately to emulate their homelands despite the climatic extremes of the Rock Springs area. (Courtesy New Studio.)

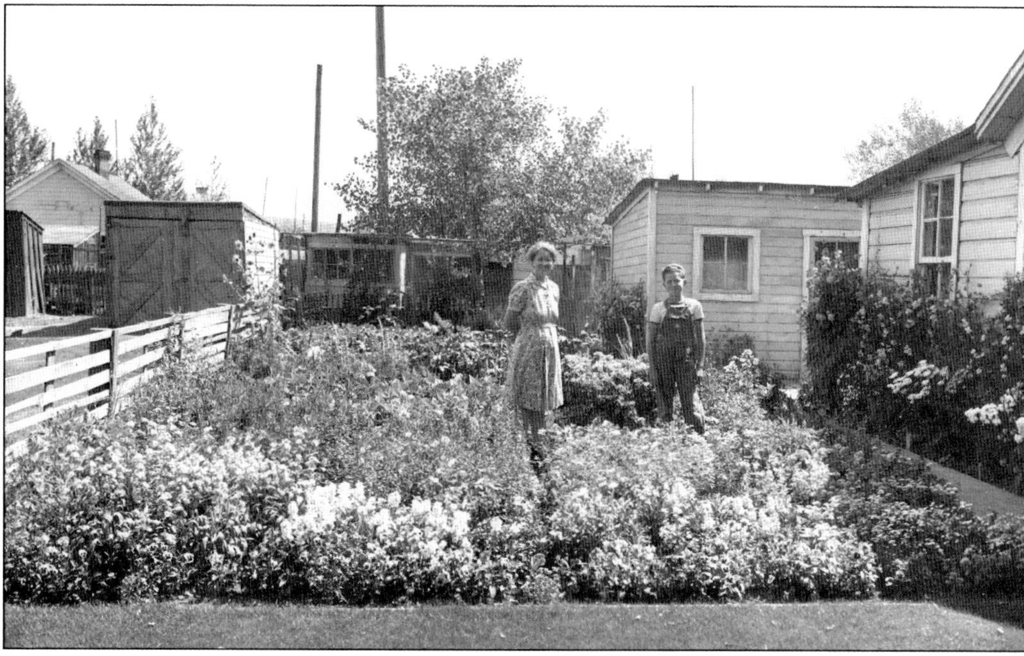

Where there is a will, there is a way. The Union Pacific Coal Company sponsored garden contests among residents of the various coal communities along the railroad. Here Mrs. Erzen and son Ben, who lived on Ninth Street in 1943, proudly look over their prize-winning efforts. (Courtesy New Studio.)

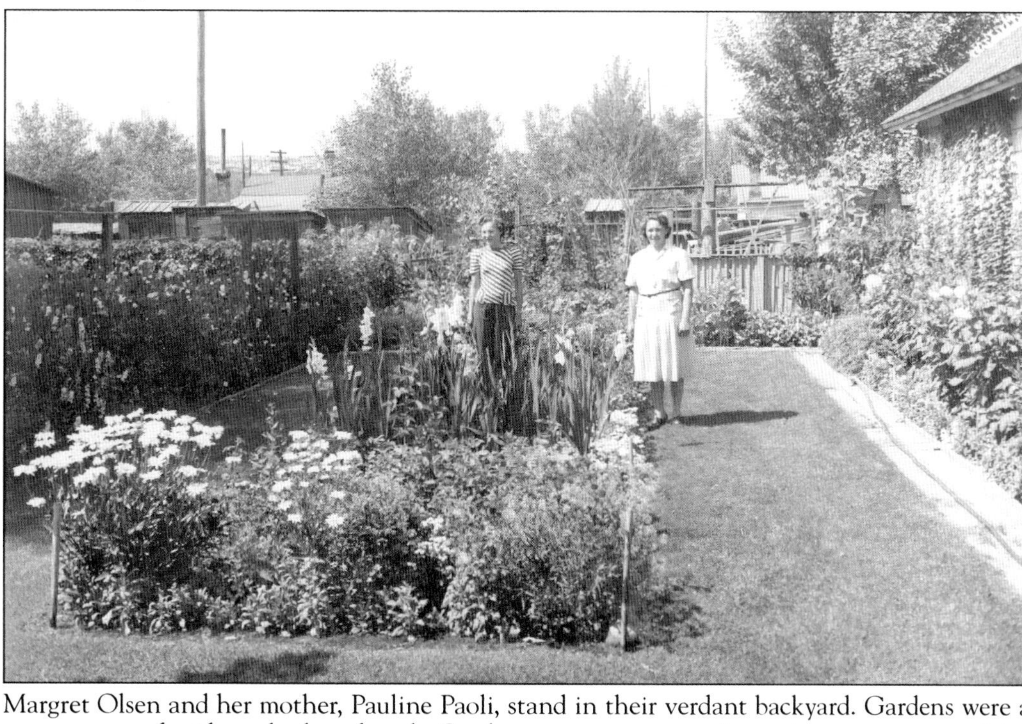

Margret Olsen and her mother, Pauline Paoli, stand in their verdant backyard. Gardens were a great source of pride and a lot of work. Garden contests were an incentive to grow something where others said it could not be done. (Courtesy New Studio.)

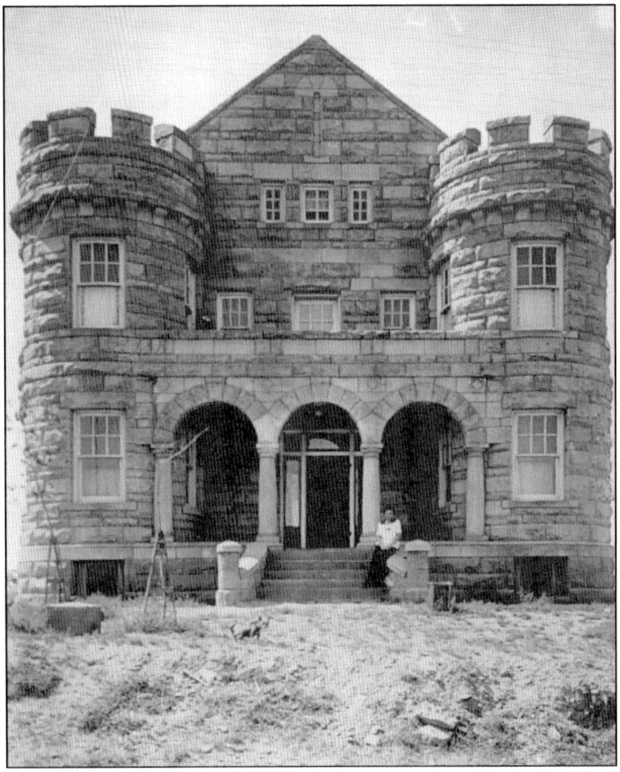

The building often called "the castle," on Cedar Street, was built by a German stonecutter and was constructed between 1909 and 1914. Joseph Schlacter also built several other buildings in the oldest part of Rock Springs, including the Carnegie Public Library on Blair Avenue. (Courtesy New Studio.)

This well-equipped kitchen has both a coal stove and a modern gas stove. By the 1940s, some residents of Rock Springs were able to afford a telephone. The customer was offered the choice of a private or public line. (Courtesy New Studio.)

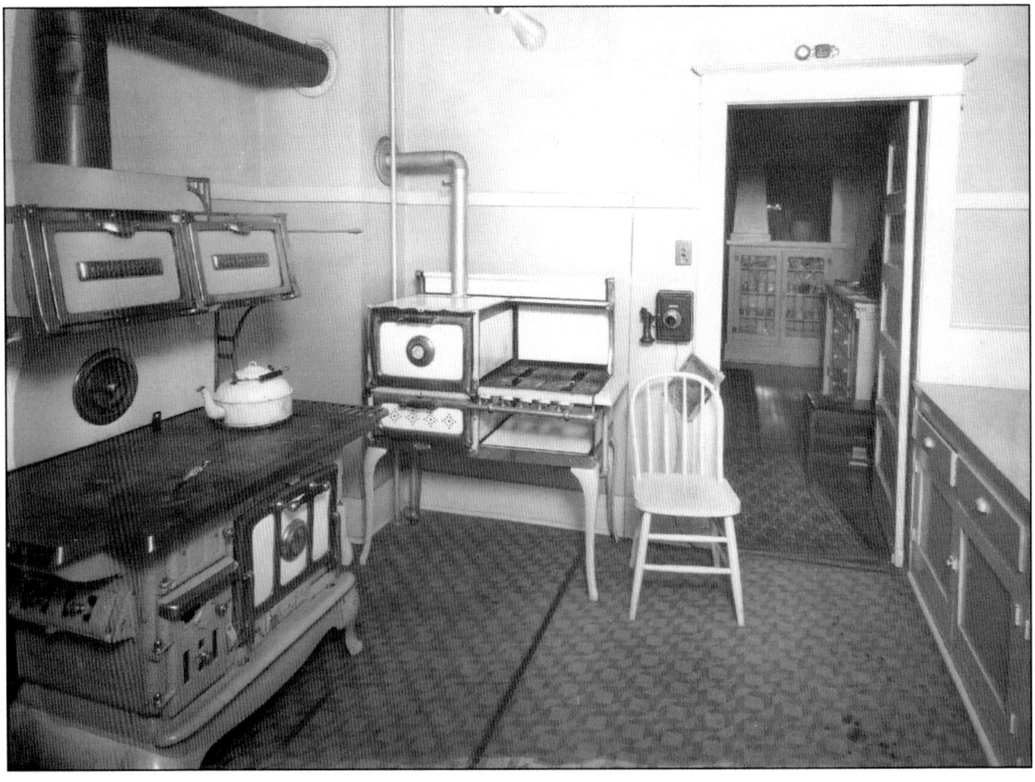

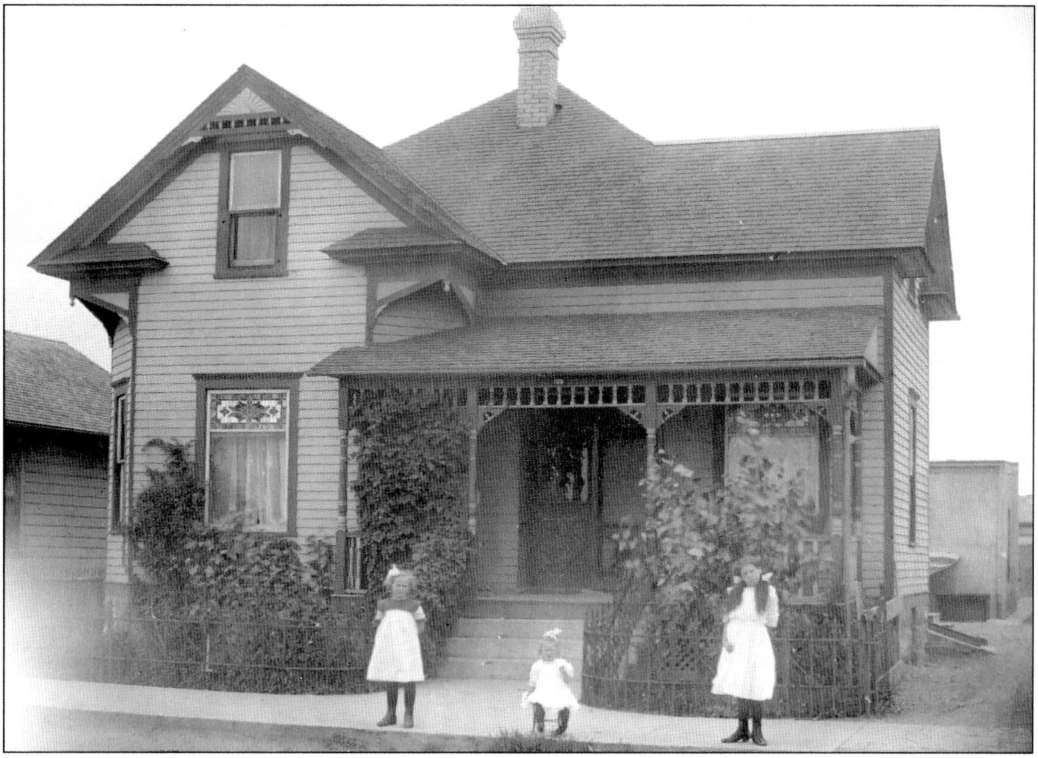

From left to right, Dora, Oretha, and Connie Bunning, daughters of Mayor P. C. and Marianne Bunning, stand in front of their home on Sherman Street. Bunning had this two-story house built while he and his family lived next door. There were four bedrooms upstairs for the children. On the main floor, there was a bedroom, office, kitchen, dining room, front room, and porch. (Courtesy New Studio.)

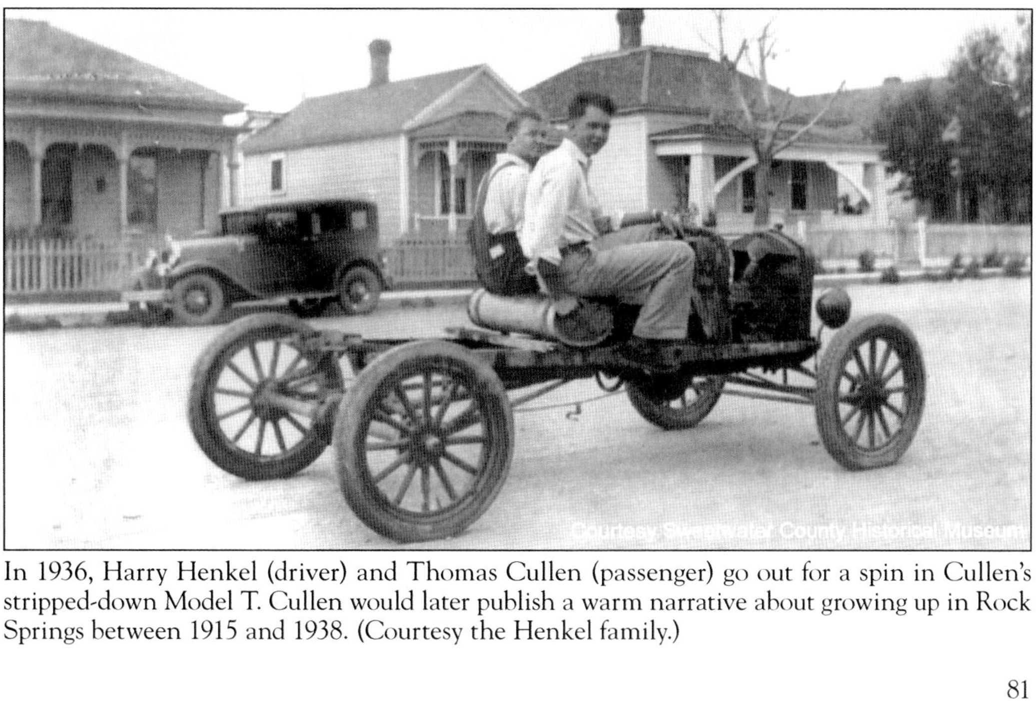

In 1936, Harry Henkel (driver) and Thomas Cullen (passenger) go out for a spin in Cullen's stripped-down Model T. Cullen would later publish a warm narrative about growing up in Rock Springs between 1915 and 1938. (Courtesy the Henkel family.)

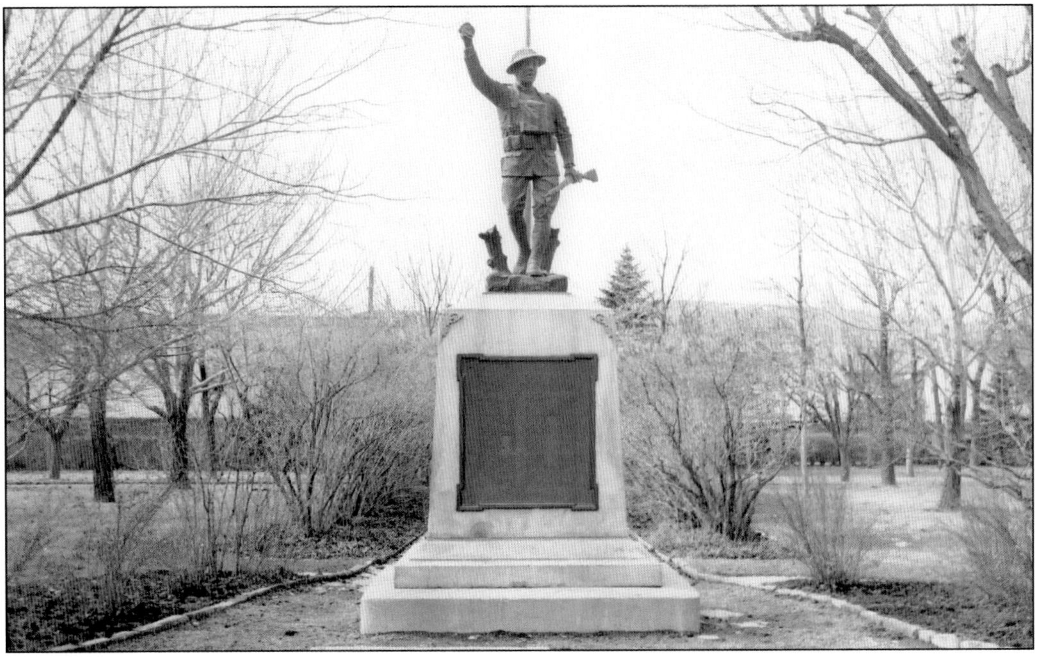

The "Spirit of the American Doughboy" statue was placed in at least 135 communities across America, including Rock Springs, following the First World War. The statue was first located at the intersection of Broadway Avenue and B Street in downtown Rock Springs. It is now located in Bunning Park, and the names of local soldiers who died in "the war to end all wars" are listed on a plaque at the base of the statue. (Courtesy New Studio.)

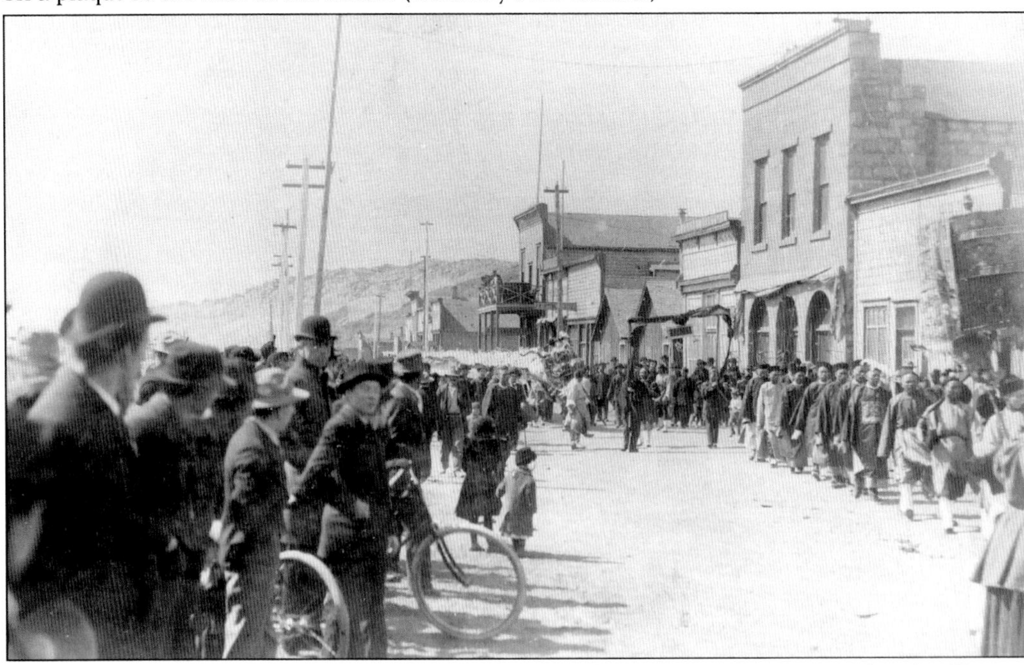

This Chinese parade was photographed in 1886 on North Front Street, one year after the Chinese massacre. It is apparent that the Chinese now felt secure enough to carry on with their traditional activities. (Courtesy RSHM.)

Five

LOCAL MERCHANTS

COMMERCE AND SERVICES IN EARLY ROCK SPRINGS

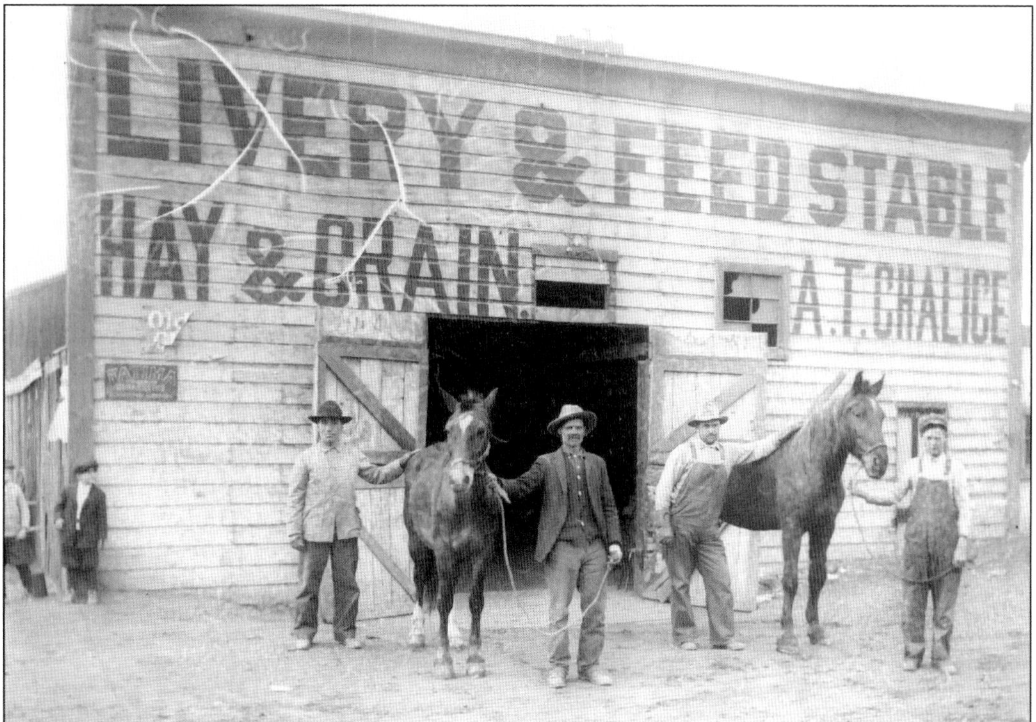

The livery stable conducted a lively business in Rock Springs in 1915 when this photograph was taken. Pete Dorrence (second from left) and liveryman A. T. Chalice (third from left) pose with two unidentified men in front of the livery stable. Two curious boys look around the corner to see what is going on. (Courtesy New Studio.)

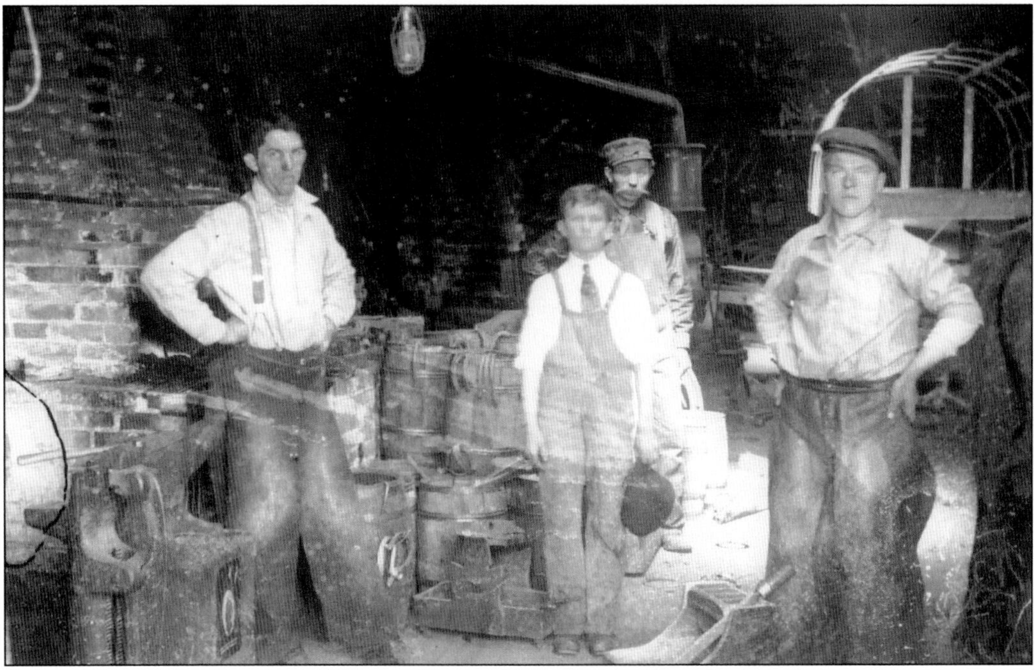

Inside the blacksmith shop, John Putz (the mustached man in the back) is pictured with three of his employees around 1915. It took great skill and strength to forge and shape metal, shoe horses, make and repair automobile and wagon springs, and make and repair sheep wagons. (Courtesy New Studio.)

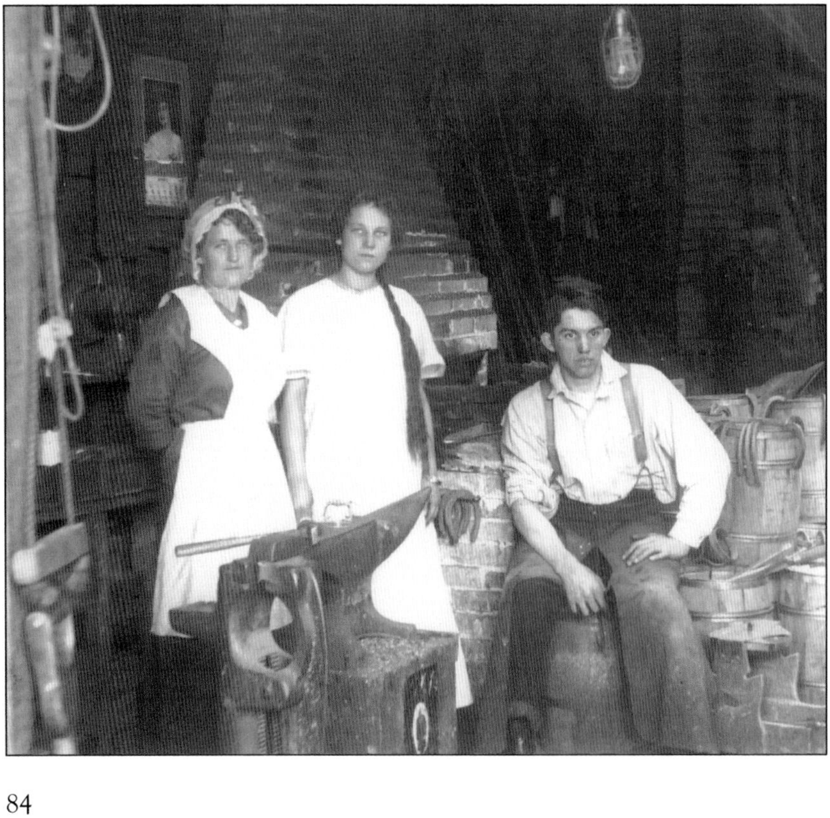

In 1915, it was unusual to see women in a blacksmith shop. Perhaps these women were visiting the young blacksmith sitting on the barrel. The anvil and horseshoes are evidence of one of the most important functions of the blacksmith shop, the manufacture and fitting of horseshoes. (Courtesy New Studio.)

A page from a 1933 Putz ledger details transactions made with W. H. Gottsche, a well-known rancher. John Putz kept track of all costs when he shod horses and made and fixed wagons, springs, and wheels. It cost 50¢ for two pounds of horseshoe nails. (Courtesy the Chadey family.)

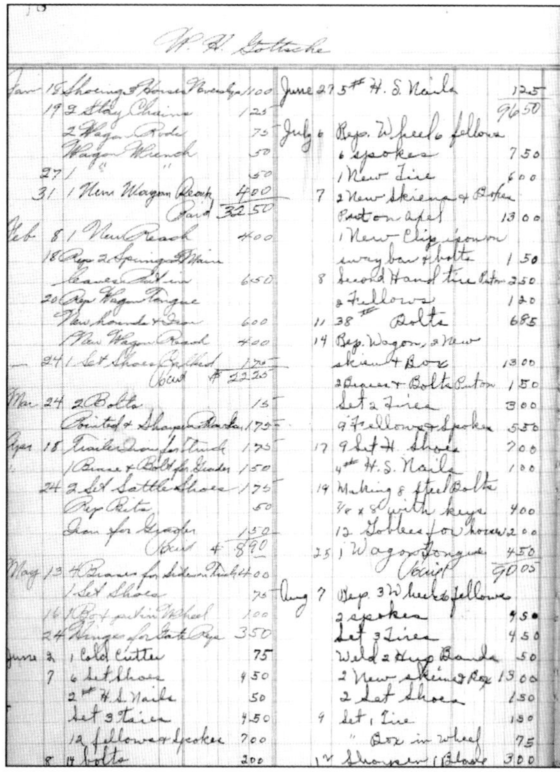

John Putz moved his blacksmith shop to this location on J Street in 1926. The wooden building with a corrugated metal roof was originally the Parker Wholesale Building. After making branding irons, the blacksmith would burn the brands into the wooden shop doors. When the building was demolished in the 1970s, these doors were salvaged and are now located in the lobby of the Point of Rocks Café and Saloon. (Courtesy the Chadey family.)

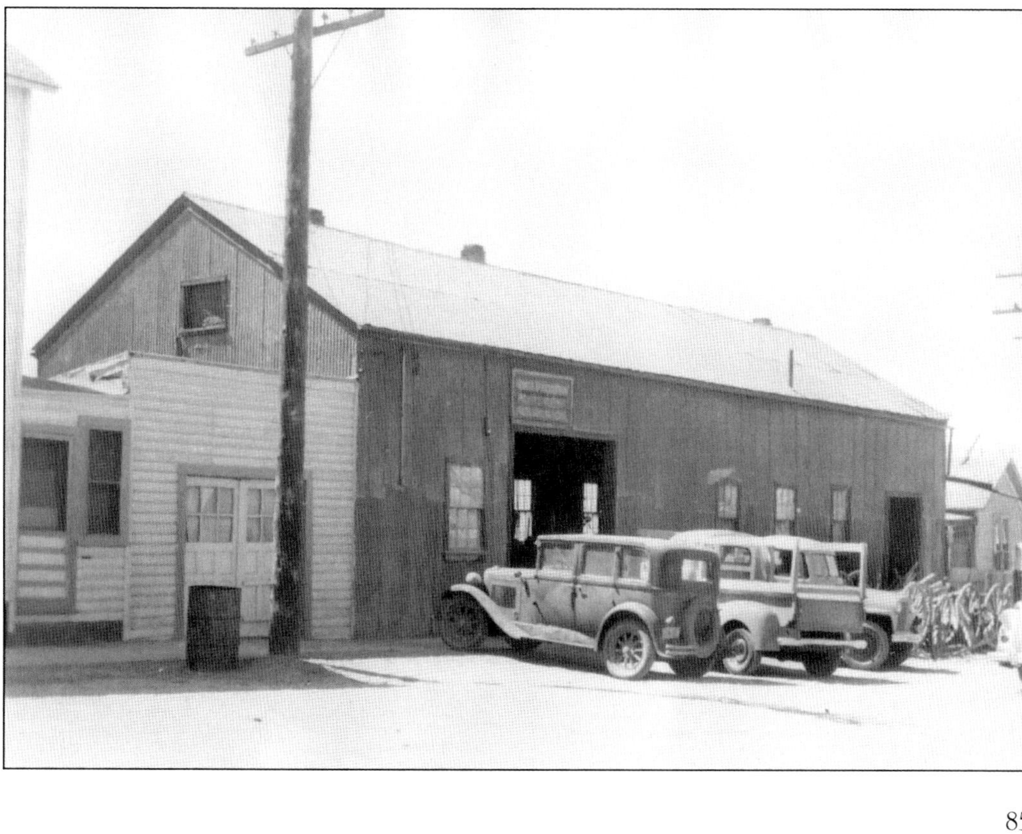

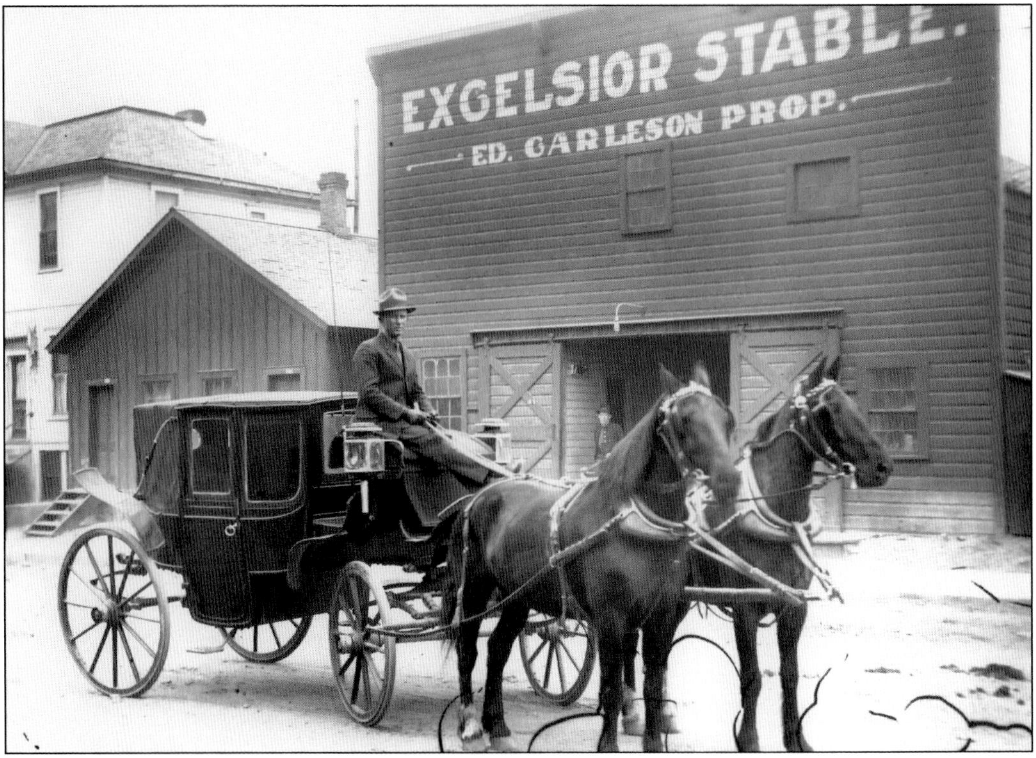

Photographed in 1915 in front of the Excelsior Stable, a matched pair of horses are hitched to a coach. It was not uncommon for stables to become automobile dealerships, which the Excelsior did soon after this photograph was taken. (Courtesy New Studio.)

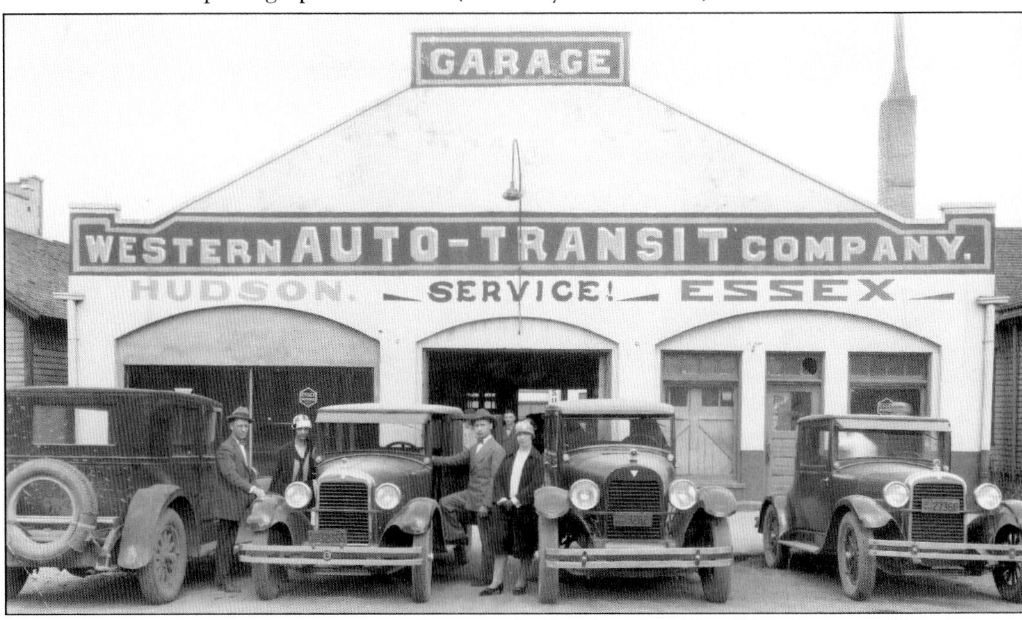

The Western Auto Transit Company, photographed in April 1927, sold and serviced Hudson and Essex cars. The stockholders for this company included prominent Rock Springs names like Hay, Gottsche, Rife, and Taliaferro. (Courtesy New Studio.)

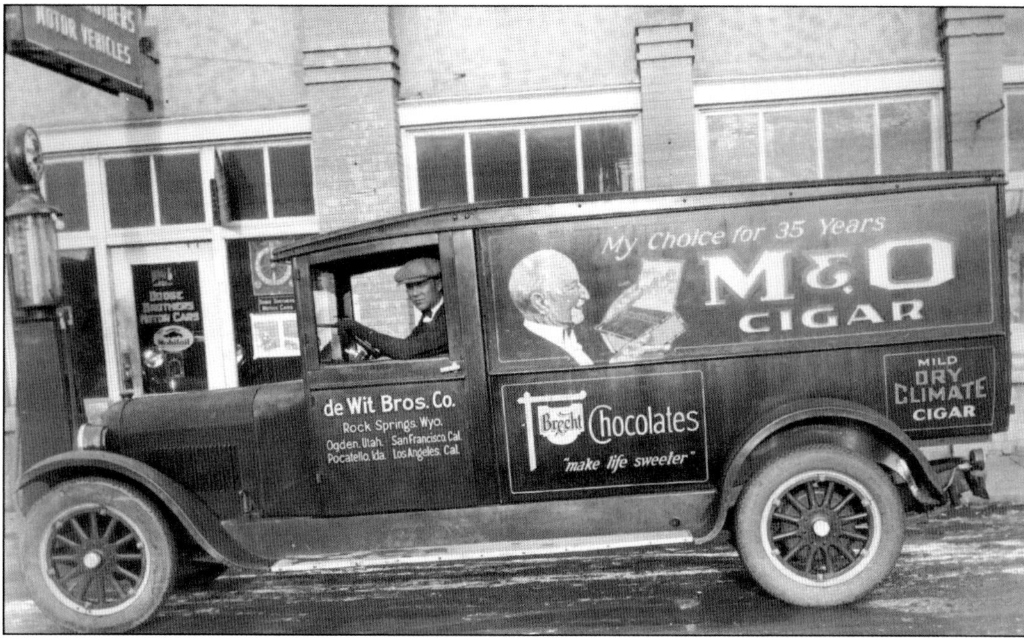

In this undated photograph, the deWit Brothers Company delivery truck is parked outside the Dodge Brothers Motor Cars dealership. The company sold Brecht chocolates in addition to "mild dry climate" cigars. The deWit Brothers Company had outlets in Ogden, Utah; Pocatello, Idaho; and San Francisco and Los Angeles, California. (Courtesy New Studio.)

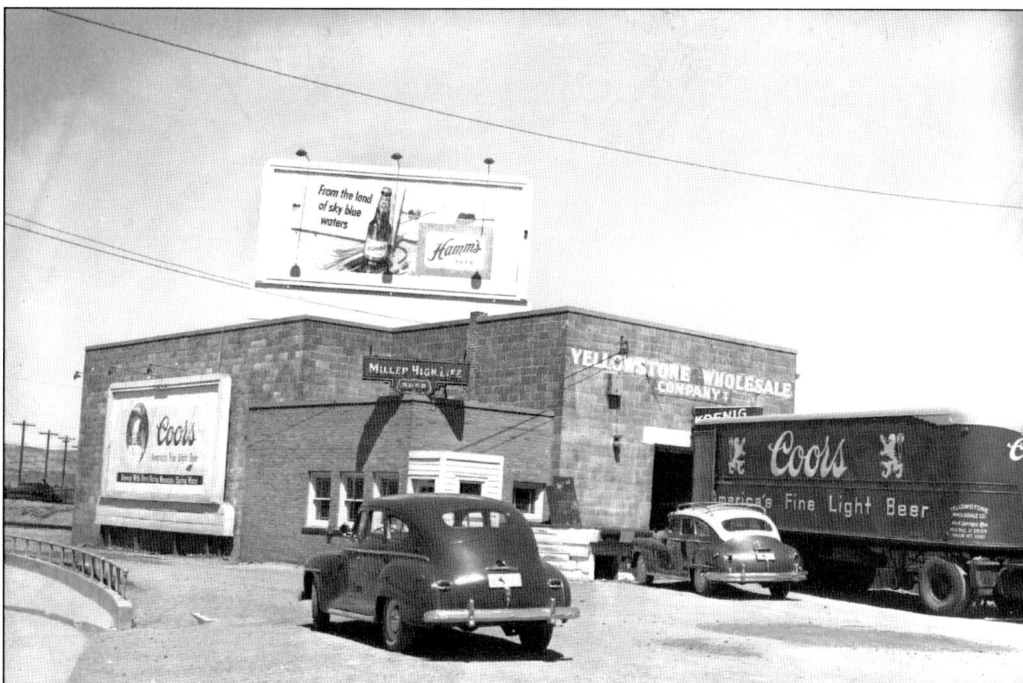

Yellowstone Wholesale Company, located on the south side of the underpass, supplied Hamms, Coors, and Miller High Life brands of beer. This photograph was taken in 1947. (Courtesy New Studio.)

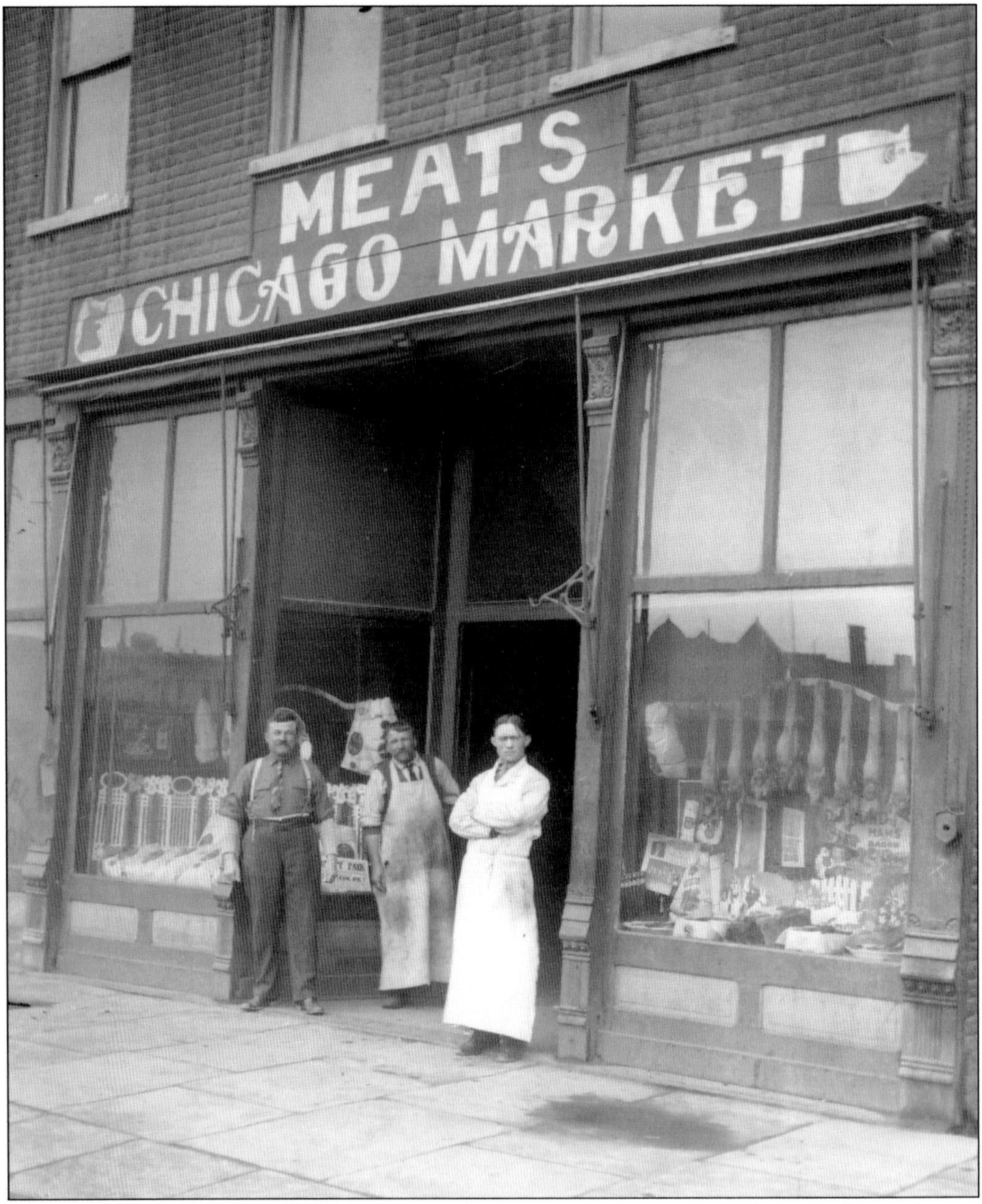

The Chicago Meat Market was located on North Front Street. It was the largest of several meat markets in Rock Springs that catered to the needs of European immigrant families. The proprietor and two employees stand in front of the store. (Courtesy New Studio.)

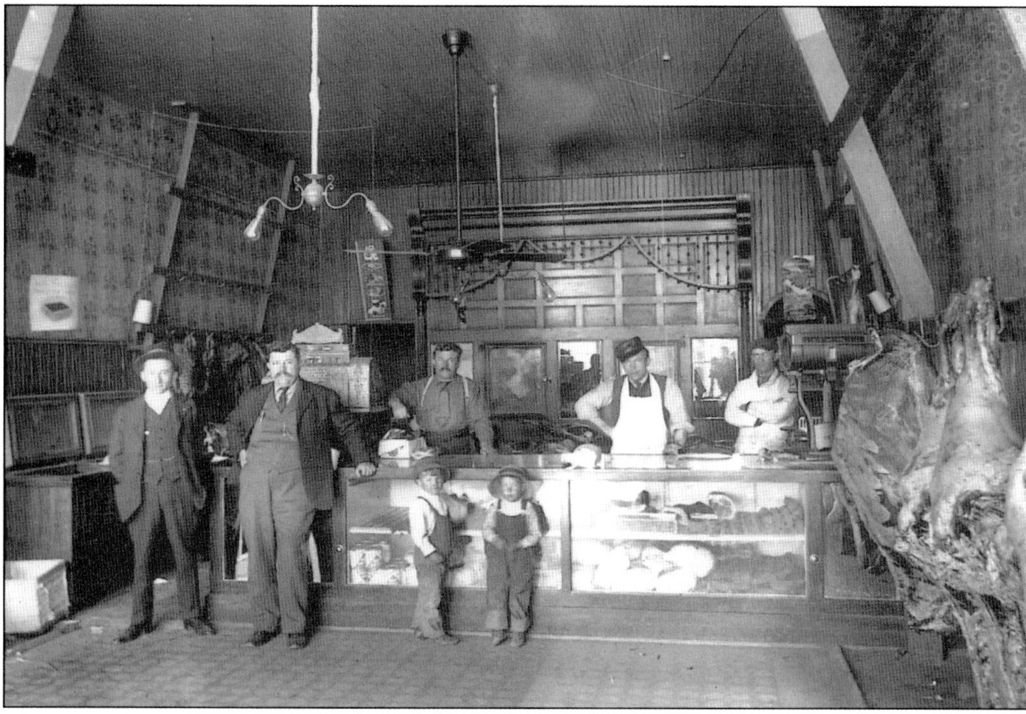

These gentlemen and children pose for this photograph inside the Chicago Meat Market. Beef, pork, lamb, and chicken did not come in a plastic-wrapped package displayed in a refrigerated case. People were closer to the source of their food in those days. Looking closely, one can see the reflection of the photographer in the window in the back right-hand side of the photograph. (Courtesy New Studio.)

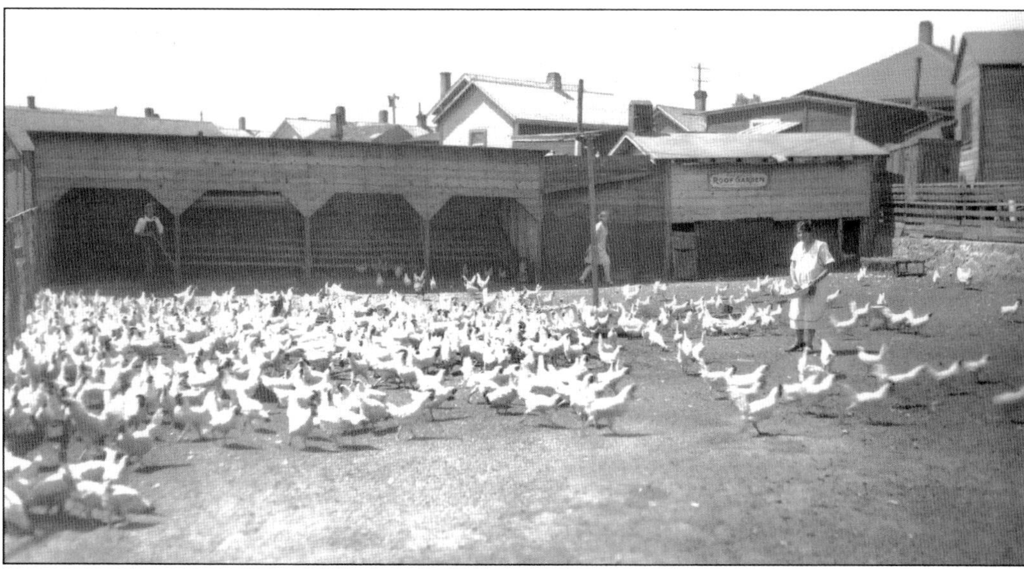

These chickens, shown in a 1930s photograph, were raised for sale at the Lincoln Meat Market. Owners Frank and Joe Gosar operated this market, which was located on Pilot Butte Avenue across the street from the Union Pacific company store. The market was where the World Famous Astro Lounge, a local nightclub, is now located. (Courtesy New Studio.)

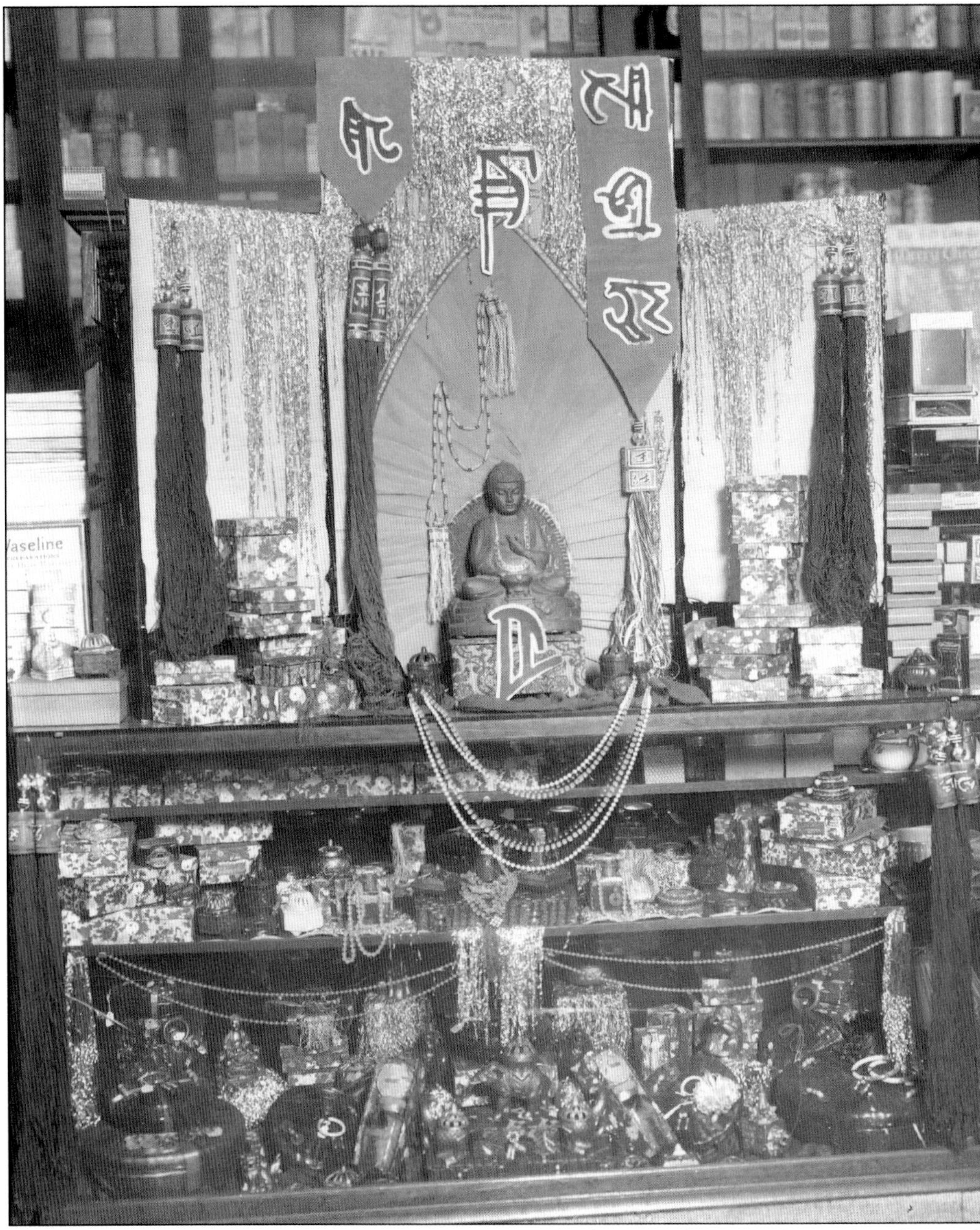

The Beckwith and Quinn Store, shown here in 1912, had a special section devoted to the needs of Chinese patrons and included such items as medicines, incense, and specially preserved food items. (Courtesy New Studio.)

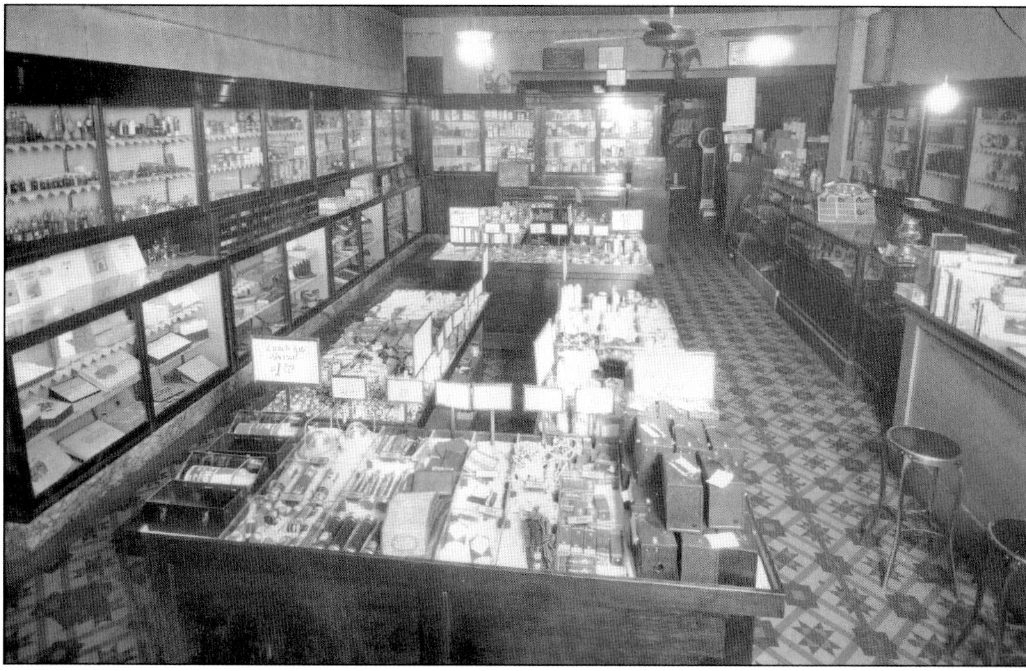

Many of the buildings still housing stores in downtown Rock Springs date to the early 1900s or even earlier. Gilded ceilings and tile floors added a hint of big-city elegance to many Rock Springs stores. This store offered Kodak box cameras for $2.19 and lunch kit specials for $1.39, as seen in the central aisle display. (Courtesy New Studio.)

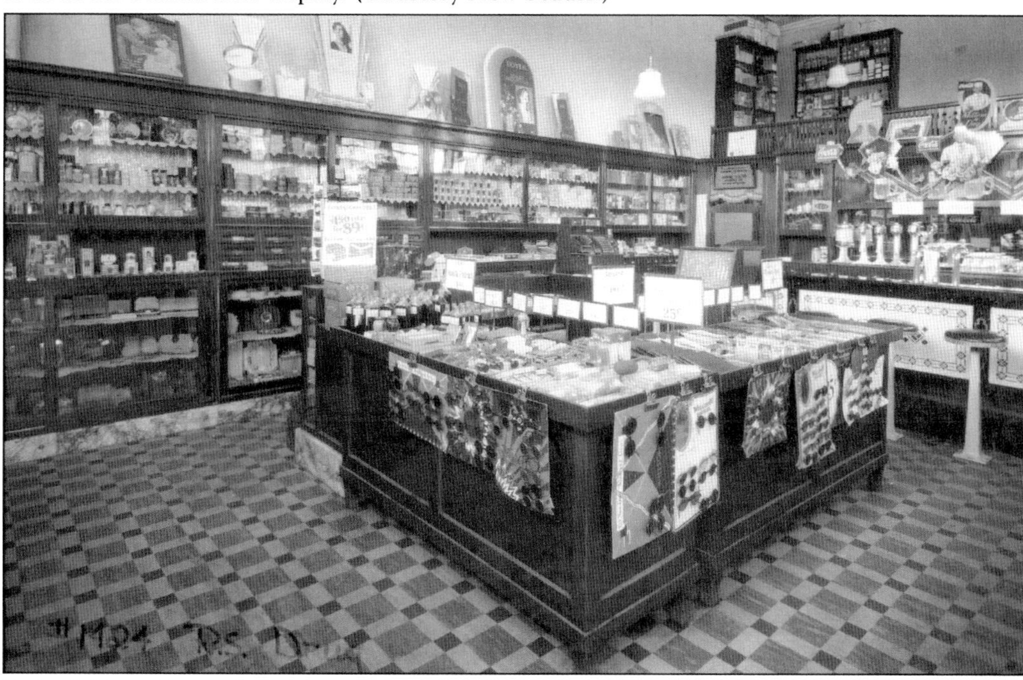

Parker's Drug Store, shown here, was located at the corner of North Front and K Streets. The store featured a soda fountain at the back, which no doubt attracted young customers with its emblematic Coca-Cola sign. (Courtesy New Studio.)

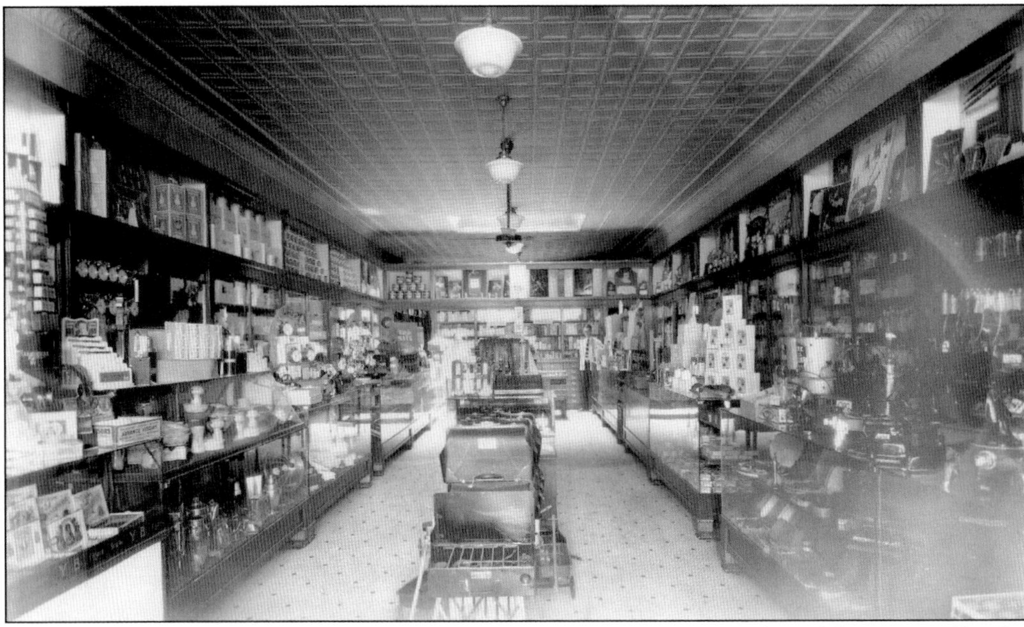

Clocks, lanterns, cigars, and Coleman-brand camping stoves are just a few of the items offered at this store, photographed in 1926 in downtown Rock Springs. Before the "big box" stores of today, variety stores like this one offered a broad spectrum of goods to shoppers. The proud proprietor stands at the back of the store on the right side. (Courtesy New Studio.)

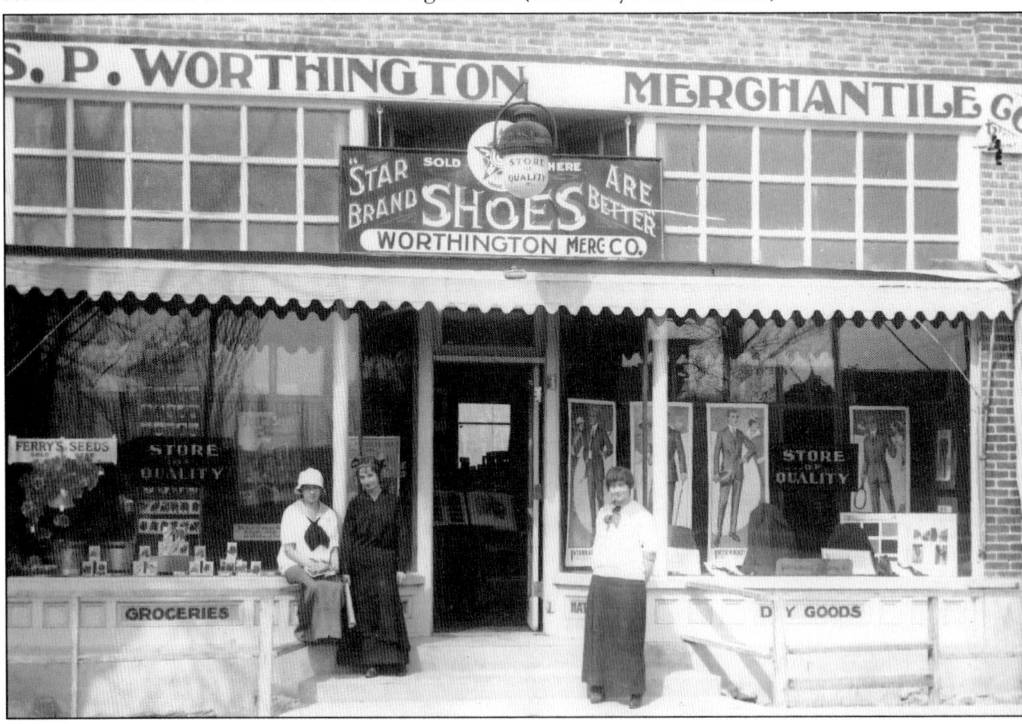

The S. P. Worthington Merchantile Company store in 1915 offered groceries, dry goods including shoes, and even garden seeds. "Quality" obviously is the motto of this store. And quality always attracts good customers, like the three young ladies outside the store. (Courtesy New Studio.)

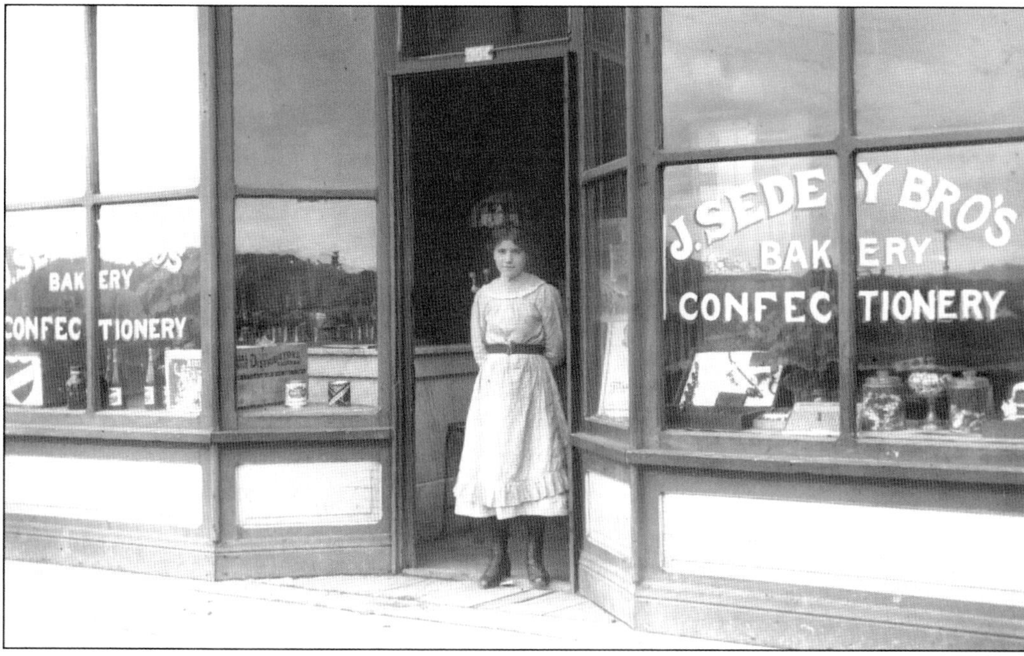

J. Sedey Brother's bakery and confectionery, operated by Slovenian immigrants, was situated at 304 Pilot Butte Avenue. The store offered baked goods, such as potica and baklava, favored by Slovenians and other Europeans. (Courtesy New Studio.)

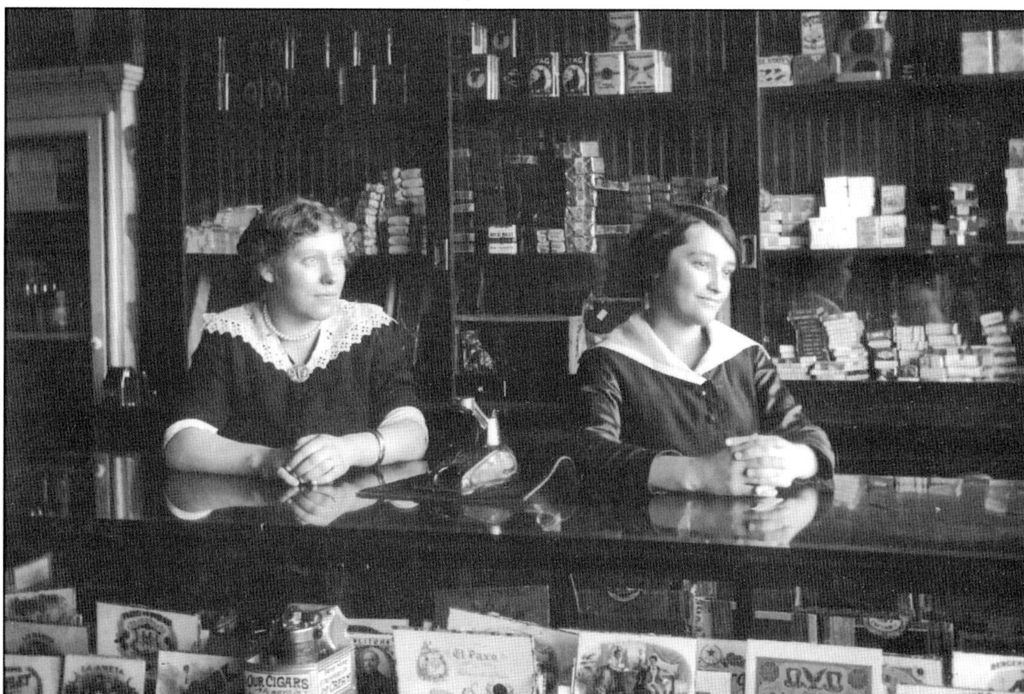

The Tom Thum confectionery on North Front Street sold fine quality cigarettes and Cuban cigars as well as confections. Rose Gras is the clerk on the left in this photograph taken in about 1915. (Courtesy New Studio.)

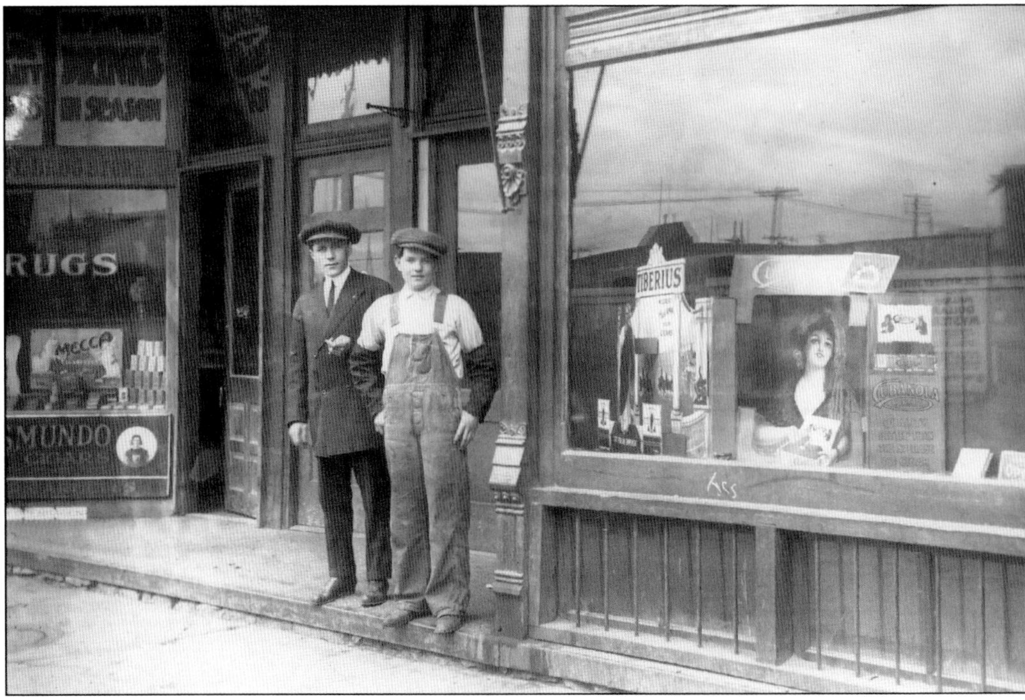

Two young men pose outside the Owl Drugstore around 1915. At this time, factory-made cigarettes were expensive and not nearly as popular as cigars. (Courtesy New Studio.)

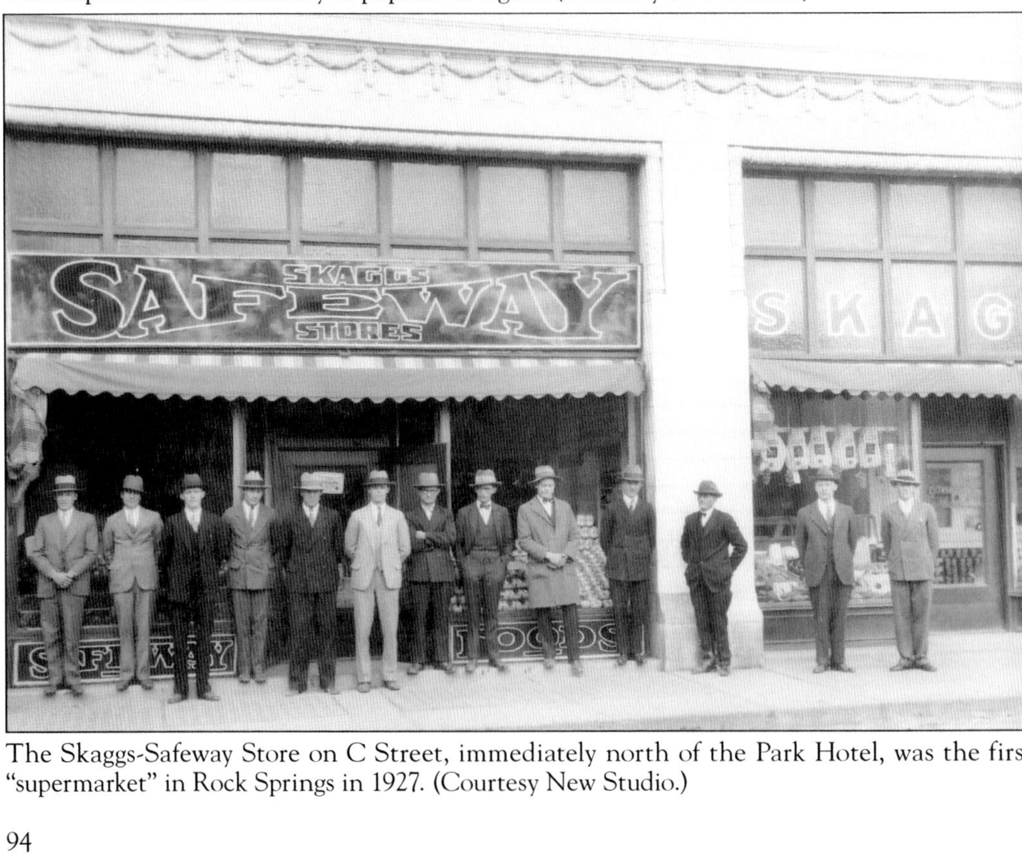

The Skaggs-Safeway Store on C Street, immediately north of the Park Hotel, was the first "supermarket" in Rock Springs in 1927. (Courtesy New Studio.)

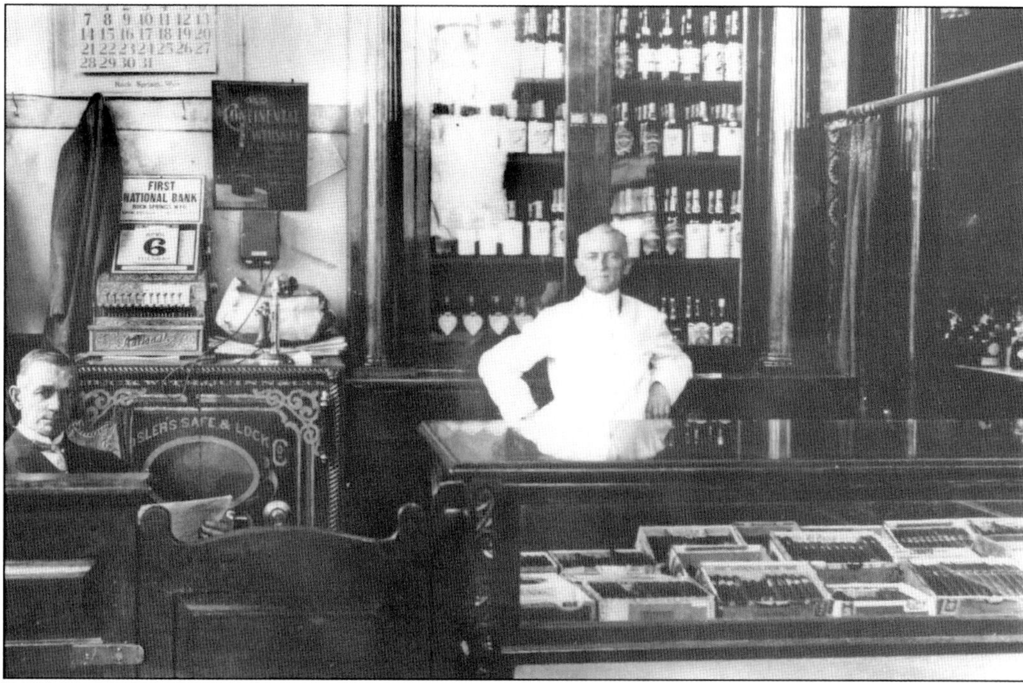

The Park brothers, shown here in 1915, operated the Park Hotel, a first-class hostelry at the corner of C and North Front Streets in downtown Rock Springs. The Park building still stands at this location but no longer operates as a hotel. (Courtesy New Studio.)

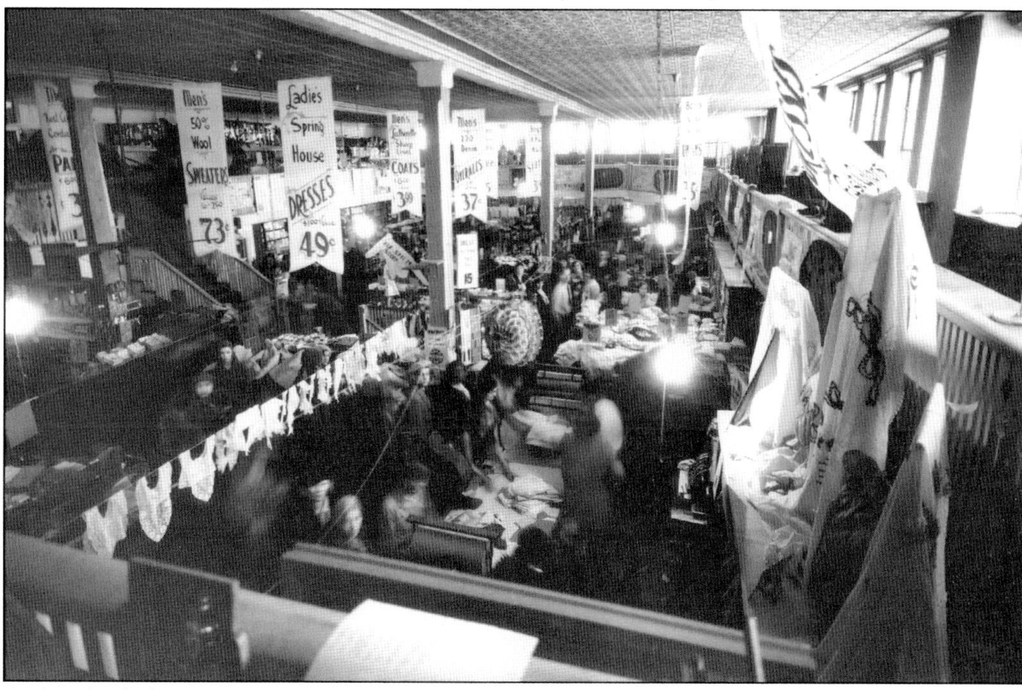

A close look shows many customers at Hudak's family clothing store in January 1932. Prices have sure changed since those days, when men's overalls were 37¢ and ladies' spring house dresses were on sale for 49¢. The store was located on K Street. (Courtesy New Studio.)

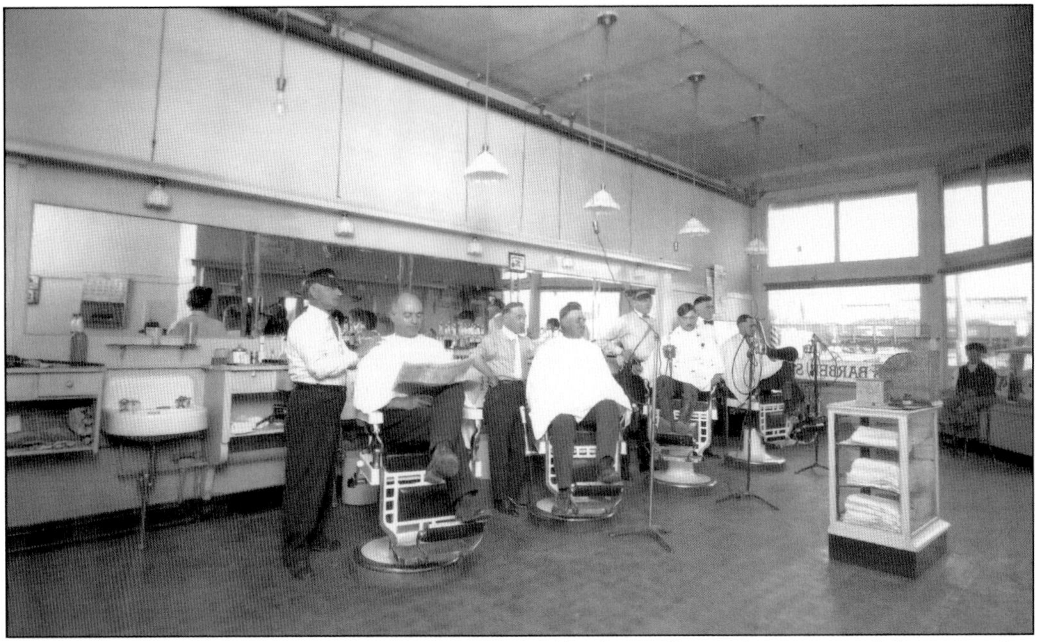

A barbershop at 319 B Street had four experienced barbers offering haircuts and shaves in this modern shop in 1921. Notice that the barber's electric shears plug into outlets in the ceiling and the shop had indoor plumbing, as evident from the sink at the left. (Courtesy New Studio.)

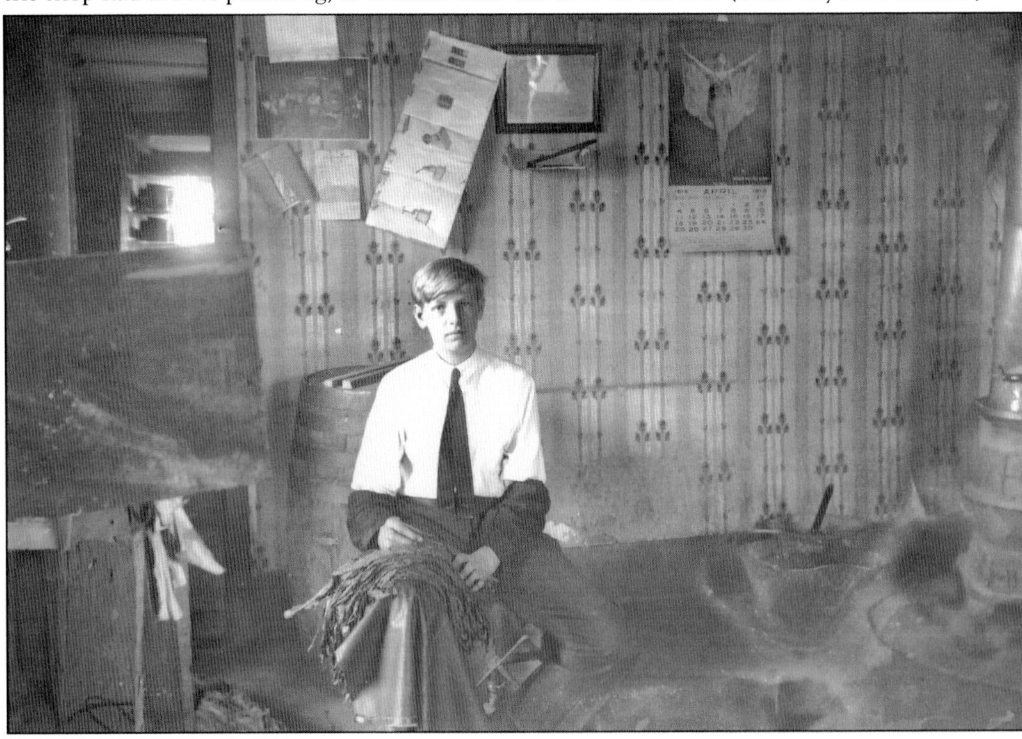

A young leather craftsman apprentice at Patterson's Leather Shop poses for a photograph in April 1915, according to the calendar featuring Isadora Duncan. A kitsch classic painting of dogs playing poker decorates the wall. (Courtesy New Studio.)

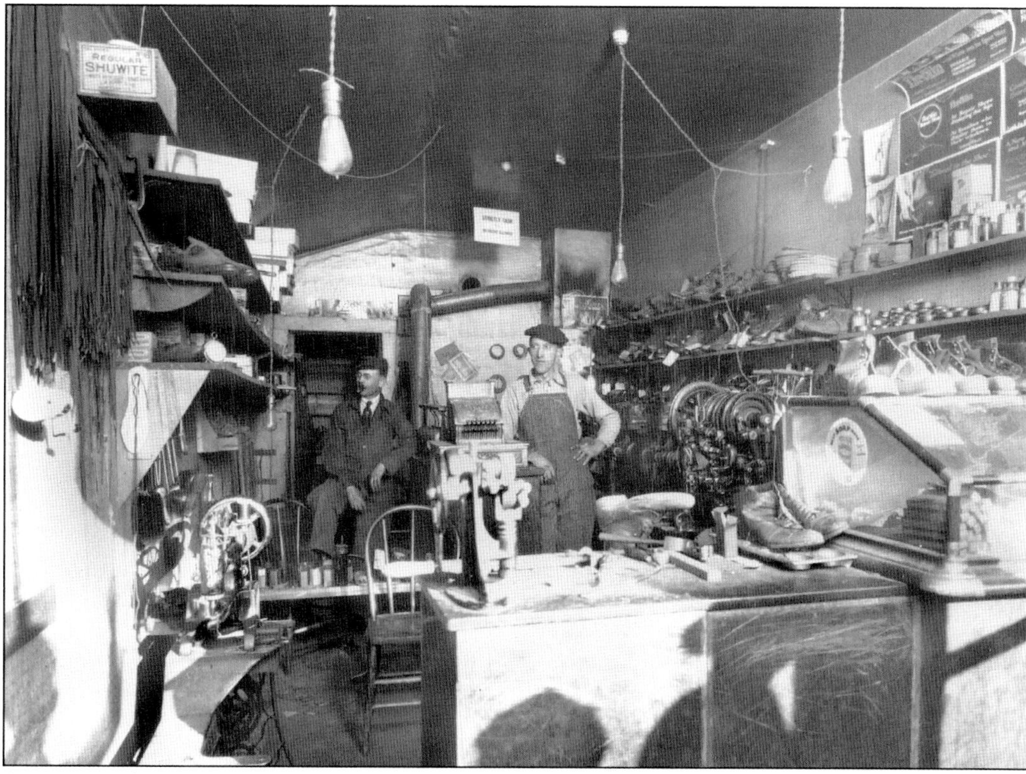

At a time when manufactured goods cost a lot and wages were low, shoe repair shops were some of the most important service businesses in any town. Shoe repair required good lighting, as is apparent from the many lights hanging from electrical cords around this shop. (Courtesy New Studio.)

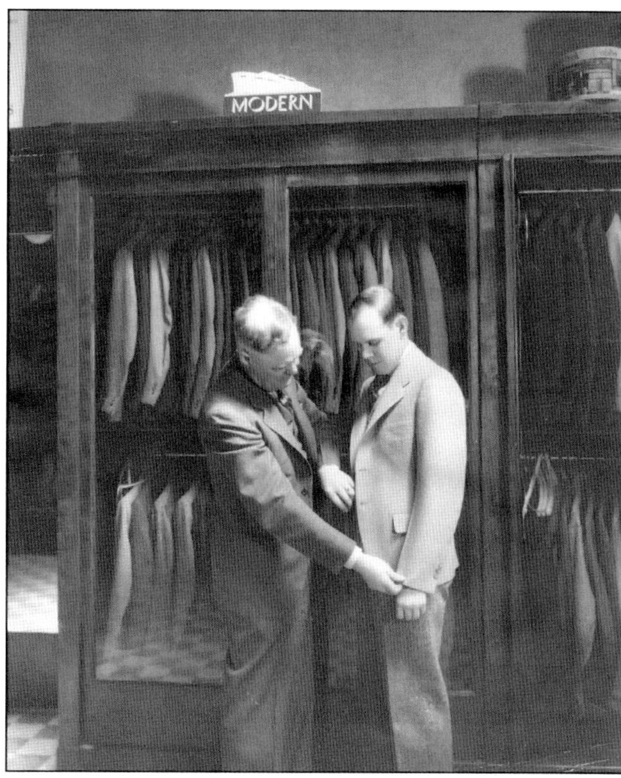

Keiths Men's Store was located on South Front Street and offered fine suits and other clothing for gentlemen as well as tailoring services. (Courtesy New Studio.)

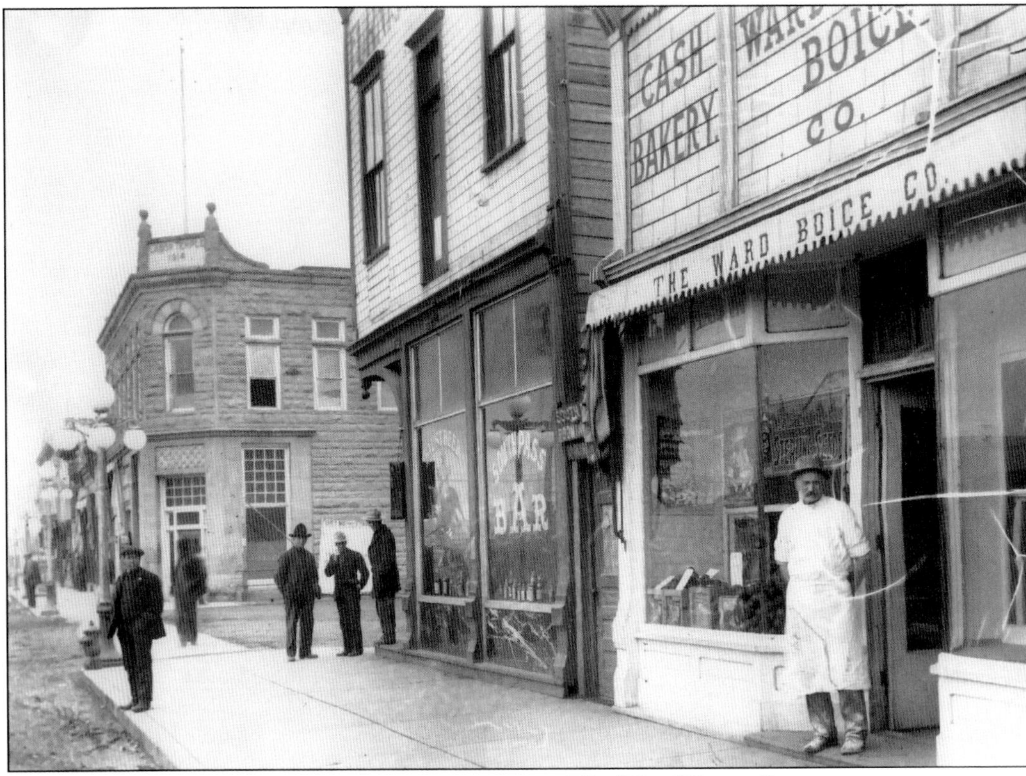

The Ward Boice Company was one of several bakeries operating in downtown Rock Springs in the early 1900s. The Labor Temple built in 1914 is the prominent building at the corner of North Front and J Streets, while the South Pass Bar is next to the bakery. (Courtesy New Studio.)

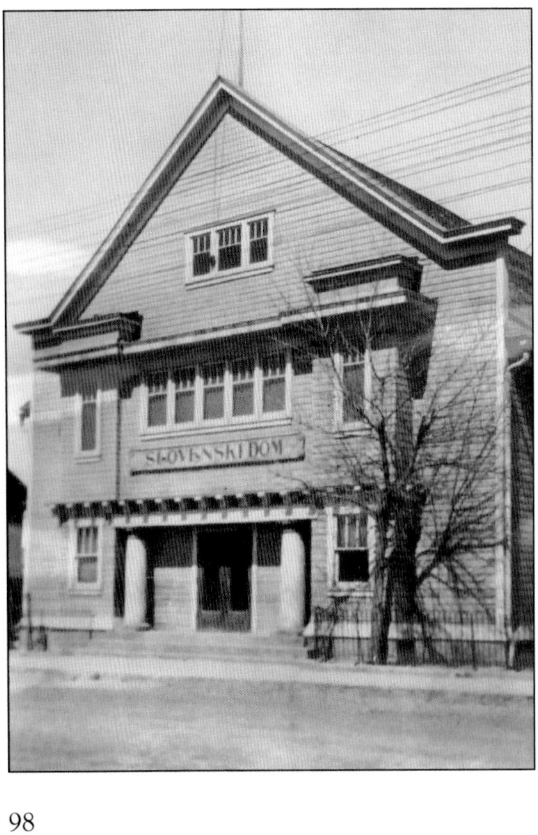

The Slovenski Dom, or Slovenian National Home, built in 1913, played a significant role in retaining the ethnic legacy that defines Rock Springs. The Dom was a center of community activities and was host to the popular Grape or Wine Arbor Festival. The hall was decorated like an orchard, and then a Slovenian skit would be performed followed by polka music and dancing. The building, now an artist co-op, has retained its character and draws visitors and locals alike.

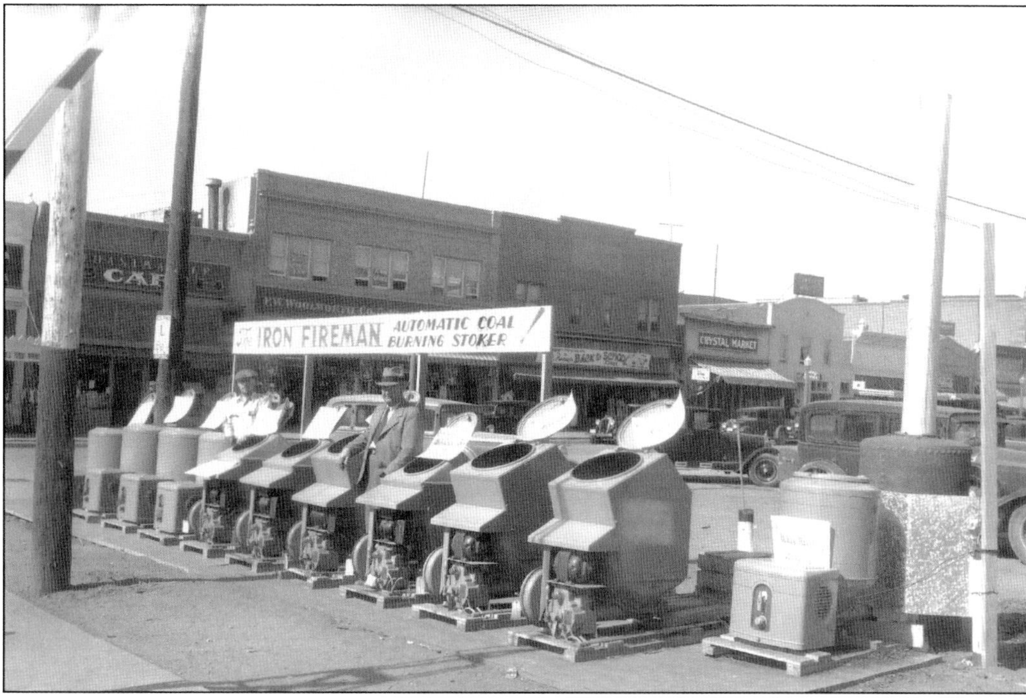

This display of Iron Fireman automatic coal-burning stokers shows an important 1933 innovation. These modern furnaces relieved owners of the need to carry buckets of coal to feed the fire and, more importantly, prevented over stoking of stoves that sometimes lead to deadly explosions and fires. (Courtesy New Studio.)

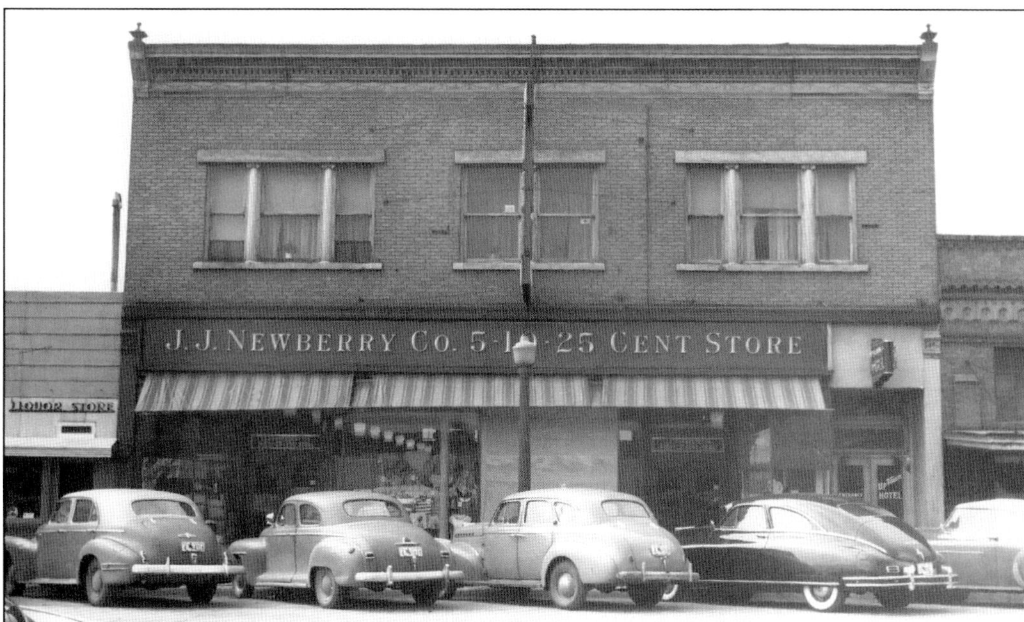

The J. J. Newberry Store on North Front Street, shown here in the late 1940s, offered clothing and other goods at low cost. The Up Town Hotel rented rooms in the space above the store, and there was a liquor store next door. (Courtesy New Studio.)

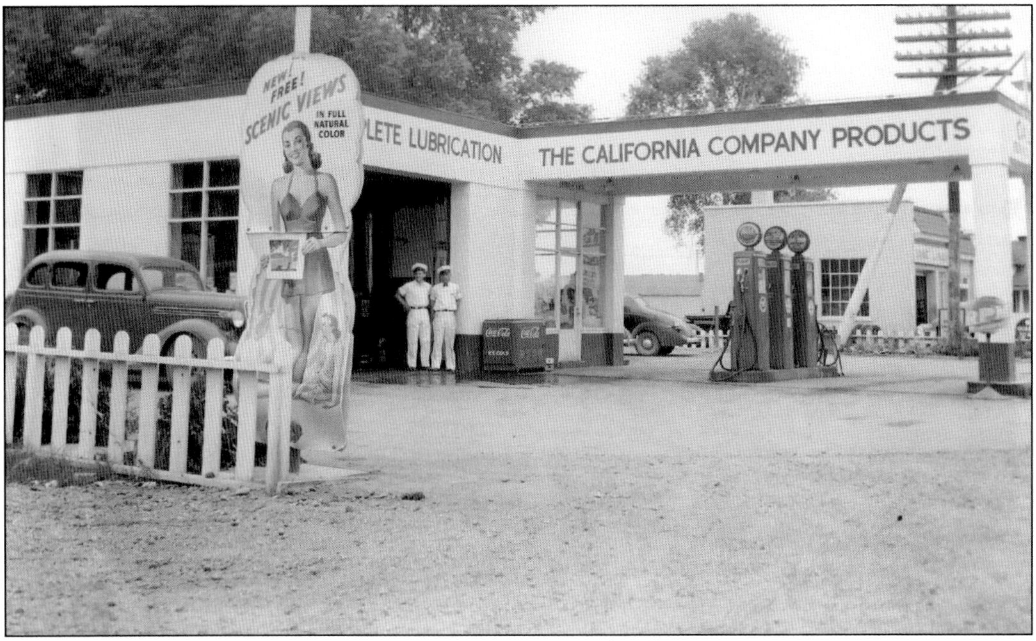

The California Company gas station in the 1940s offered full-service automotive care. Vacation destinations were advertised on the sign in the foreground, while white-uniformed attendants tended the station. (Courtesy New Studio.)

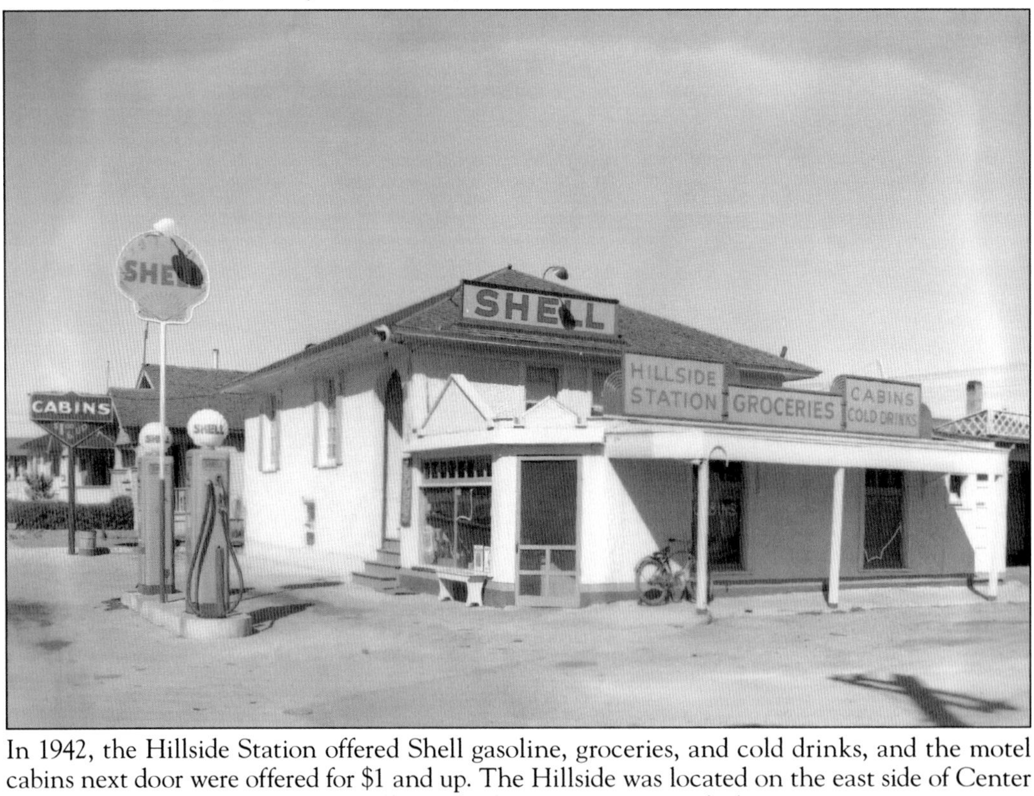

In 1942, the Hillside Station offered Shell gasoline, groceries, and cold drinks, and the motel cabins next door were offered for $1 and up. The Hillside was located on the east side of Center Street, near the intersection with Elk Street. (Courtesy New Studio.)

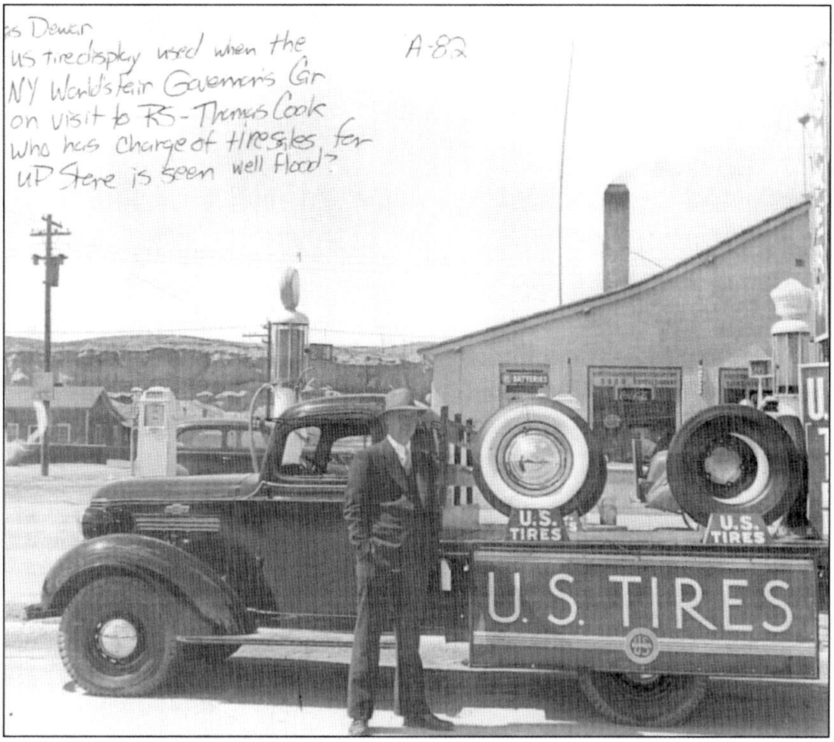

Whitewall tires, all the rage in the late 1940s and early 1950s, were offered by Thomas Cook, who was in charge of tire sales for the Union Pacific Store. The U.S. Tire display was used when the New York World's Fair Governor's Car visited Rock Springs. (Courtesy New Studio.)

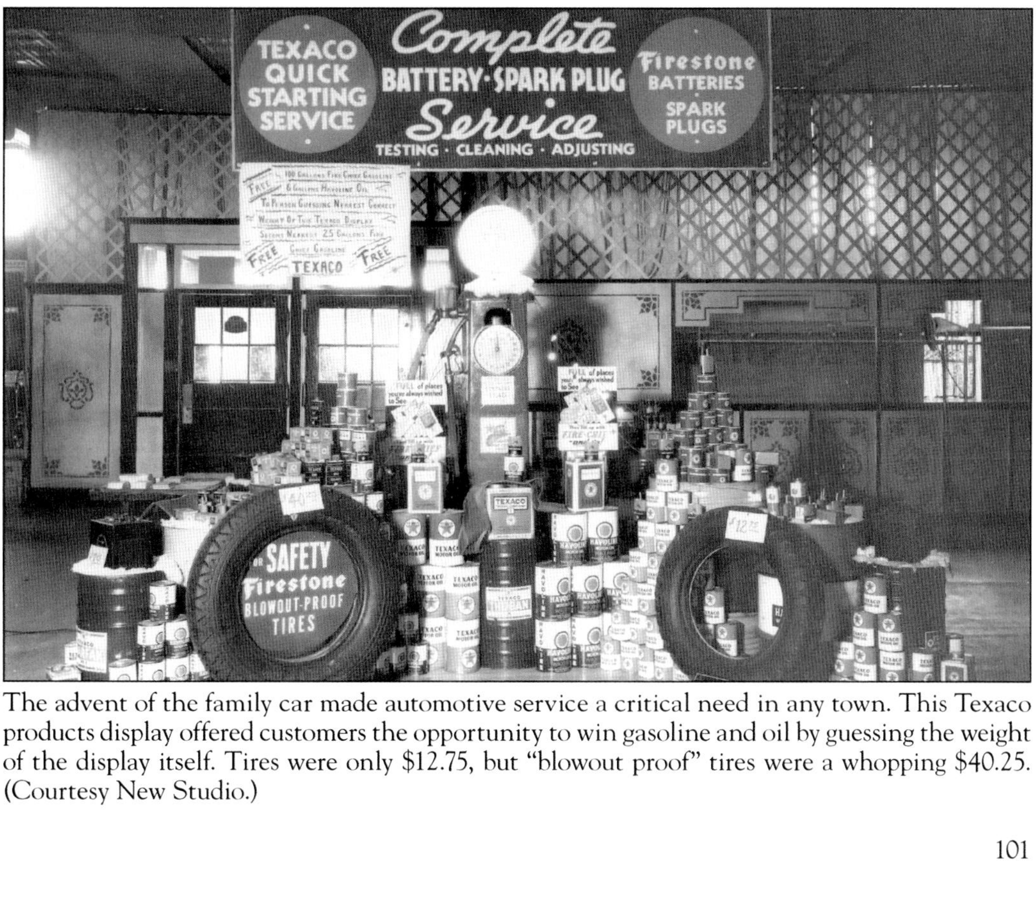

The advent of the family car made automotive service a critical need in any town. This Texaco products display offered customers the opportunity to win gasoline and oil by guessing the weight of the display itself. Tires were only $12.75, but "blowout proof" tires were a whopping $40.25. (Courtesy New Studio.)

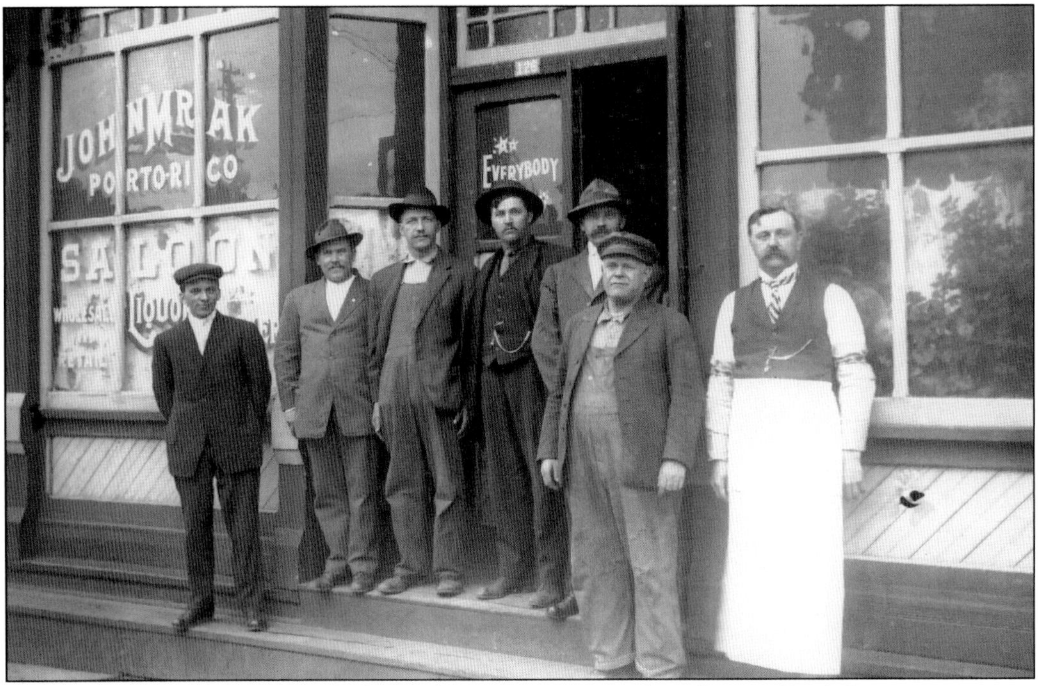

John Mrak, the gentleman in the long white apron, operated a saloon in Rock Springs as seen in this 1915 photograph. Mrak was of Slovenian descent, and new immigrants were often guided to saloons where their native language was spoken. (Courtesy New Studio.)

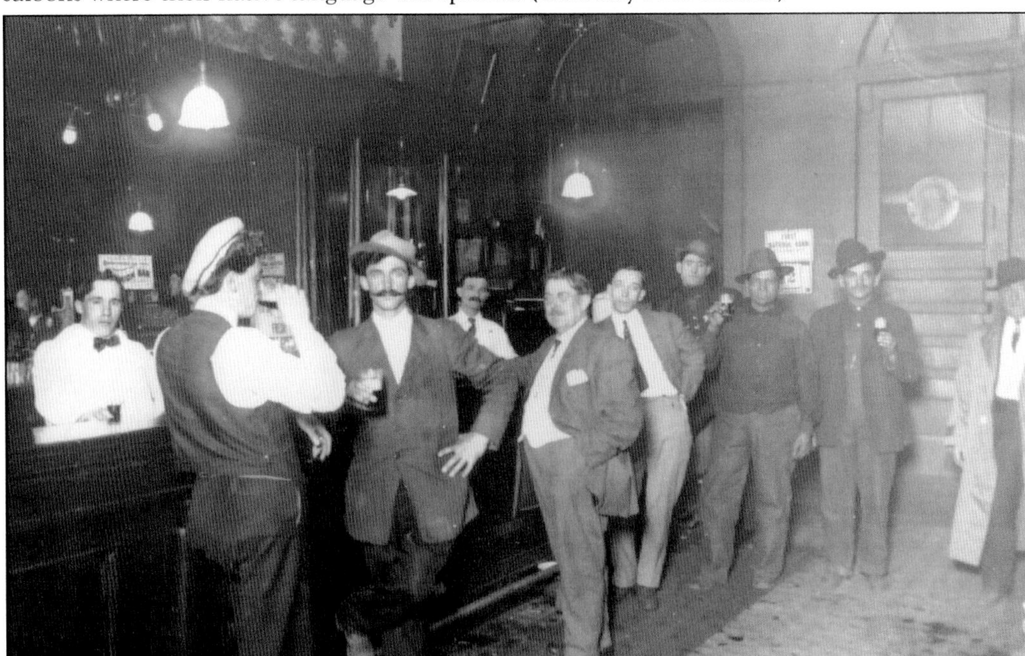

The Roosevelt Bar on K Street proudly displayed a sign proclaiming it is a "union bar." Labor unions were very strong in early Rock Springs, and a union establishment would attract working-class clientele like coal miners. (Courtesy New Studio.)

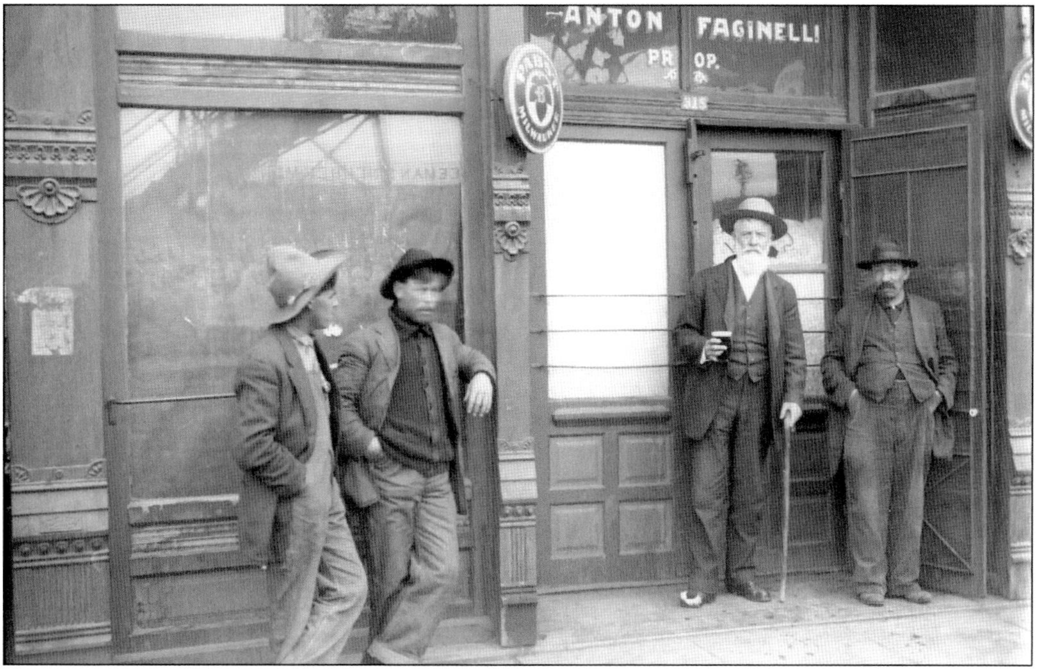

Anton Facinelli, the fellow with a glass of beer seen here, operated a bar and short-order restaurant near the pedestrian viaduct in the 1910s. The viaduct can be seen in the reflection in the window of the establishment. The sign proclaims that Facinelli sold Papst Milwaukee beer, a very popular brand. (Courtesy New Studio.)

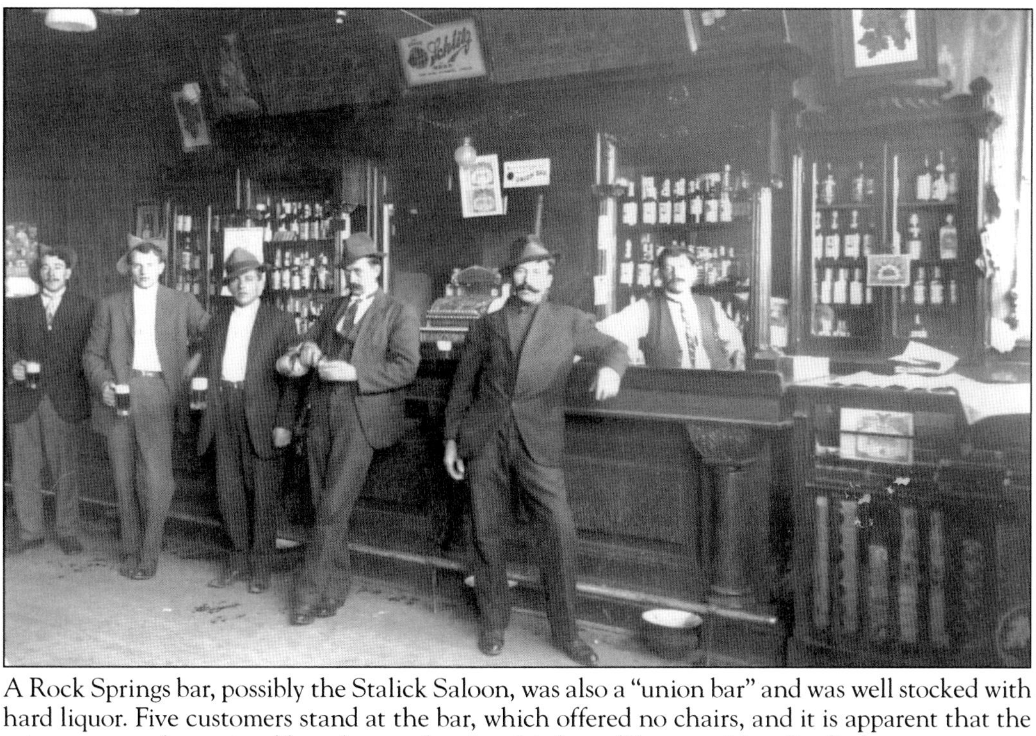

A Rock Springs bar, possibly the Stalick Saloon, was also a "union bar" and was well stocked with hard liquor. Five customers stand at the bar, which offered no chairs, and it is apparent that the spittoon was often missed by tobacco-chewing drinkers. (Courtesy New Studio.)

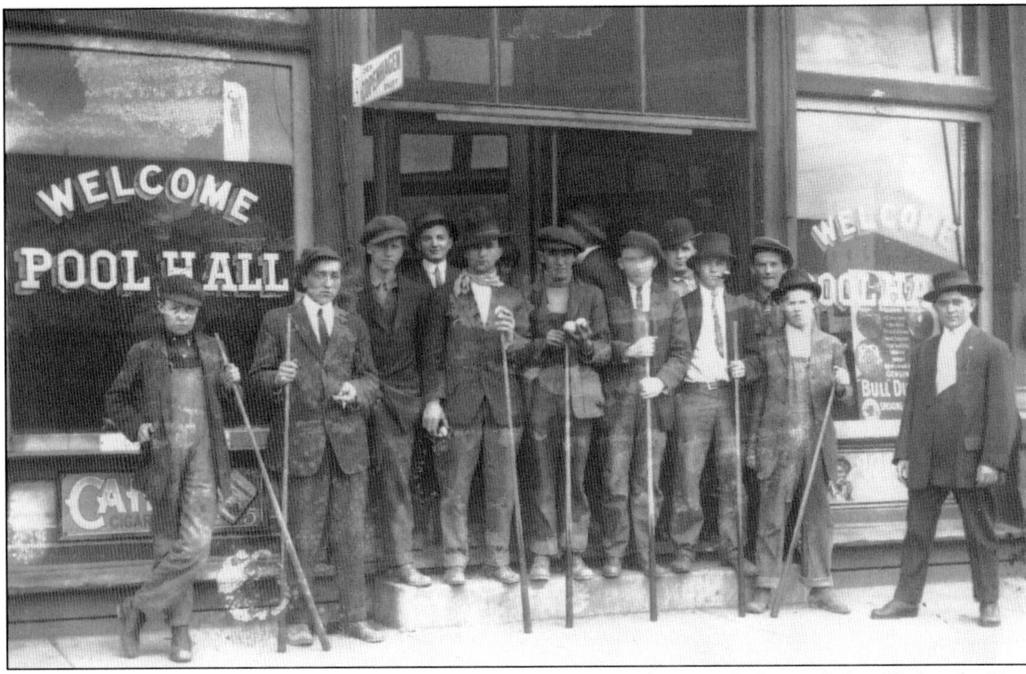

Six of the customers at this pool hall are identified as G. Behun, Bill Oyett, John Yedinak, Tiny Mike Steffin, Jackie Moon, and Mario Evanovich, although it is not known which person is which. The business advertised Copenhagen snuff, 5¢ cigars, and genuine Bull Durham smoking tobacco. Like many of the photographs from the New Studio, this picture was taken in 1915. (Courtesy New Studio.)

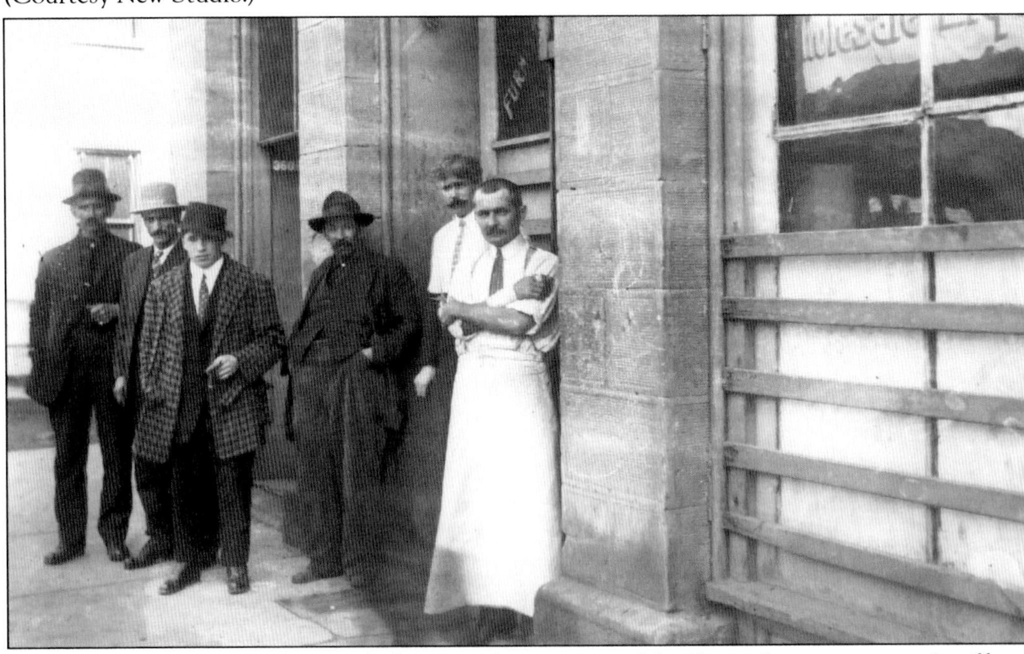

Branch's Bar, shown in this 1915 photograph, was owned by Spanish immigrants. It offered furnished rooms upstairs, which were rumored to serve as a brothel. It was located on South Front Street. (Courtesy New Studio.)

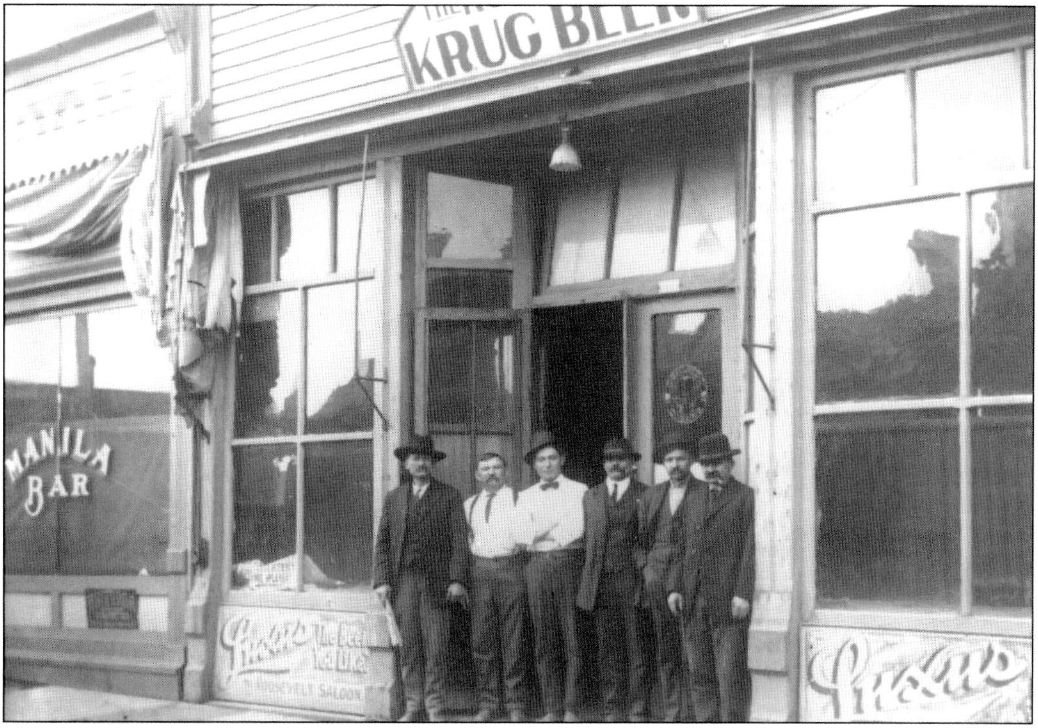

The Roosevelt Saloon featured beer from the Krug Brewing Company, including their finest Luxus, "the beer you like," according to the advertisement. The Roosevelt, pictured here in 1915, was on North Front Street. (Courtesy New Studio.)

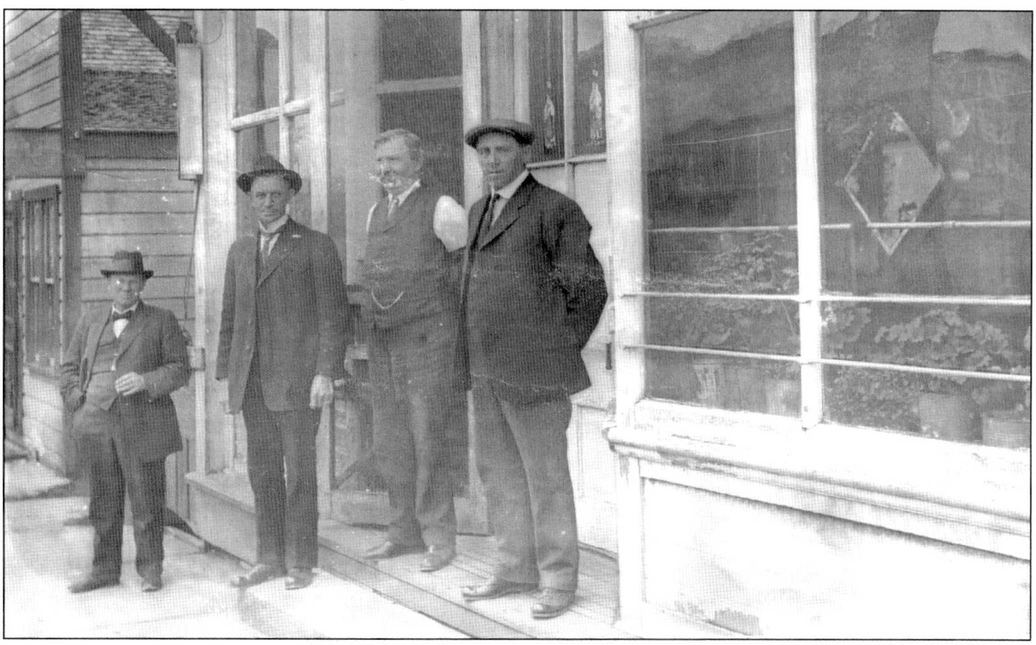

This photograph taken in the 1910s is of the Cottage Beer Club and Sandwich Shop located in downtown Rock Springs. As in several of the bars recorded from this era, there are plants in the window. (Courtesy New Studio.)

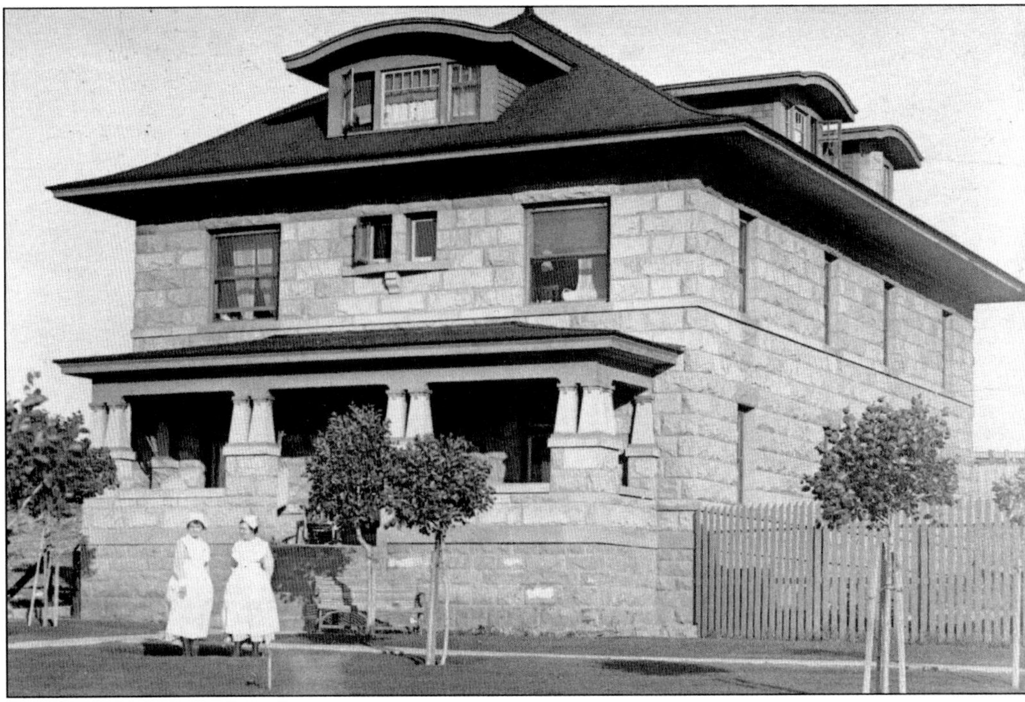

Two nurses stand outside the Nurses School at the Miner's Hospital. Newly planted trees are staked so they will not blow over or lean because of the prevailing westerly winds. The two-story building with dormers was made of locally quarried sandstone. The Nurses School offered educational opportunity for local women in the early 20th century. (Courtesy New Studio.)

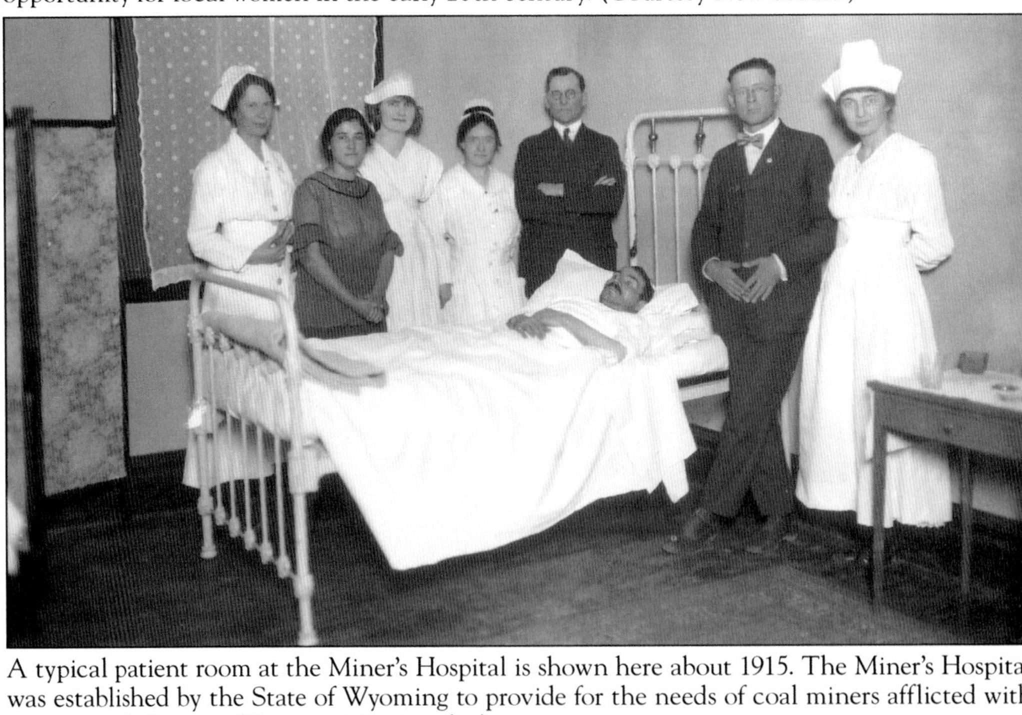

A typical patient room at the Miner's Hospital is shown here about 1915. The Miner's Hospital was established by the State of Wyoming to provide for the needs of coal miners afflicted with injuries and diseases. (Courtesy New Studio.)

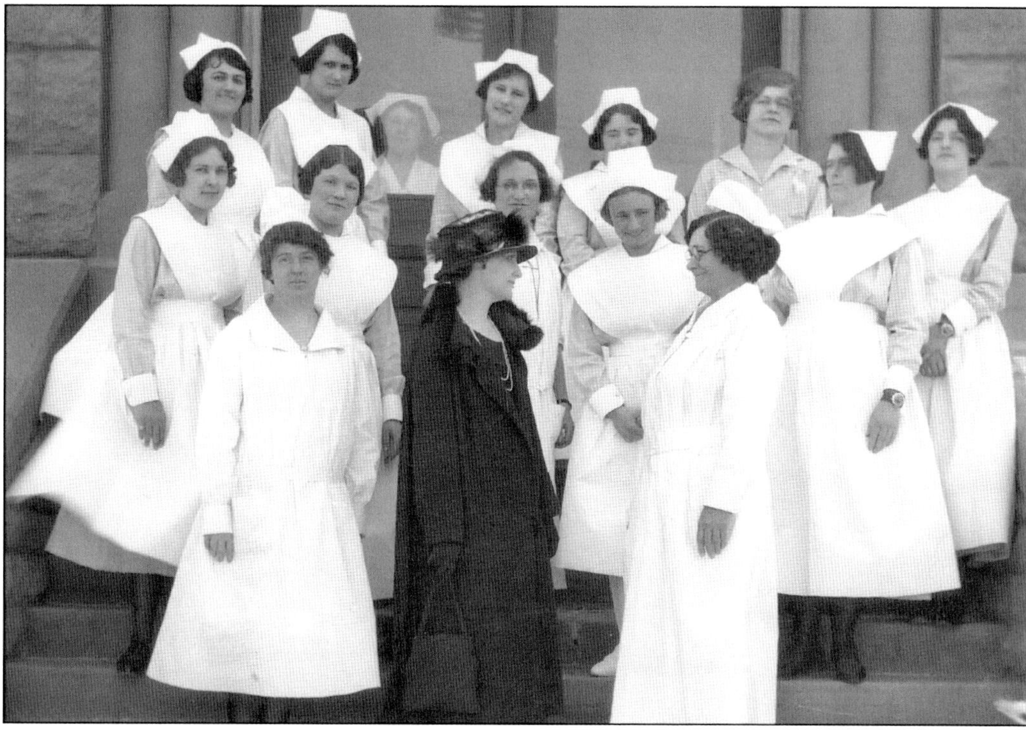

Nellie Tayloe Ross, governor of Wyoming and the first woman governor in the United States, visited with nurses in 1925. She served from January 1925 but lost her reelection bid in 1927. In 1933, FDR appointed her to the post of director of the U.S. Mint, a position she held until 1953. (Courtesy New Studio.)

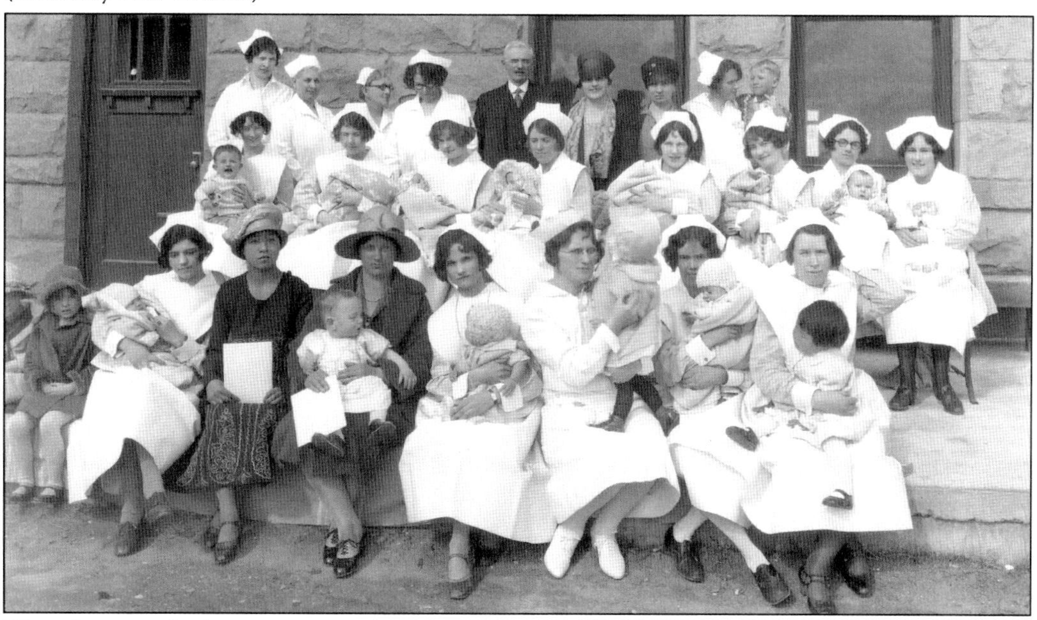

This photograph shows nurses at the Miner's Hospital holding 14 little babies and several other small children in 1926. The Miner's Hospital served the needs of miners' families as well as miners themselves. (Courtesy New Studio.)

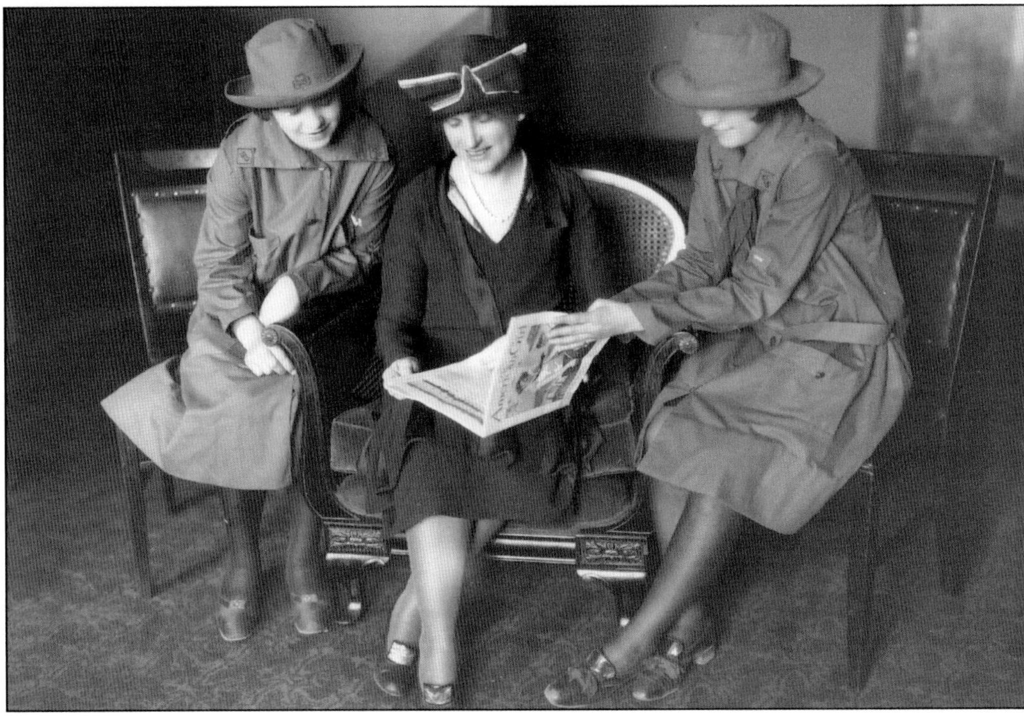

This photograph was taken of Governor Ross and two Girl Scouts at the Park Hotel in 1926. Nellie Tayloe Ross retired from government service in Washington, D.C. She died in 1977 when she was 101 years old. (Courtesy New Studio.)

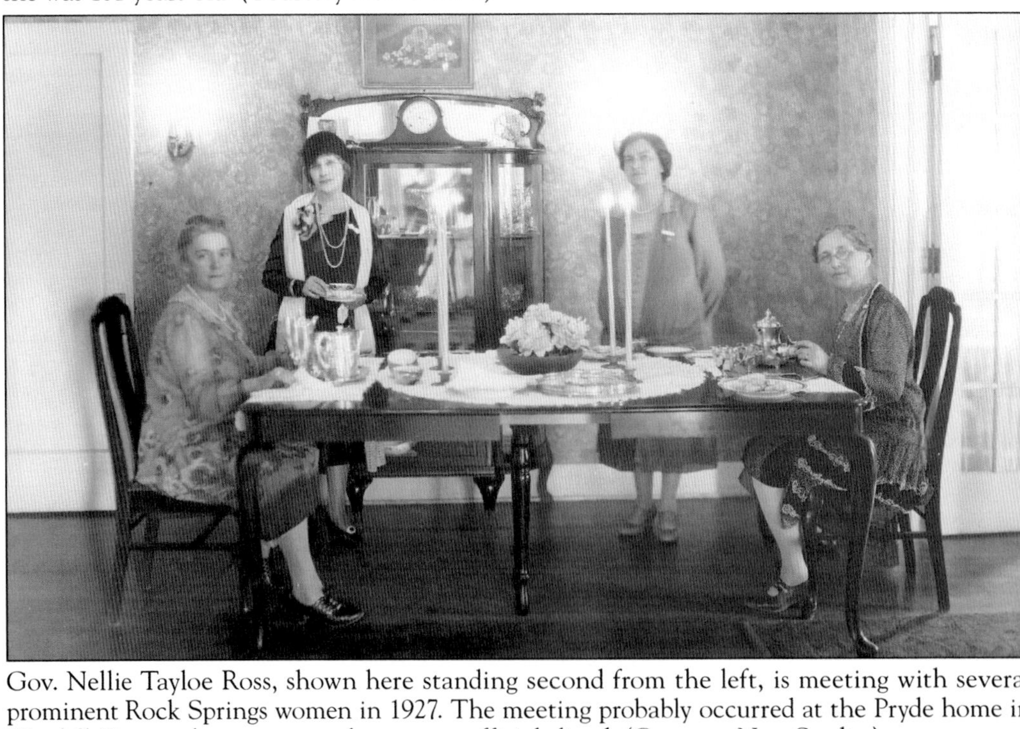

Gov. Nellie Tayloe Ross, shown here standing second from the left, is meeting with several prominent Rock Springs women in 1927. The meeting probably occurred at the Pryde home in Wardell Court, where many coal company officials lived. (Courtesy New Studio.)

Six

Faces of Rock Springs

People Make the Place

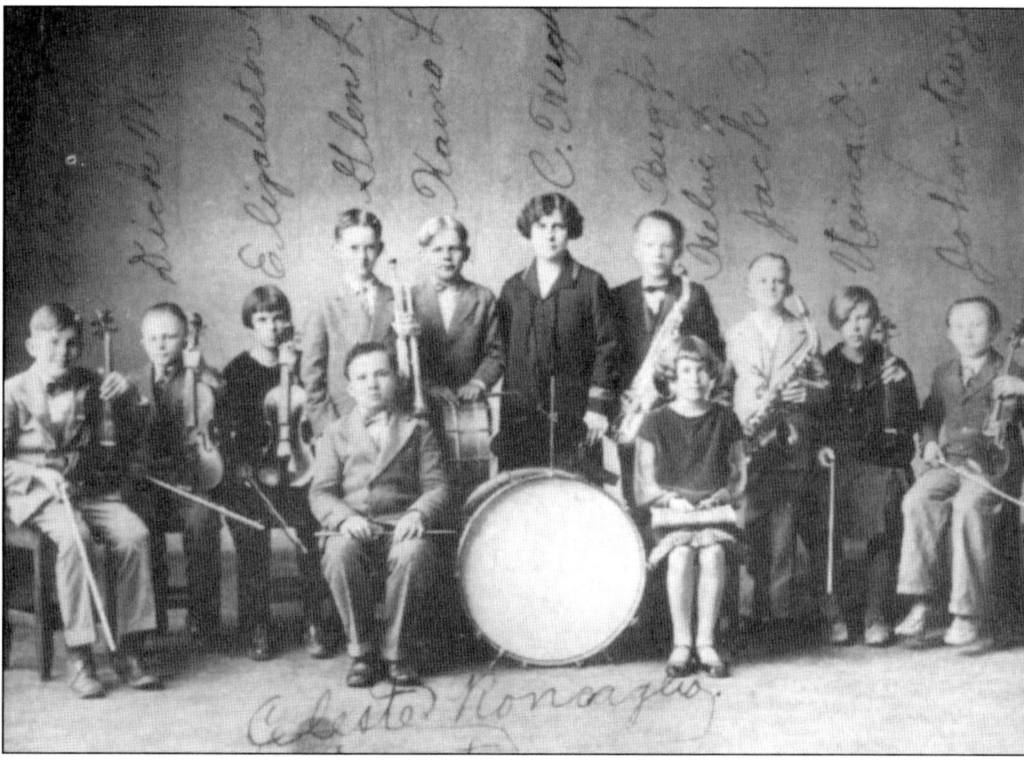

Celeste Roncaglio, the schoolboy conductor of this orchestra, apparently exhibited leadership potential even at this early age. Better known as Teno Roncalio, he went on to earn a Silver Star for valor during the Normandy Invasion. Teno later served five terms as Wyoming's lone representative in the U.S. House of Representatives. Among his significant accomplishments in Congress were the return of 50 percent of federal mineral royalties to the state and the creation of Fossil Butte National Monument. As one of his school friends recalls, his career could have taken a different course; he used to "dress up as a hunchback and carry a sandwich board sign" advertising events at the Rialto Theater, and he nearly joined Mickey Daniels of "Our Gang" fame as a child actor. The U.S. Post Office in Rock Springs is named in Teno's honor. (Courtesy Rock Springs U.S. Postal Service.)

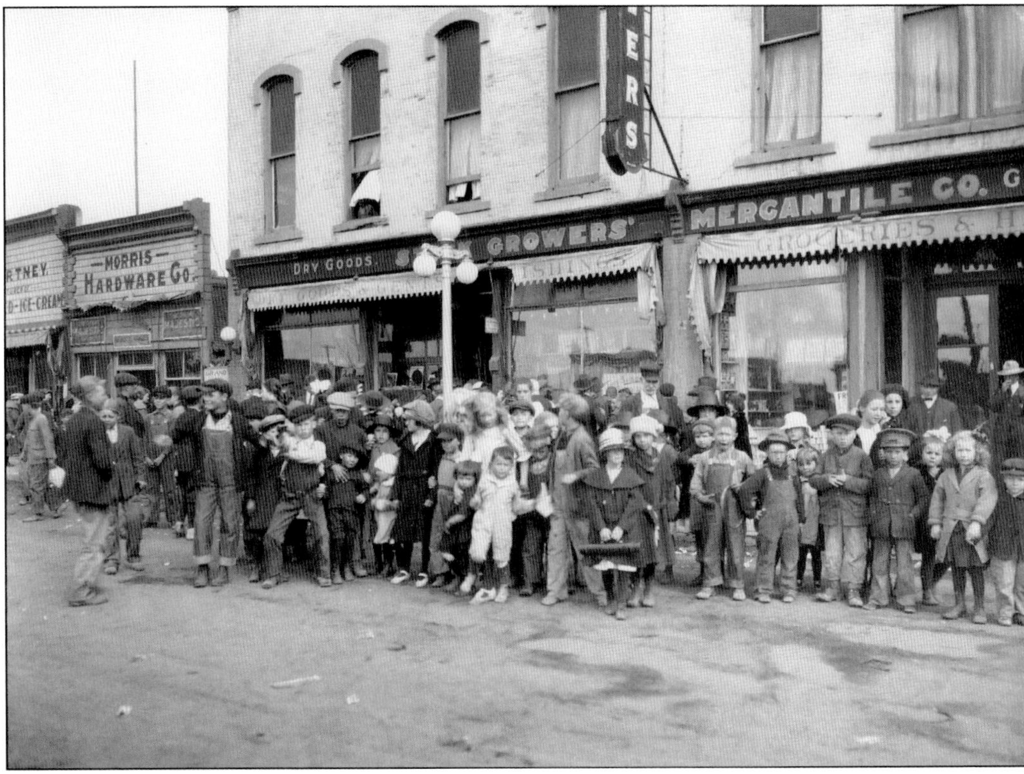

A crowd of children line up on the dirt street in front of the Stock Growers Mercantile Company on South Front Street. The event that prompted these children to be here is not known. This photograph was taken in May 1922. (Courtesy New Studio.)

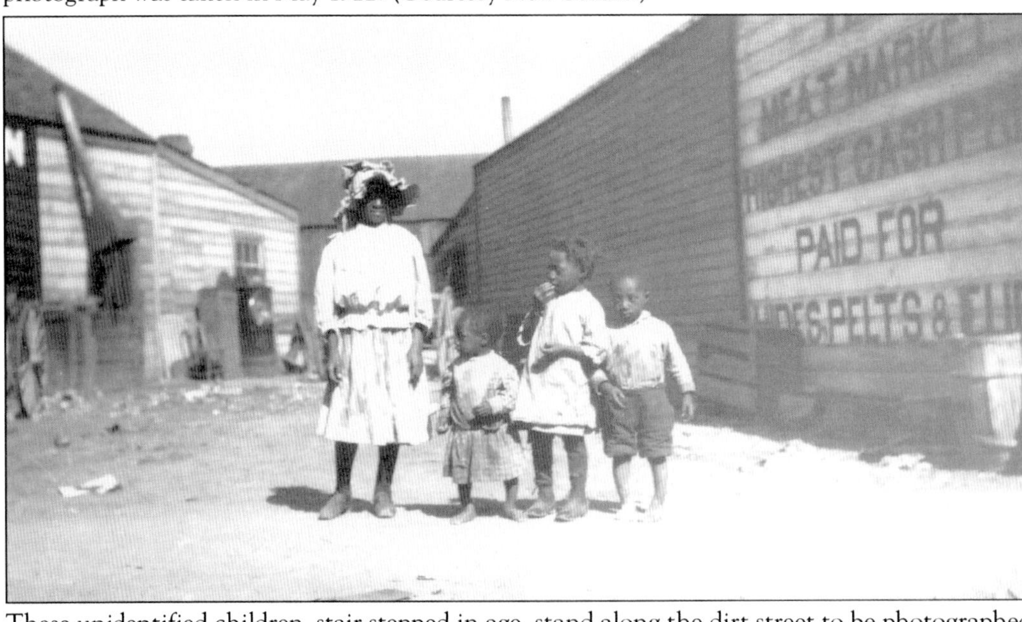

These unidentified children, stair-stepped in age, stand along the dirt street to be photographed in the early 1900s. Coal mining towns are notoriously dirty, with slag from mining activity all around and coal-burning stoves used to heat homes and cook. (Courtesy RSHM.)

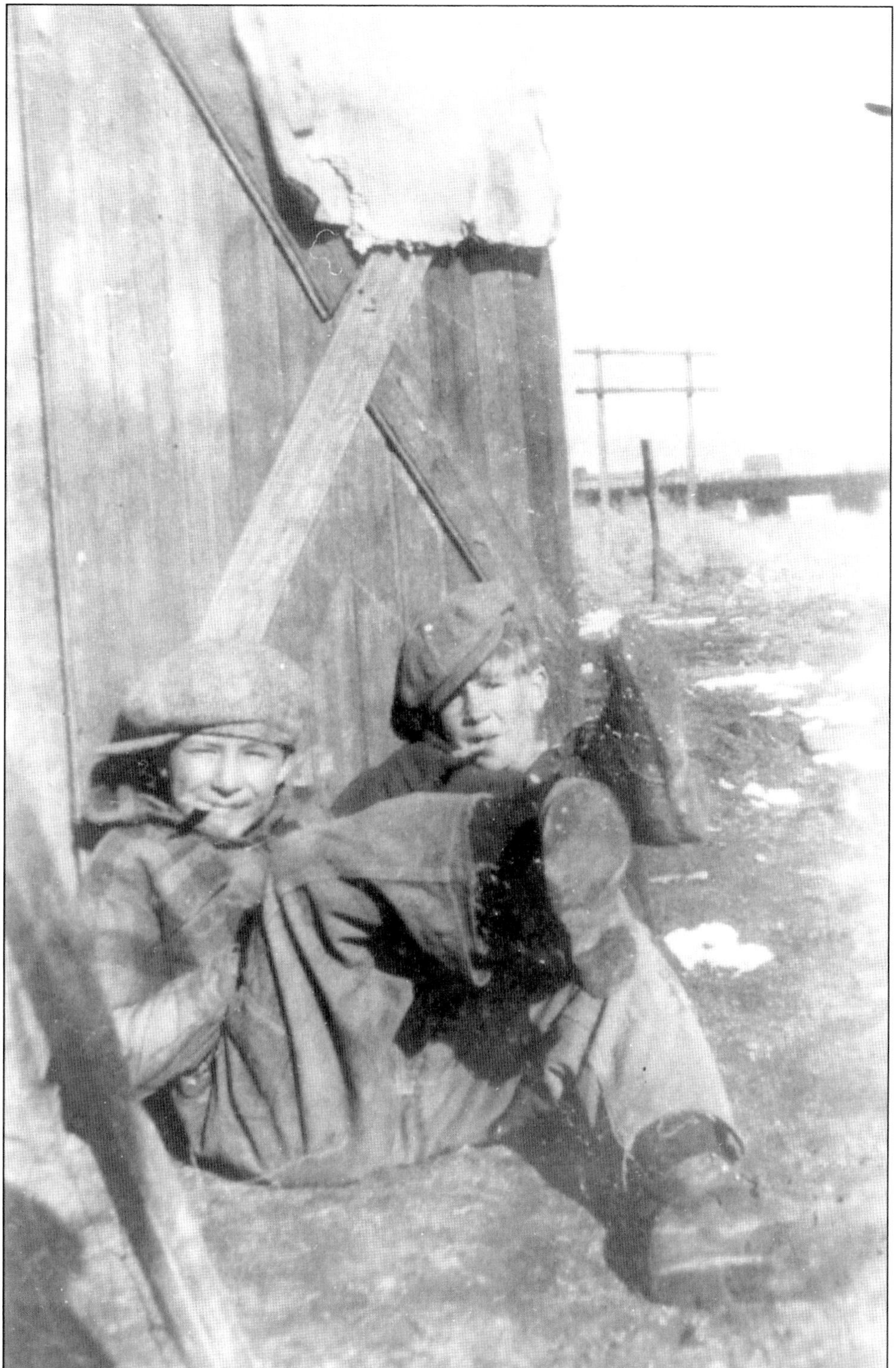

These young men behind the shed mimic undesirable adult behavior. It was not uncommon for children about this age to smoke or work in the mines. (Courtesy RSHM.)

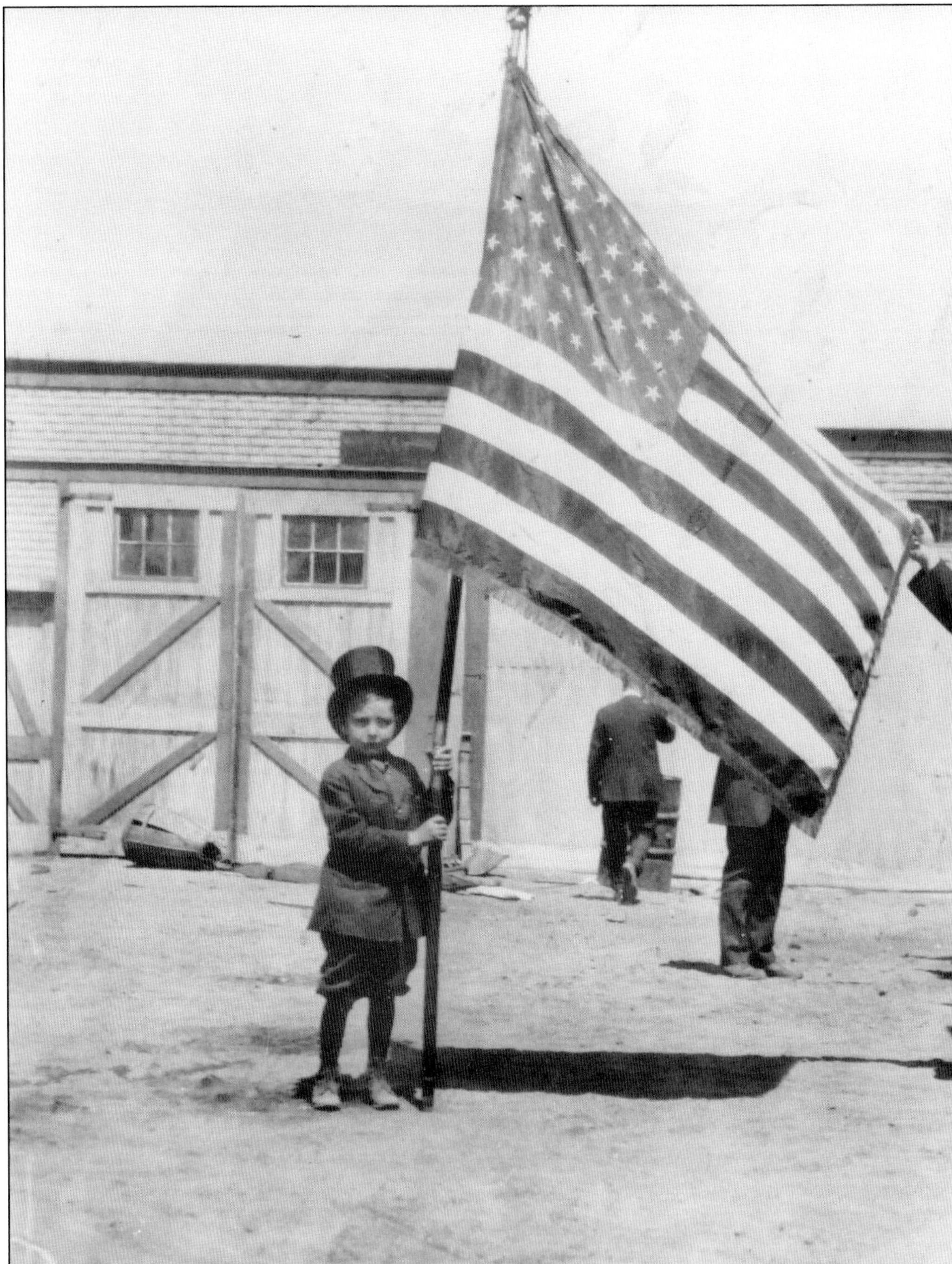

On July 4, 1921, at the west end of North Front Street, near Kellogg Lumber, young Thomas P. Cullen holds an American flag that is bigger than he is. The Patrick Henry Chapter of the American Association for the Recognition of the Irish Republic participated in Rock Springs's big Fourth of July Parade. Cullen was the only kid to participate, as he just tagged along with his dad and the other Irish men. (Courtesy the Cullen family.)

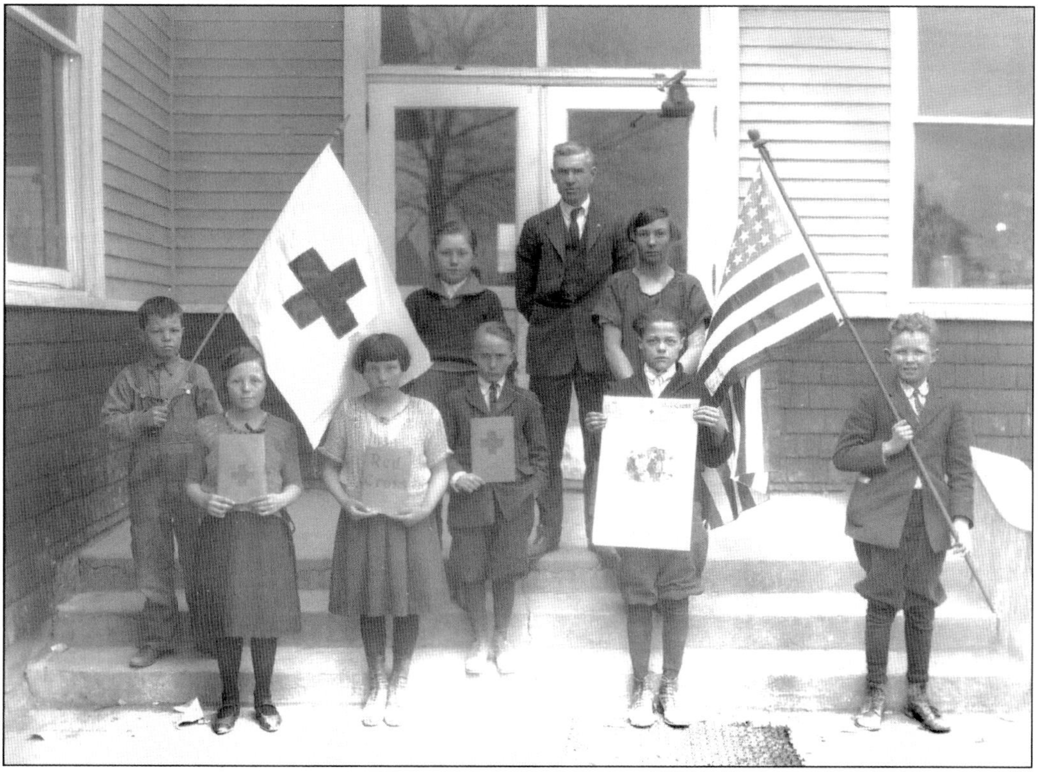

Members of the Junior Red Cross Council were photographed in 1924. These children displayed the Red Cross and U.S. flags in front of Washington Elementary School on Bridger Avenue. (Courtesy New Studio.)

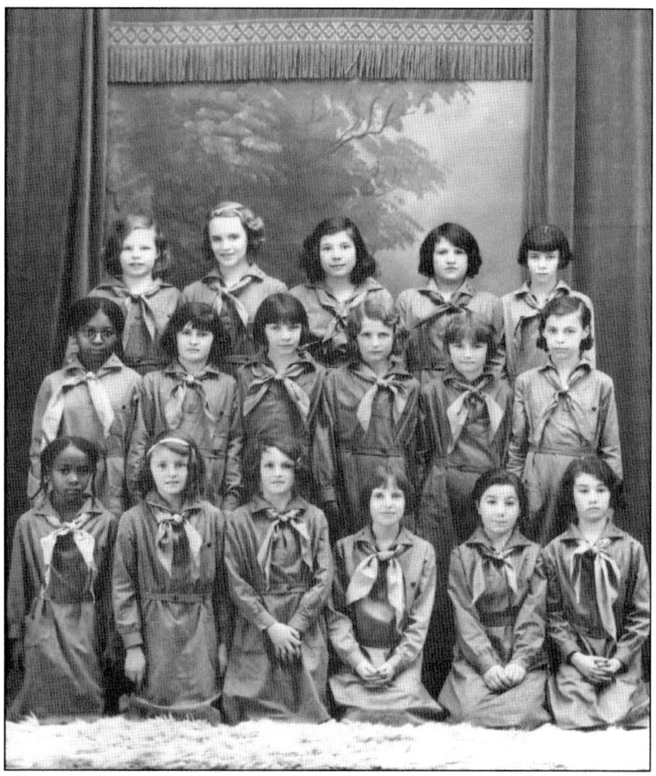

In 1933, these girls, members of the Girl Scouts, pose for a professional group portrait. Associations for the youth of the community also included church groups, Boy Scouts, and organizations affiliated with the different ethnic lodges. (Courtesy New Studio.)

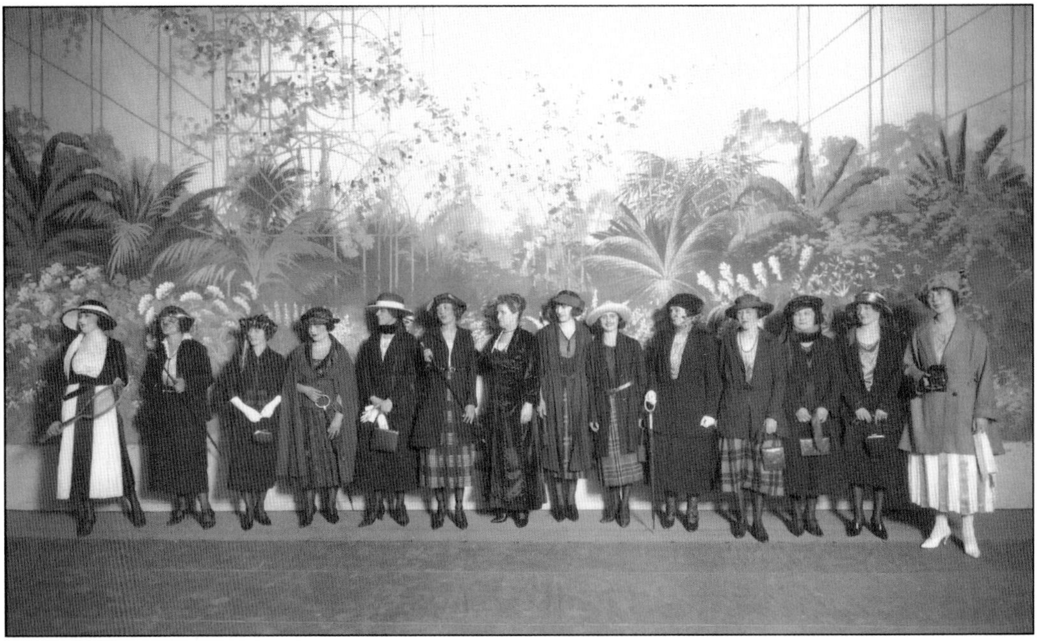

These stylish women presented a fashion show at the Stock Growers Mercantile Company. With ankles showing, these models donned trendy hats, pocketbooks, and gloves. Women rarely wore trousers, even at home. (Courtesy Dr. Bernadine Craft.)

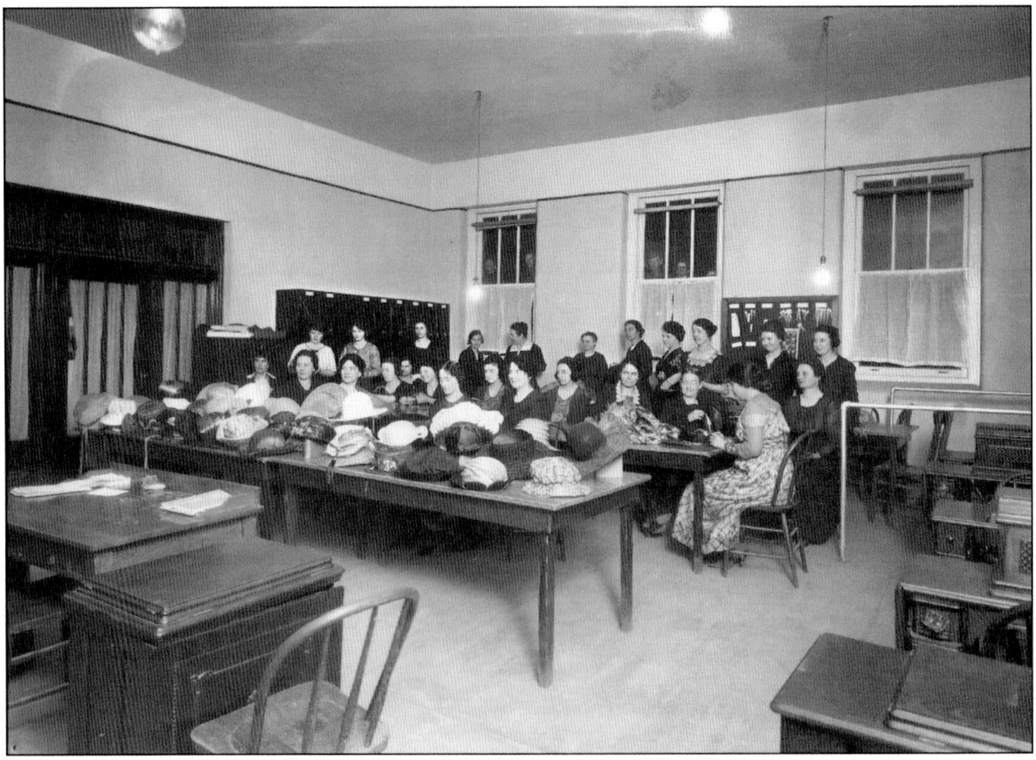

In 1921, women seeking a trade could attend this millinery night school. Millinery is a term rarely used now, and it refers to the making or selling of hats. (Courtesy New Studio.)

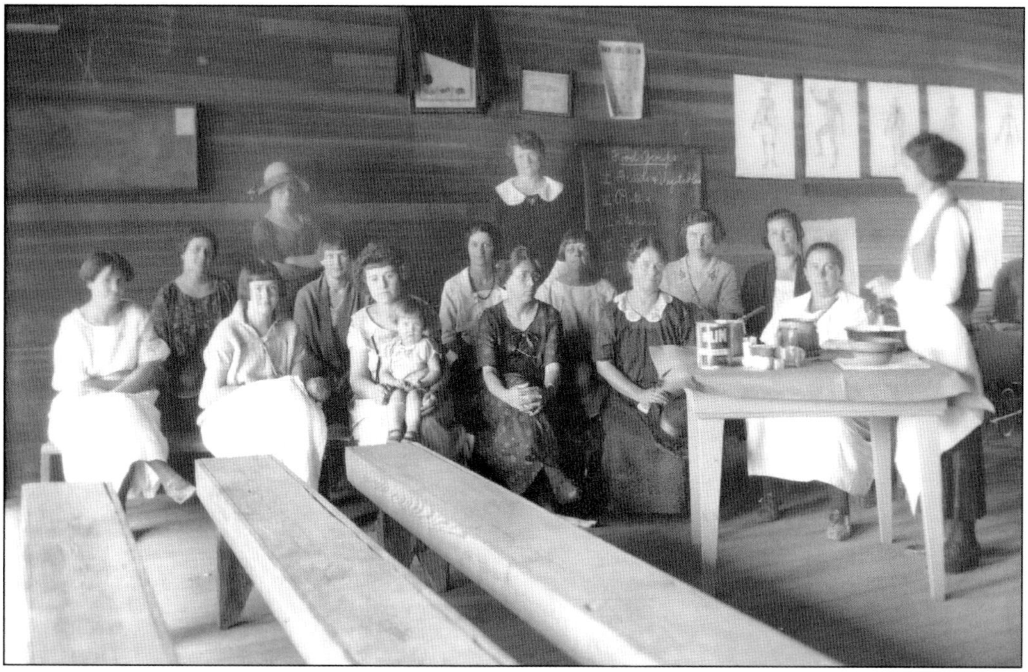

The Union Pacific Cooking Club is pictured here in 1921. Women could hone their cooking skills and learn techniques that could help them at home. Adult education was valued, and women from different cultural backgrounds could associate and learn from each other. (Courtesy New Studio.)

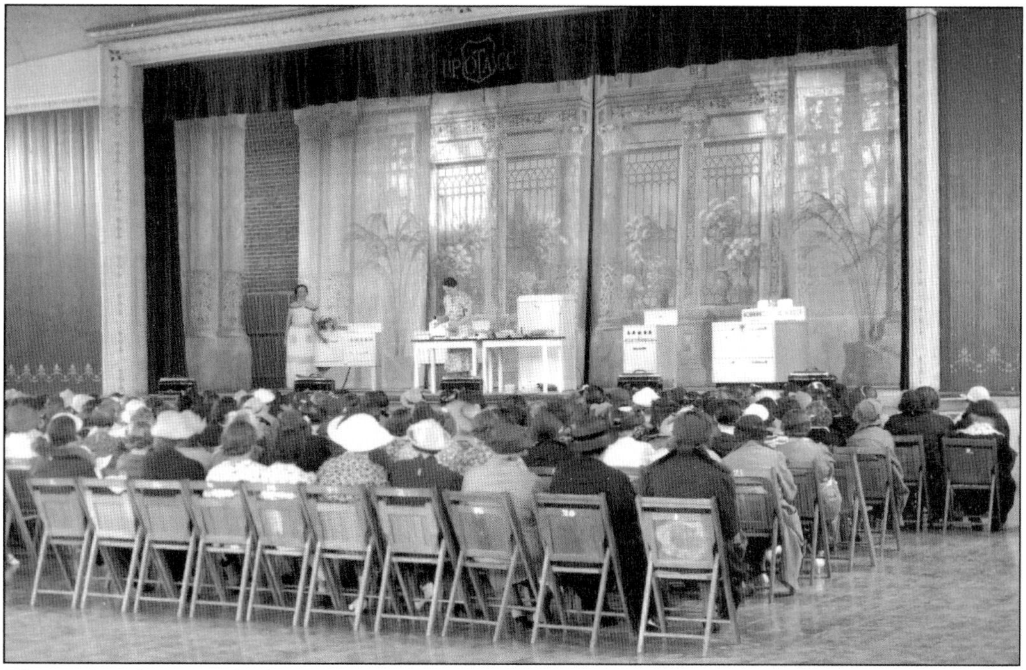

This 1938 photograph shows a Union Pacific Railroad cooking class held in the Old Timer Building. Several stoves and other appliances are being demonstrated for the women attending. (Courtesy New Studio.)

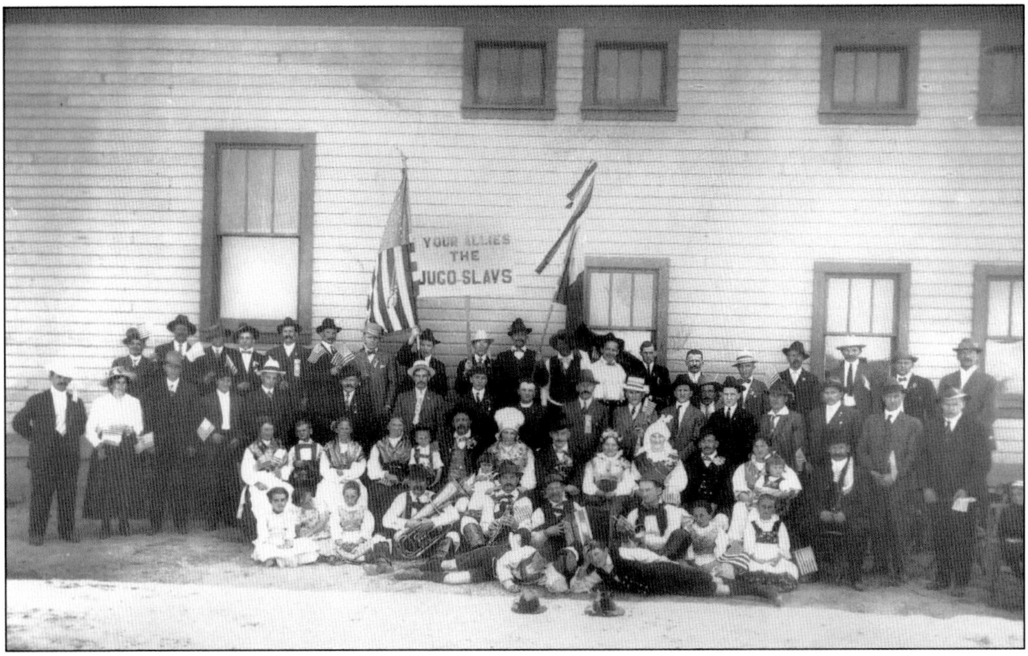

This is a photograph of the Jugo-Slav Republican Alliance No. 79 with a sign proclaiming "Your Allies the Jugo-Slavs." The group sent a letter to Sen. Frances E. Warren in June 1919, which contained their "Twenty-eight Ultimo," a declaration of allegiance to the United States to present to the Senate. (Courtesy New Studio.)

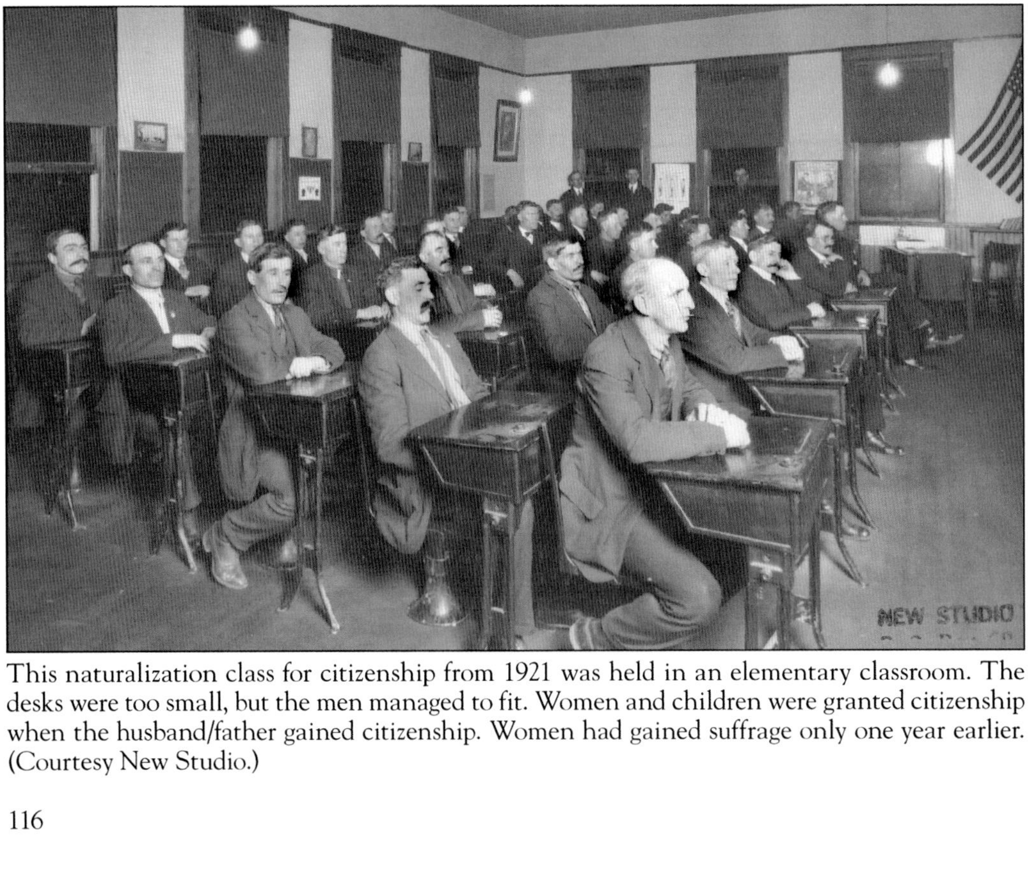

This naturalization class for citizenship from 1921 was held in an elementary classroom. The desks were too small, but the men managed to fit. Women and children were granted citizenship when the husband/father gained citizenship. Women had gained suffrage only one year earlier. (Courtesy New Studio.)

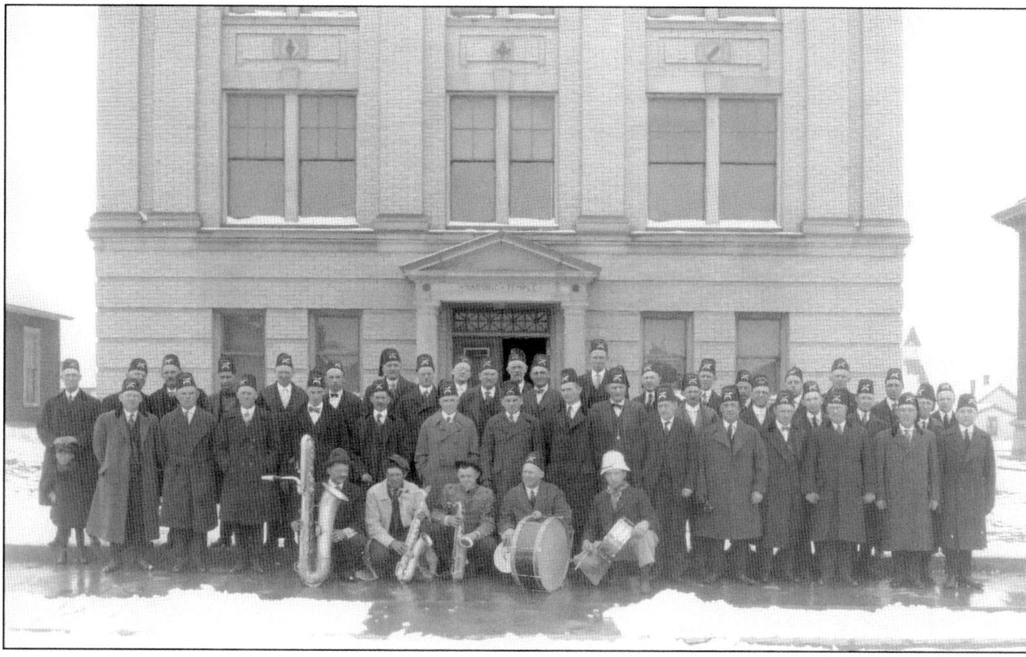

These Shriners pose in front of the Masonic Temple on B Street in 1921. The Shriner organization is an international fraternity requiring members to have the title of master mason in Freemasonry. In 1922, they opened Shriners Hospitals for Children. (Courtesy New Studio.)

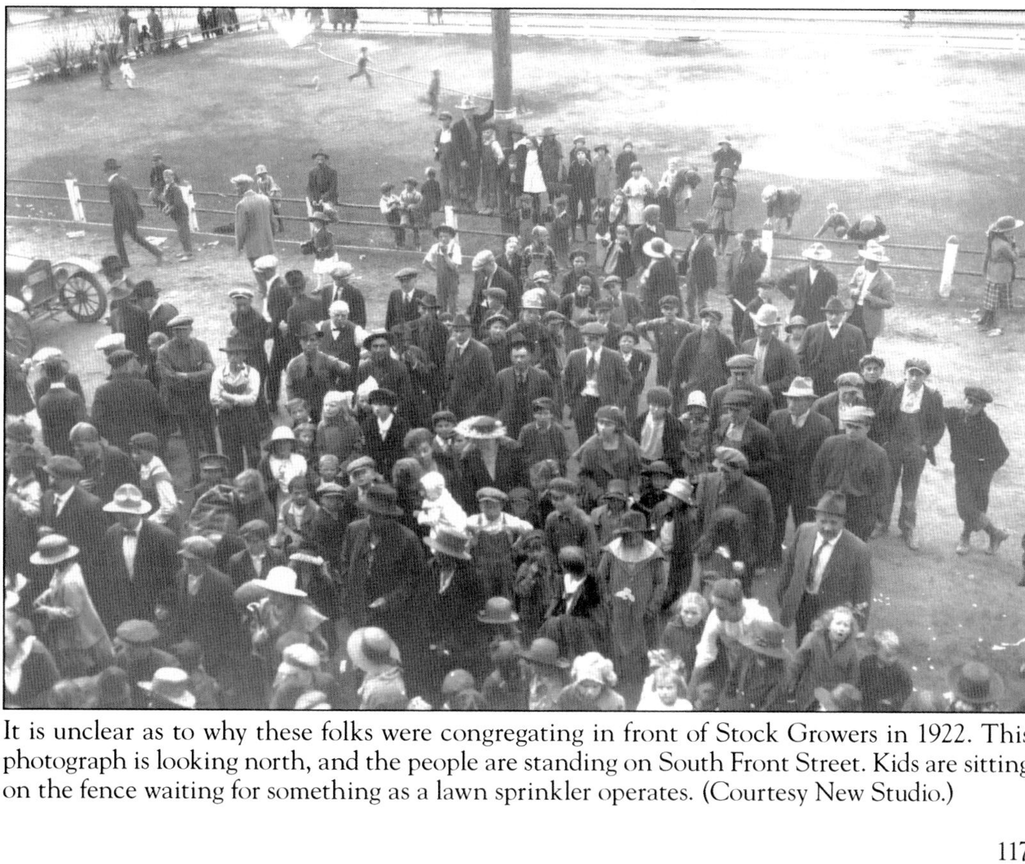

It is unclear as to why these folks were congregating in front of Stock Growers in 1922. This photograph is looking north, and the people are standing on South Front Street. Kids are sitting on the fence waiting for something as a lawn sprinkler operates. (Courtesy New Studio.)

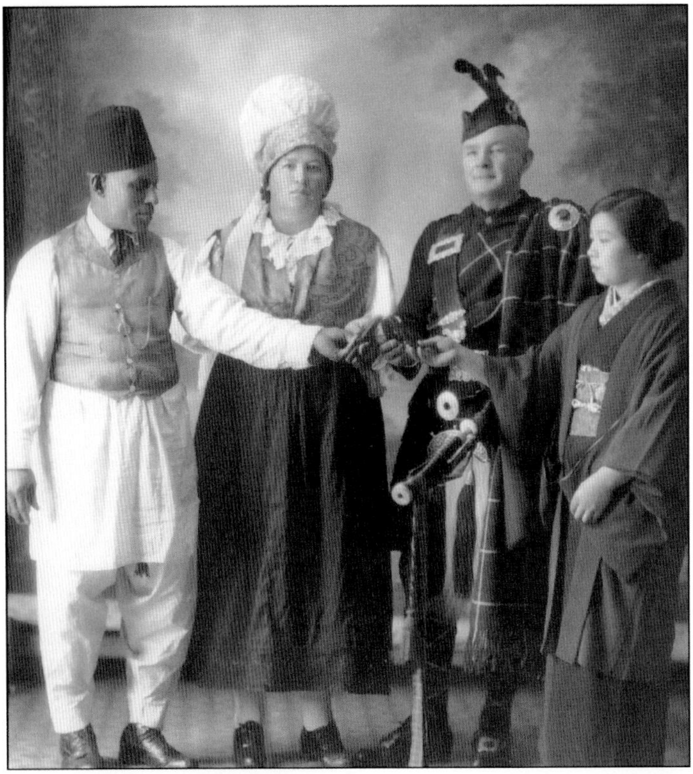

This photograph captures the candle-lighting ceremony performed at International Days in 1928. This traditional celebration would bring the diverse cultures of Rock Springs together. Participants all hold an unlit candle until one person lights his neighbor's candle and recites in his native language, "As light begets light, so love begets love the world around." The ritual would be repeated until everyone's candle was burning. This event continues today. (Courtesy New Studio.)

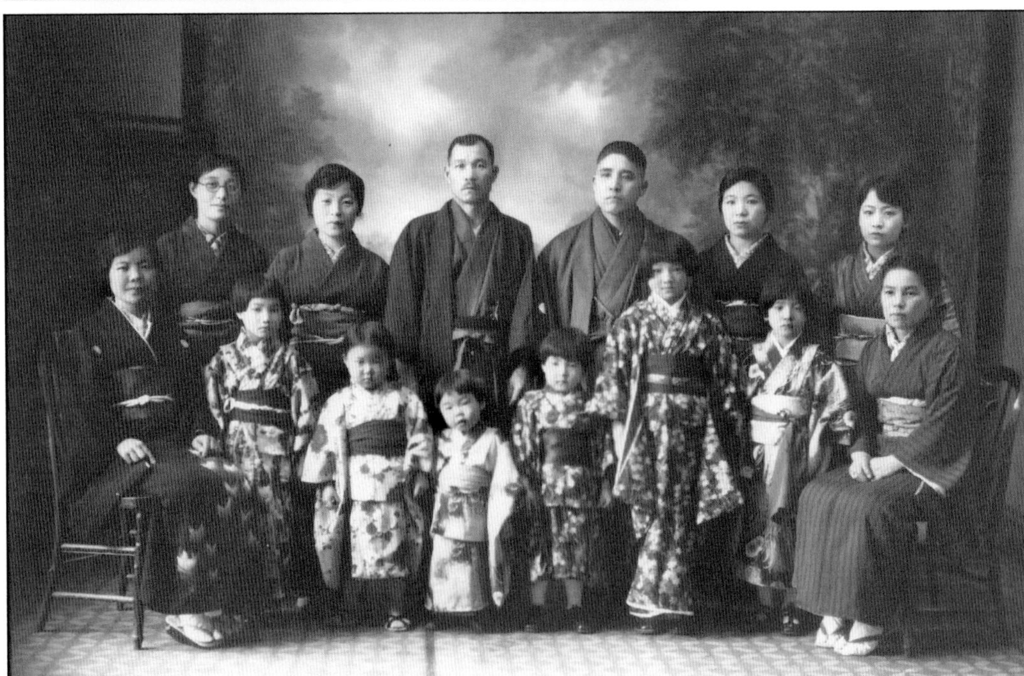

These unidentified people of Japanese descent wore the clothes of their homeland and participated in the 1928 International Days. Different ethnic groups celebrated their individuality yet recognized the similarities between disparate cultures. (Courtesy New Studio.)

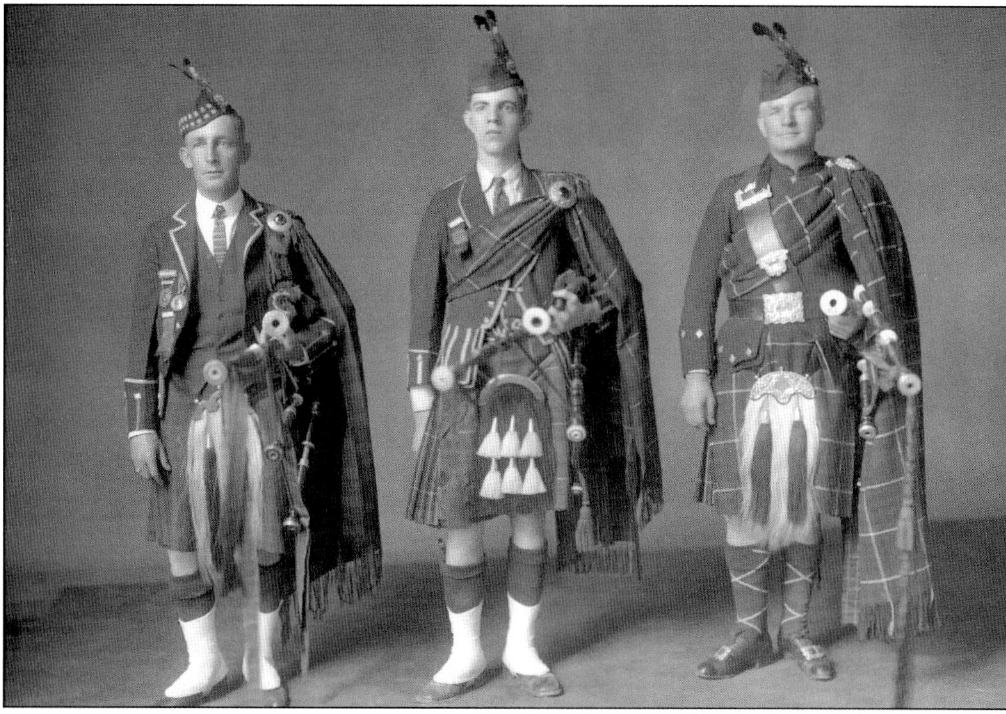

Three Scottish men wore their traditional kilts and other regalia during the 1928 International Days. Bagpipes were an integral part of Rock Springs parades, and the Kilty Band played and marched for the enjoyment of the crowd. (Courtesy New Studio.)

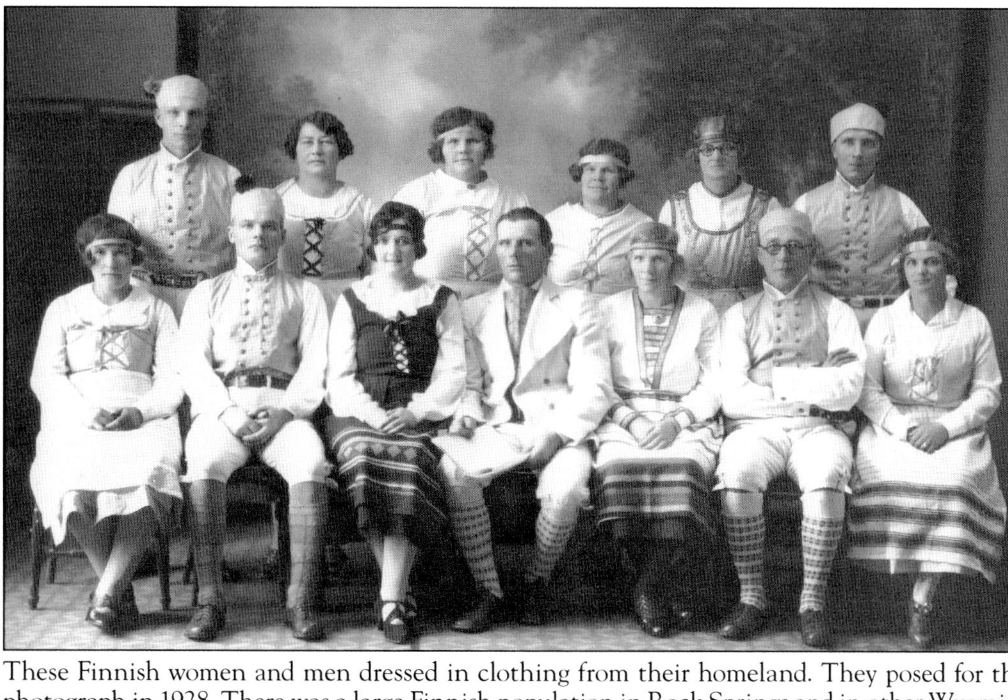

These Finnish women and men dressed in clothing from their homeland. They posed for this photograph in 1928. There was a large Finnish population in Rock Springs and in other Wyoming coal towns. (Courtesy New Studio.)

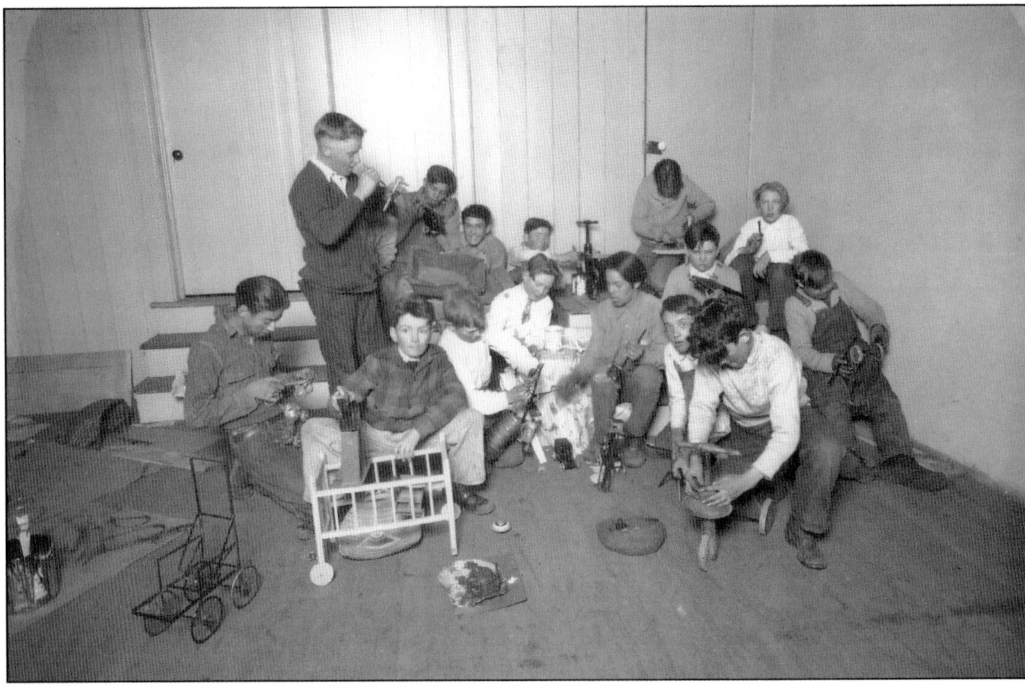

These young men were photographed in December 1928 at the First Baptist Church. They are cleaning and refurbishing used roller skates, tricycles, and other toys. Perhaps some lucky child would get something nice for Christmas. (Courtesy New Studio.)

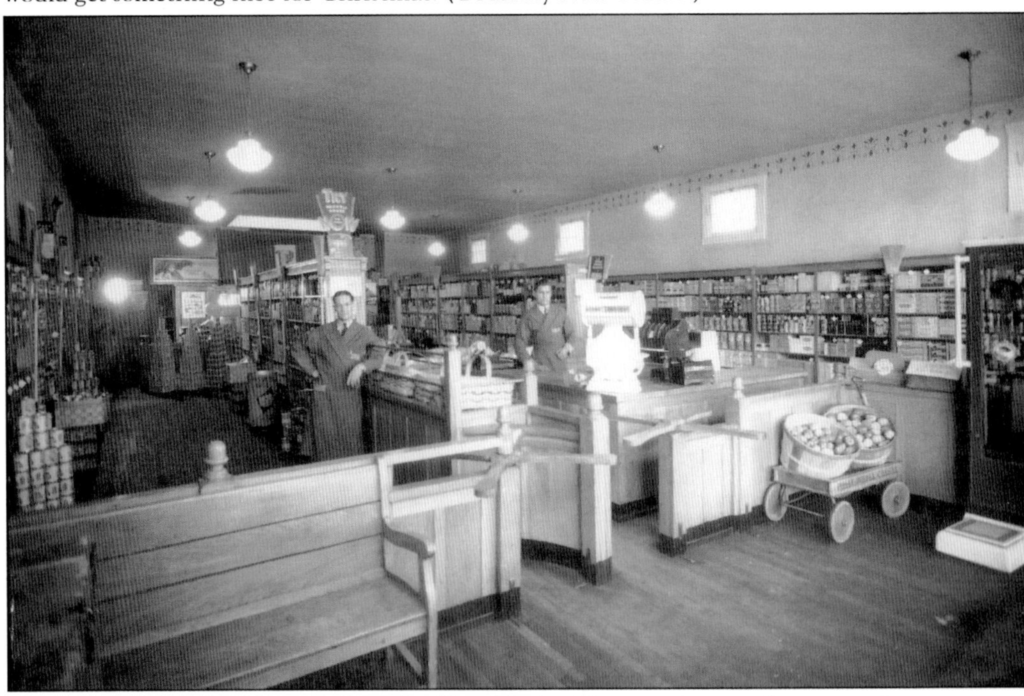

This Piggly Wiggly store located in the Klondike building used turnstiles to regulate customers in 1932. Dry goods and fresh produce could be purchased here. Money was in such short supply that businesses had a difficult time remaining afloat. (Courtesy New Studio.)

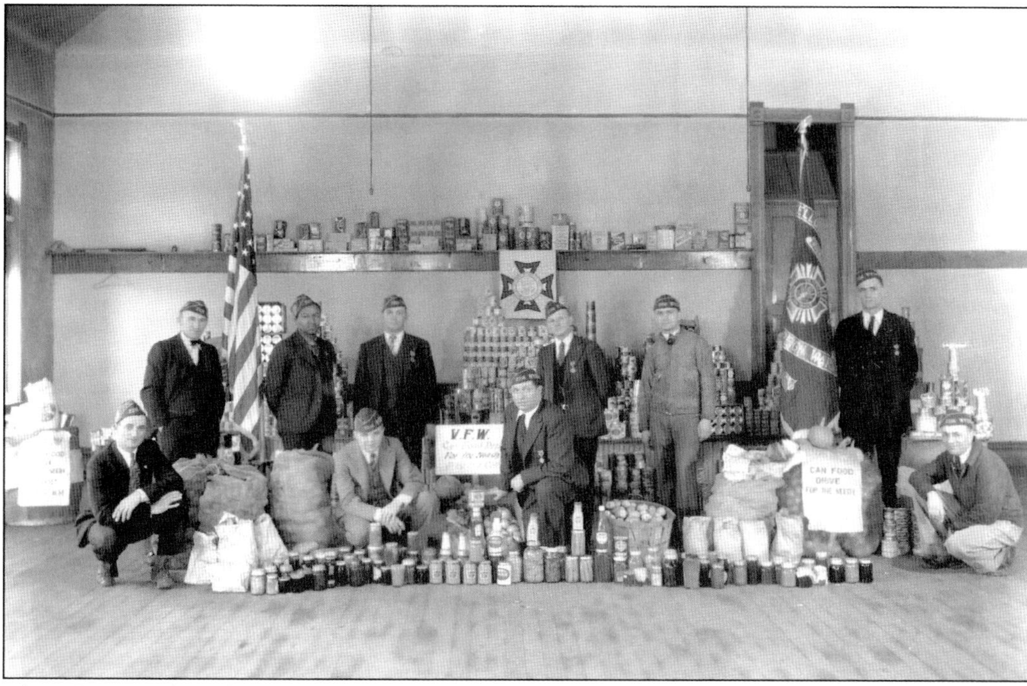

The VFW conducted a canned food drive in 1933 for the needy. Rock Springs was in the depths of the Depression, and the community was attempting to care for their own citizens. One man said of the Depression, "We always had food, just sometimes not enough." (Courtesy New Studio.)

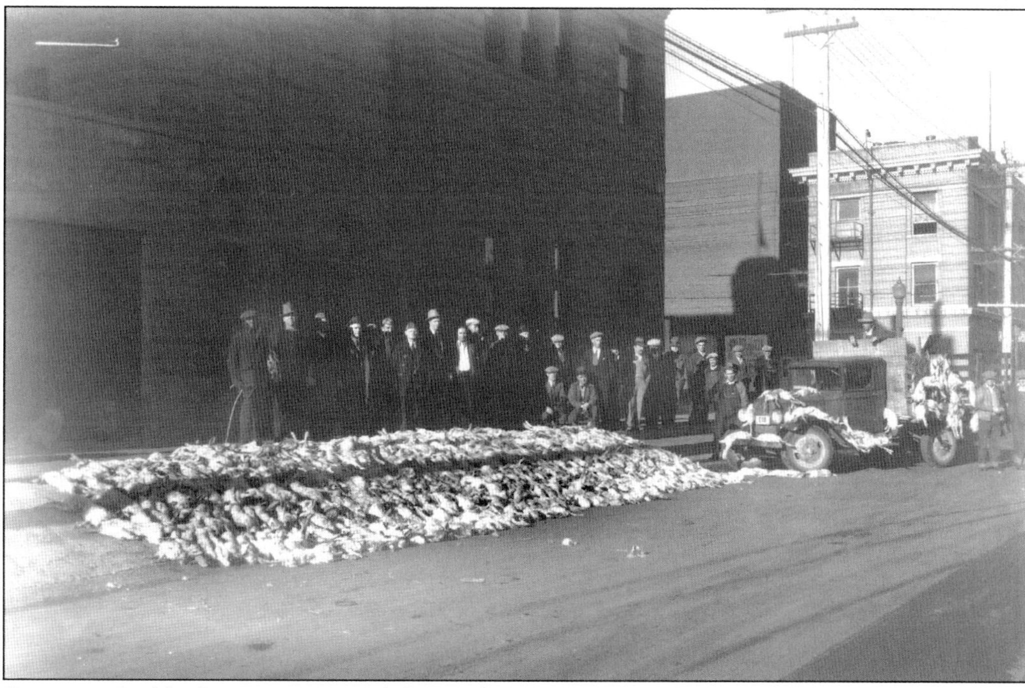

Communal rabbit hunts were staged during the Depression in an effort to ease the food shortage. The bounty from this effort was given to the Relief Committee to help the needy families. Rabbits from the Ramsey rabbit hunt were displayed on Broadway Avenue. (Courtesy New Studio.)

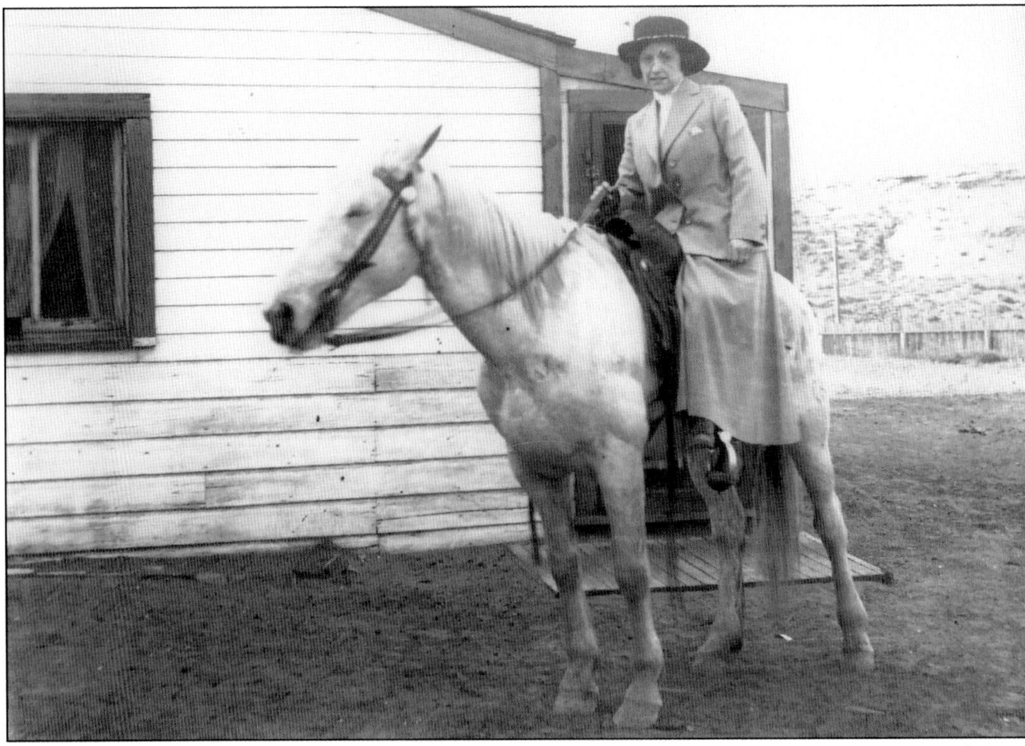

Mary L. Muir sits astride a horse in this 1915 photograph. Women in Western coal towns did not feel compelled to ride sidesaddle. (Courtesy New Studio.)

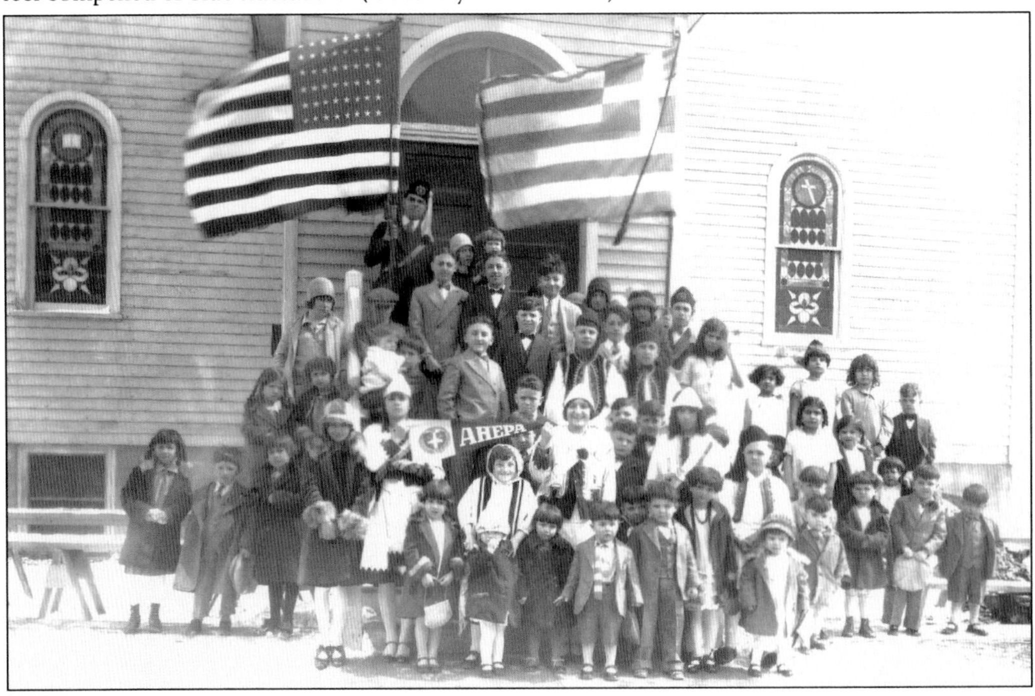

This group of Greek youth stood in front of the Trinity Greek Orthodox Church on the corner of Pilot Butte and N Streets in 1929. (Courtesy New Studio.)

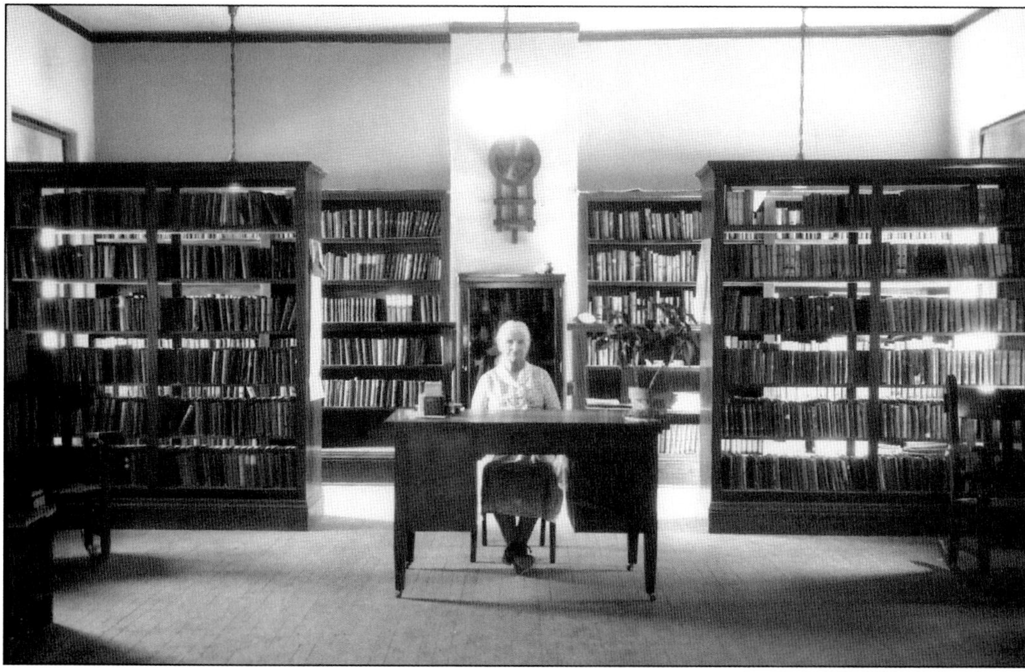

The library was built with money donated by Scottish American businessman Andrew Carnegie. He claimed that books and libraries provide the opportunity to acquire knowledge to improve oneself. This 1931 photograph shows Mary Clark and open stacks of books to encourage people to browse. (Courtesy New Studio.)

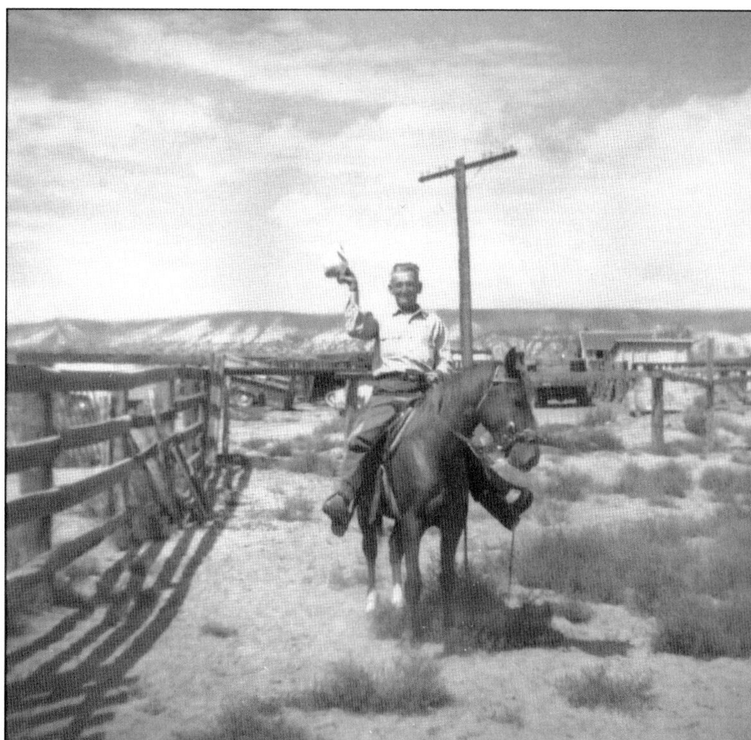

Hugh "Chappie" Roberts is pictured here on his Morgan horse in corrals near the Number Six mine. He came to Rock Springs around the dawn of the 20th century with his family and left school very young to work in the mines to help support them. Roberts was a World War I veteran, a freighter, and a railroader. He served as a Sweetwater County commissioner in the 1940s. (Courtesy the Roberts family.)

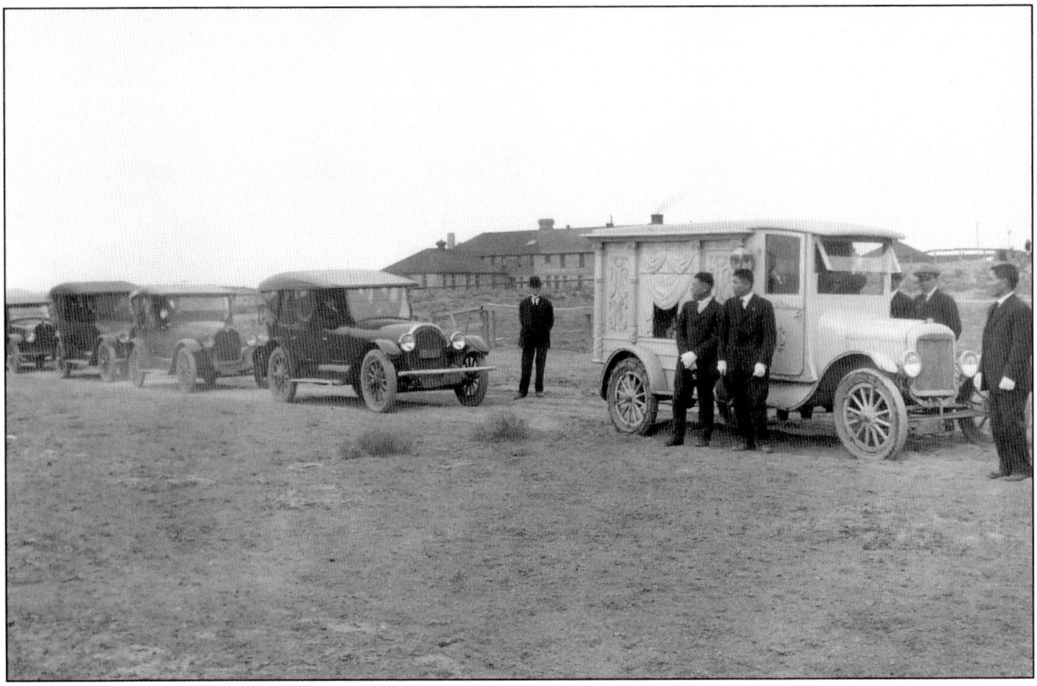

This 1921 funeral procession was for S. Yamasaki. The Miner's Hospital is in the background. Many Rock Springs people were afraid to go to the hospital because the poor house was right up the hill and the cemetery was within a stone's throw. (Courtesy New Studio.)

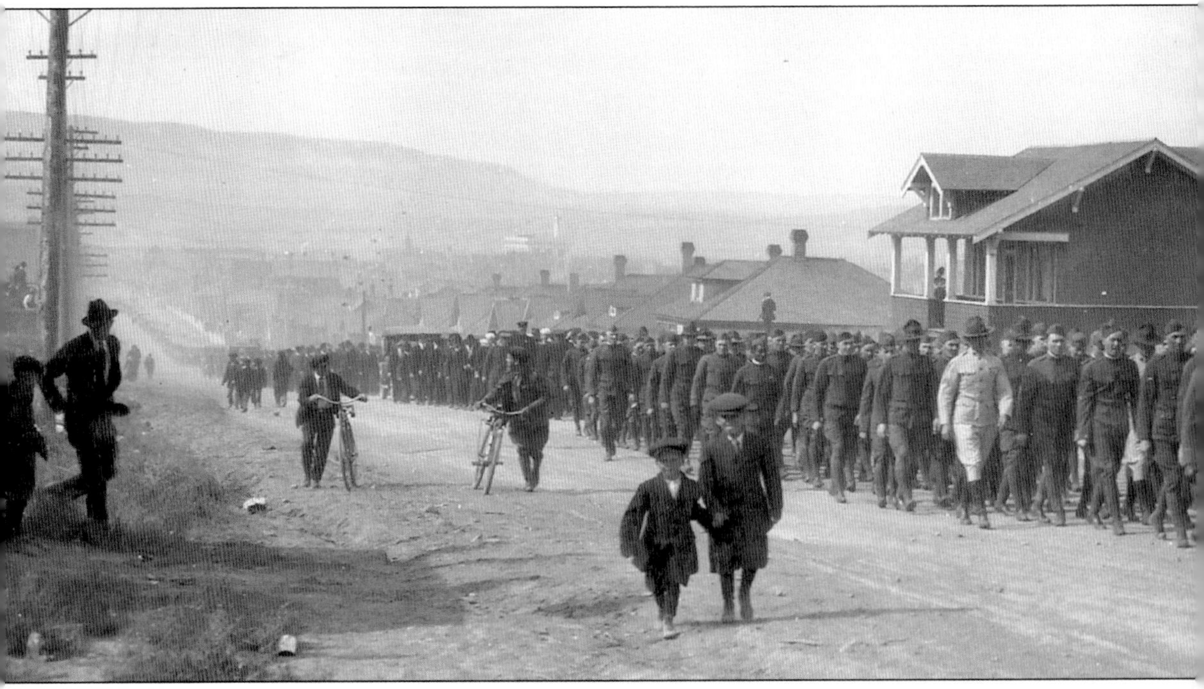

On April 3, 1921, funeral services were held for Thomas Whelan, the first Sweetwater County boy to be killed in the First World War. Whelan's body had been transferred to Rock Springs from a cemetery in France where he had been interred since May 1918. Over 300 men in uniform

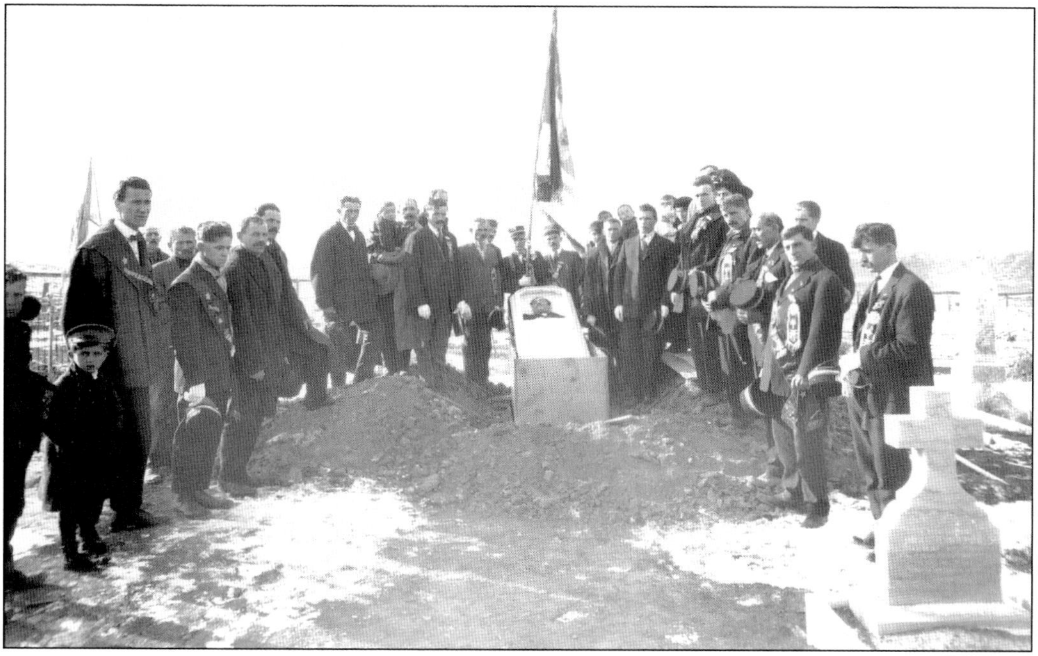

This funeral is likely for a Slovakian man based on the Cyrillic lettering on the regalia worn by mourners. Rock Springs is especially known for having a large population of Eastern Europeans, including members of both Catholic and Orthodox faiths. Traditions from many of these cultures are still a part of Rock Springs society. (Courtesy New Studio.)

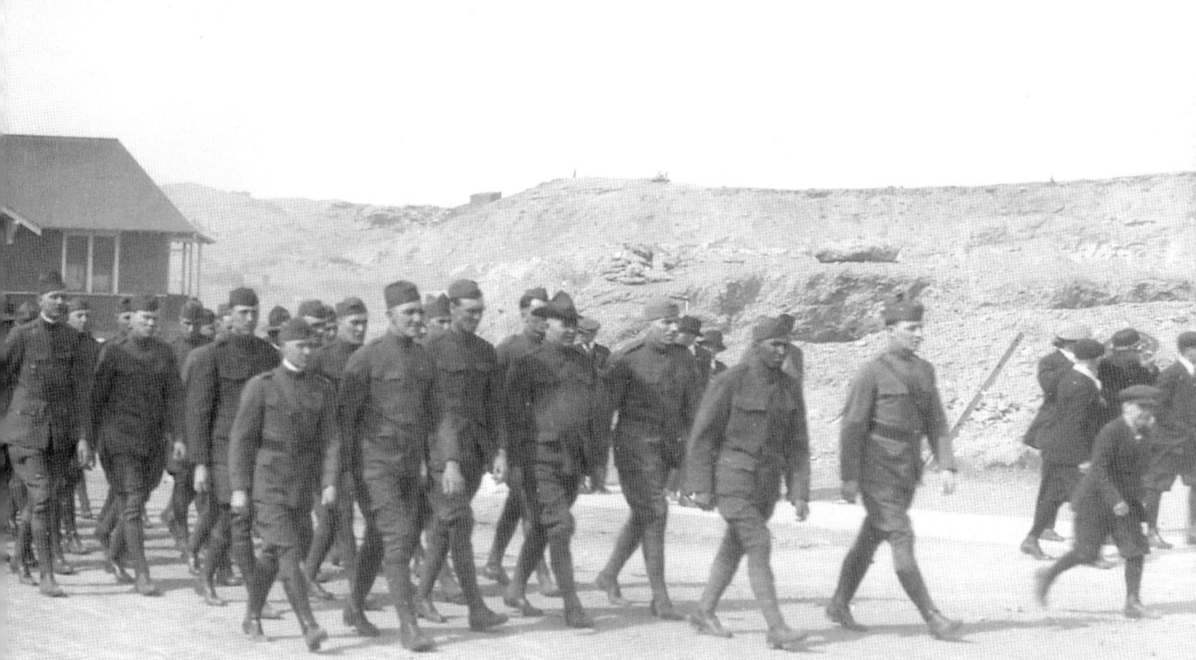

and hundreds of citizen paid their last respects to their fallen hero. It was reported to be the most impressive ceremony ever held in the city and perhaps the state. (Courtesy New Studio.)

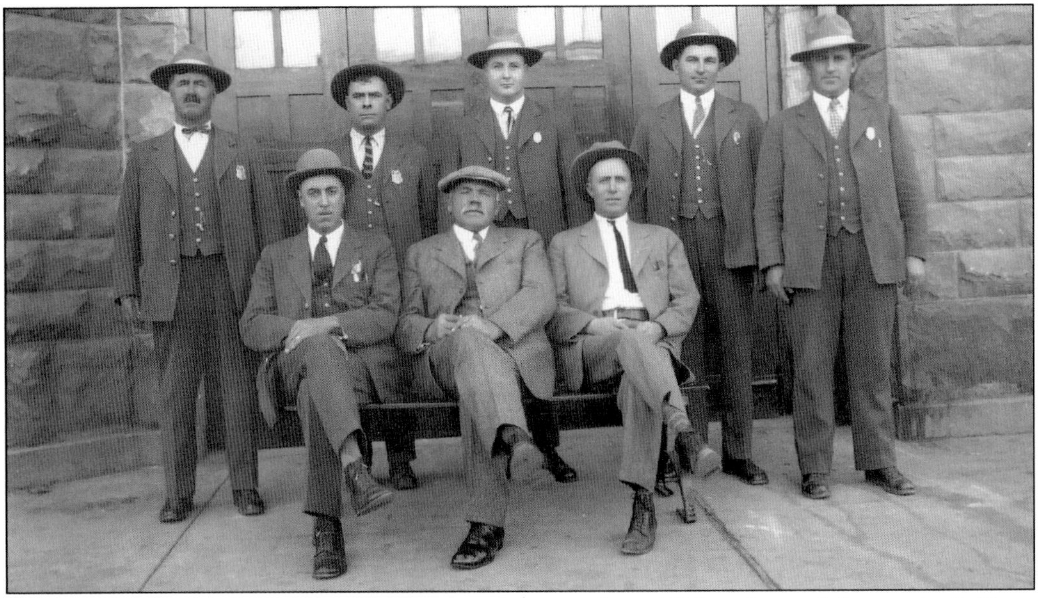

The Rock Springs mayor and police force are seen in about 1925 in front of the city hall. From left to right are (first row) chief of police James Harris, Mayor P. C. Bunning, and George Harris; (second row) Joe Davenport, Sam Ryder, William J. Harvey, Val Marcina, and John Veranda. (Courtesy New Studio.)

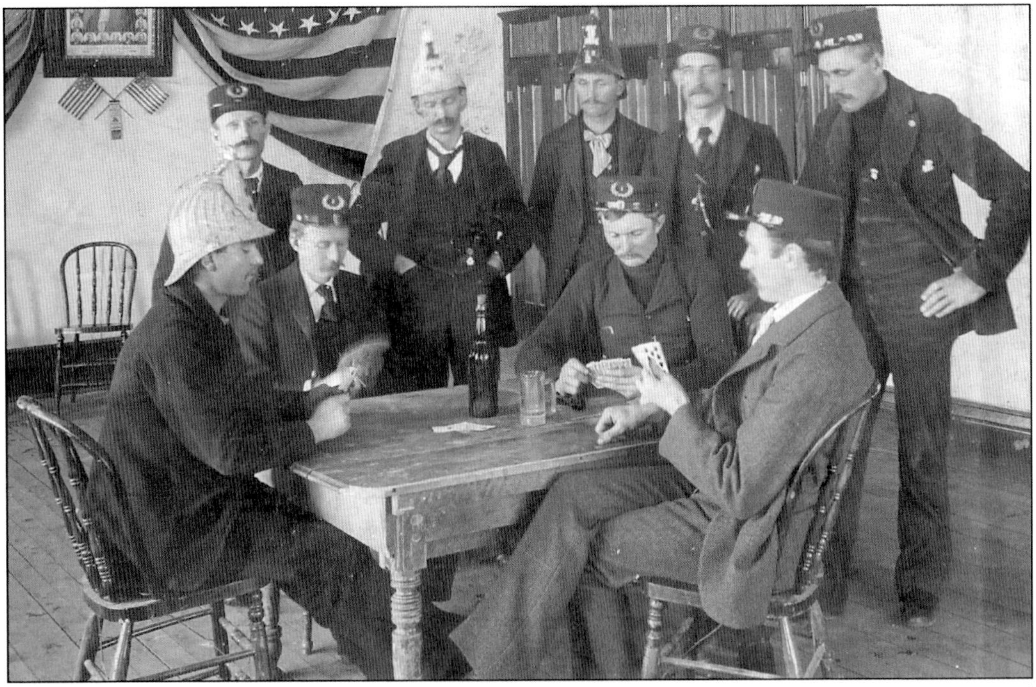

It may seem unusual by today's standards, but drinking and gambling seem to have been accepted pastimes for Rock Springs city firemen in the fire station at city hall in the early 1900s. The firemen must have been a very patriotic bunch with a picture of the presidents on the wall and several American flags. The photograph appears to be staged, so perhaps the drinking was all in jest. (Courtesy RSHM.)

BIBLIOGRAPHY

Brinkerhoff, Val, and A. Dudley Gardner. An American Place: A Centennial Portrait of Rock Springs, Wyoming Then and Now 1889–1989. Rock Springs, WY: Pioneer Press, 1990.
Chadey, Henry. The Chinese Story and Rock Springs, Wyoming. Green River, WY: Sweetwater County Museum.
Cullen, Thomas. Rock Springs: Growing up in a Wyoming Coal Town 1915–1938. Green River, WY: Sweetwater Museum Foundation, 2005.
Gardner, A. Dudley, and Verla Flores. Forgotten Frontier: A History of Wyoming Coal Mining Boulder, CO: Westview Press, 1989.
Hendrickson, Gordon Olaf, ed. Peopling the High Plains: Wyoming's European Heritage. Cheyenne, WY: Wyoming State Archives and Historical Department, 1977.
Krza, Margie F. Oral history interview with Robert Fletcher. Manuscript in the possession of the author. Rock Springs, WY: 1984.
Lindmier, Tom, and Steve Mount. I See by Your Outfit: Historic Cowboy Gear of the Northern Plains. Glendo, WY: High Plains Press, 1996.
McLean, Karen Spence, and Marjean Telck. Coal Camp Reunion: Dines, Stansbury, Reliance, and Winton. Rock Springs, WY: Sweetwater County Travel and Tourism Board, 2006.
Rhodes, Robert B. Booms and Busts on Bitter Creek: A History of Rock Springs, Wyoming Boulder, CO: Pruett Publishing Company, 1987.
Robbins, Norma Jean. Rock Springs Historic Downtown Walking Tour. Rock Springs, WY: Rock Springs Historical Board.
Rock Springs Historic Preservation Board. Downtown Rock Springs Historic District National Register of Historic Places nomination. On file at Western Archaeological Services, Rock Springs, WY: 1993.
Smith, Barbara, ed. Rock Springs Stories: Adult Writers Project. Rock Springs, WY: Western Wyoming Community College, 1992.
Storti, Robert. Incident at Bitter Creek: The Story of the Rock Springs Chinese Massacre. Ames, IA: Iowa State University Press, 1991.
Union Pacific Coal Company. History of the Union Pacific Coal Mines: 1868–1940. Omaha, NE: The Colonial Press, 1940.
Wilde, Gisela Bertagnolli. "Memories and Facts." Unpublished manuscript in the possession of Ernestine Magagna Baker. Rock Springs, WY: 1982.